Mobilizing
Restraint

Mobilizing Restraint

Democracy and Industrial Conflict in Post-Reform South Asia

Emmanuel Teitelbaum

ILR PRESS
an imprint of Cornell University Press,
Ithaca and London

FOUNDATION® BOOKS

Delhi • Bengaluru • Mumbai • Kolkata • Chennai • Hyderabad
Pune • Thiruvananthapuram

Published by
Cambridge University Press India Pvt. Ltd.
under the imprint of Foundation Books
Cambridge House, 4381/4 Ansari Road, Daryaganj, **New Delhi** 110 002

Cambridge University Press India Pvt. Ltd.
C-22, C-Block, Brigade M.M., K.R. Road, Jayanagar, **Bengaluru** 560 070
Plot No. 80, Service Industries, Shirvane, Sector-1, Nerul, **Navi Mumbai** 400 706
10 Raja Subodh Mullick Square, 2nd Floor, **Kolkata** 700 013
21/1 (New No. 49), 1st Floor, Model School Road, Thousand Lights, **Chennai** 600 006
House No. 3-5-874/6/4, (Near Apollo Hospital), Hyderguda, **Hyderabad** 500 029
Agarwal Pride, 'A' Wing, 1308 Kasba Peth, Near Surya Hospital, **Pune** 411 011
T.C. 25/ 2731 Lukes Lane, Ambujavilasam Road, **Thiruvananthapuram** 695 001

This edition has been published by Cambridge University Press India Pvt. Ltd. by arrangement with Cornell University Press.

First South Asia Edition 2012

ISBN 978-93-82264-08-8

Published by Manas Saikia for Cambridge University Press India Pvt. Ltd. and printed at Sanat Printers, Kundli, Haryana

For Lauren

The same repressive face that makes the developmental state an anathema to labor makes it useful to capital. Useful, that is, as long as traditional repressive methods work. Once labor gains enough power to make peace depend on more sophisticated forms of industrial relations, the absence of legitimate ties to labor becomes a disadvantage. The developmental state may begin to look more like an albatross than a valued protector of entrepreneurial interests.

—Peter Evans, *Embedded Autonomy*

Contents

Tables and Figures

Tables

Figures

Preface

This book is about the politics of industrial conflict and industrial peace in South Asia. Contrary to conventional wisdom, it argues that democracies are better at managing industrial conflict than authoritarian regimes. This is because democracies have two unique tools at their disposal for managing worker protest—mutually beneficial union-party ties and worker rights.

Political competition provides incentives to political parties to mobilize the support of the working-class as part of a strategy for winning elections, resulting in ties between parties and unions. At the same time, the pressure to win elections also encourages parties to restrain and institutionalize the protest of affiliated unions in support of broader developmental goals. This is especially true of major political parties, which are encompassing organizations that internalize the militant behavior of affiliated unions.

Democracies also afford workers with rights such as the right to form unions, the right to strike, and the right to engage in collective bargaining. These rights—typically referred to by scholars as freedom of association and collective bargaining (FACB) rights—form the bedrock of institutionalized grievance resolution. FACB rights enable workers to air their grievances in such institutions as labor courts, labor tribunals, and arbitration proceedings without being co-opted or coerced. FACB rights also provide workers with the tools they need (the right to strike chief among these) to effectively press their demands at the collective bargaining table.

By contrast, authoritarian governments have tended to keep unions at arms length and to sever mutually beneficial ties. Historically, the repression and exclusion of unions has had extremely deleterious effects on labor relations throughout the developing world. Not only have authoritarian regimes systematically eroded synergistic ties and worker rights, their repressive tactics have provoked a backlash among workers who increasingly view the state and employers with hostility and suspicion and engage in ever-more aggressive protest tactics to challenge their authority.

Throughout this book I test these arguments using a mixed-methods approach with evidence from the industrial sector in South Asia. I focus mainly on India but contrast India with Sri Lanka as a comparison case. I draw heavily on original qualitative interviews and survey evidence from Sri Lanka and three Indian states—Kerala, Maharashtra, and West Bengal—to test the political theory of union behavior described above. I also analyze panel data from fifteen Indian states to evaluate the relationship between political competition and worker protest and to study the effects of protective labor legislation on economic performance.

The book's main finding—that democracy promotes industrial relations and economic performance—has profound implications for debates about democracy and economic growth. Scholars have not found a straightforward relationship between democracy and economic growth; however, they have noted the many ways in which political and social stability matter for investment, productivity, and output. For many years the "developmental state approach" within political economy promoted the view that authoritarian regimes were better at providing this stability than democracies. This view was largely based on the experience of East Asia, where so-called "plan-rational bureaucracies" subdued labor in favor of broader economic objectives. Although the third wave of democratization may have rendered this perspective obsolete, few theories about how states can control labor in the absence of repression have emerged. This book fills this gap by showing how democratic governments in India manage organized labor and industrial conflict.

The results uncovered in this book also have substantial implications for public policy. Although many countries have adopted the institutional trappings of democracy, many newly democratic countries continue to repress organized labor. I suggest that the continued exclusion and suppression of unions is not conducive to growth. I also suggest that countries must undergo further political liberalization to achieve the more sophisticated types of growth-enhancing management of industrial protest seen throughout many parts of South Asia.

While the book finds much to be lauded in the South Asian context, it also suggests some areas where governments could improve the quality of state-labor relations. Sri Lanka continues to rely heavily on labor-repressive tactics, such as export processing zones, to boost its production of low-end manufactured goods. And while India has some of the most robust protections of worker rights in the world, its industrial law harbors clauses that make it difficult for workers to strike in particular industries. These repressive tactics continue to serve as a major constraint on growth in the region. In recent years policymakers in Sri Lanka have made a number of antidemocratic choices, while policymakers in India have weakened worker rights by undermining employment protection provisions in industrial law. Policymakers in both countries would do well to expend more of their effort on ensuring the protection of worker rights.

Acknowledgments

In writing this book, I have incurred many more debts than I can list here, and many deeper debts than can be repaid through a simple "thank you." To those whom I fail to mention and those I owe deep debts, my apologies.

I owe a special debt of gratitude to Ron Herring for his support, guidance and energetic criticism. Ron's frequent and engaging critiques of my writing pushed me to think more broadly, helping me to link my narrow empirical interests to a much larger set of theoretical issues. Without Ron's influence, this book would have been about union protest, but not democracy or development.

Chris Way's unique gift for teaching made the quantitative analysis in this book possible. Chris also influenced the theoretical trajectory of the project by introducing me to the theories of Mancur Olson and delivering many rounds of detailed comments on early drafts of the book's core chapters. I am grateful to Jonas Pontusson for his insights into the political economy of OECD countries and patient encouragement when the going got tough. I owe Sidney Tarrow a debt of gratitude for his thoughts about social movement theory, his multiple rounds of helpful comments, and for administering a dose of reality whenever my ego got bigger than my work ethic.

I also owe a special debt of gratitude to Brent Brossmann, Verghese Chirayath, Dwight Hahn, Pamela Mason, Chris Roark, Jim Swindal, and Victoria Voytko of John Carroll University for their support.

The research for this book depended on the generous hospitality and assistance of numerous people in South Asia. In addition to room and board, Sutami Ratnavale provided countless hours of friendly conversation that made Colombo feel like a second home. I thank Kumari Jayawardena whose generous support and enthusiasm greatly facilitated my work in Sri Lanka. I am grateful to Gayani Silva, whose capable research assistance made interviews with local trade union leaders possible and to Vidya Abhayagunawardena for his friendship and support. Franklin Amerasinghe provided generous assistance for my work during his tenure as secretary-general of the Employers' Federation of Ceylon. I am also grateful for the loyalty of Abeysekera, my regular taxi driver who helped me negotiate Colombo's crowded streets from the day I arrived. In Mumbai, my research was facilitated by the generosity of the Yagnik family, who graciously allowed me to stay in their centrally located flat. In Calcutta, I benefited from the friendship and help of the Gupta family, and I am grateful to Mr. Aurobindo Ray for room, board, and many stimulating conversations. In Kerala, I was encouraged by the warm generosity of my late Malayalam instructor, Professor Andrews Kutty, and enjoyed the many hours I spent discussing politics and all-things-Kerala with my friend Patricia Swart.

Data collection was enhanced by cooperation from union leaders and company managers and directors who were extraordinarily generous with their time in interviews. The high response rates of my surveys speak to the willingness of these individuals to assist me with my work. While I hope that my work can be of use to them, I realize that my debt to the business community and trade union leaders in South Asia can never be fully repaid.

The field research for the book received support from a Fulbright fellowship, a Fulbright-Hays Doctoral Dissertation Research Abroad (DDRA) fellowship, a Social Science Research Council (SSRC) International Dissertation Research Fellowship (IDRF), and a National Science Foundation (NSF) grant. Subsequent data collection benefitted from George Washington University's Sigur Center for Asian Studies.

Since arriving in Washington, D.C., the manuscript has benefited enormously through my interaction with colleagues in GW's political science department and the Elliott School for International Affairs. I cannot imagine a more supportive or engaging group of colleagues. I owe special thanks to Eric Lawrence for his constant availability and quick responses to my methods questions. I am very grateful to Kimberly Morgan, who has served informally as a mentor to me at GW and who commented on the entire manuscript. Her encouragement and guidance were immensely important to the completion of this manuscript. I am also grateful to Jim Goldgeier, who took it upon himself to organize a book workshop that resulted in enormous feedback on the manuscript. I also thank the participants of that workshop, and especially the discussants—Teri Caraway, Henry Farrell, and Raj Desai—all of whom read substantial portions of the manuscript and provided valuable feedback. I am also grateful for the feedback I received from colleagues at the George Washington University Comparative Politics Workshop and the GW political science department's Junior Faculty Seminar. At GW, I also benefitted from the assistance of many excellent research assistants. I am especially grateful to Christopher Mitchell and Stoyan Stoyanov for their support in gathering the data and coding the labor law indices used in chapter 5.

This book also benefitted from numerous comments from colleagues at other universities. I thank Leila Agha for her tremendously helpful feedback on the analysis in chapter 5 and to Irfan Nooruddin who gave insightful comments on chapters 1–4. I am also thankful to the many participants and discussants of conferences and workshops, including the University of Chicago Comparative Politics Workshop, the Workshop on Labor Rights and Multinational Production at the University of North Carolina Chapel Hill, the Workshop on Labor and Globalization at SUNY Binghamton, the annual meetings of the American Political Science Association, and the annual meetings of the Midwest Political Science Association. While all of the feedback at these evens was useful, I am especially grateful to Graeme Robertson and Andrew Schrank for their especially incisive and thought-provoking comments.

The analysis in chapter 4 is drawn from "Mobilizing Restraint: Economic Reform and the Politics of Industrial Protest in South Asia," *World Politics* 62(4): 676–713. Copyright 2010 Trustees of Princeton University. It is reprinted here with the permission of Cambridge University Press. Parts of chapter 6 are reprinted from "Does a Developing Democracy Benefit from Labor Repression," *Journal of Developmental Studies* 43(5): 830–855, with the permission of Taylor & Francis Ltd. Parts of chapter 7 are drawn from "Recovering Class: Observations from the Subcontinent,"

Critical Asian Studies 38(4): 389–417, and reprinted with permission. See www.criticalasianstudies.org.

Finally, in writing this book, I have incurred enormous personal debts to friends and family who have provided their moral support over the years. The friendships from which I have benefitted are simply too numerous to list here, but I will always remember with special fondness my many friends from the graduate program at Cornell. I owe Steven Kelts, Eric Lawrence, John Sides, and Tom Young a debt of gratitude for many hours of conversation and encouragement in the gym and on the roads. I thank my mother, Mary Ann Teitelbaum and late father, Martin Teitelbaum, for their encouragement and inspiration. I thank my grandmother Rita Teitelbaum who has been so supportive in so many ways over so many years. I am grateful to Jenny and Allan Aronson for the ways they have enriched my life. I owe a debt of gratitude to Lauren Teitelbaum, who offered companionship and support as I wrote this book. Our three daughters, Olivia, Sophia, and Ella, have been an immeasurable source of joy that has made this process entirely bearable, even fun. This book is dedicated to Lauren, for being an amazing mom to the girls and a wonderful friend.

Abbreviations

ACW	Association of Chemical Workers
AEW	Association of Engineering Workers
AIFB	All India Forward Bloc
AITUC	All India Trade Union Congress
BCC	Bombay Chamber of Commerce
BJP	Bharatiya Janata Party
BKKM	Bharatiya Kamgar Karmachari Mahasangh
BKS	Bharatiya Kamgar Sena
BMS	Bharatiya Mazdoor Sangh
BOI	Sri Lanka Board of Investment
CACP	Commission on Agricultural Costs and Prices
CCC	Ceylon Chamber of Commerce
CFL	Ceylon Federation of Labor
CFTU	Ceylon Federation of Trade Unions
CII	Confederation of Indian Industry
CITU	Center for Indian Trade Unions
CIWU	Ceylon Industrial Workers' Union
CMU	Ceylon Mercantile Union
CP	Communist Party
CPI	Communist Party of India
CPM	Communist Party of India, Marxist
CSO	Central Statistical Organization
CTUF	Ceylon Trade Union Federation

DMK	Dravida Munnetra Kazhagam
EFC	Employers' Federation of Ceylon
EOI	Export Oriented Industrialization
EPZ	Export Processing Zones
FACB	freedom of association and collective bargaining (rights)
FCI	Food Corporation of India
FDI	foreign direct investment
GCEC	Greater Colombo Economic Commission
GDP	gross domestic product
GOI	Government of India
ICEU	Intercompanies Employees Union
ICFTU	International Confederation of Free Trade Unions
IDA	Industrial Disputes Act
ILO	International Labor Organization
INTTUC	Indian Trinamool Trade Union Congress
INTUC	Indian National Trade Union Congress
ISI	import substitution industrialization
IT	information technology
JSS	Jathika Sevaka Sangamaya
JVP	Jathika Vimukthi Peramuna
KC	Kerala Congress
KUS	Kamgar Utkarsh Sabha
LSSP	Lanka Sama Samaja Party
MDMK	Marumalarchi Dravida Munnetra Kazhagam
MGKU	Maharashtra Girni Kamgar Union
MLA	Member of the Legislative Assembly
MPU	major party union
NCP	Nationalist Congress Party
NIC	newly industrialized country
NIU	narrow interest union
NSSP	Nawa Sama Samaja Party
OECD	Organization for Economic Cooperation and Development
RJD	Rashtriya Janata Dal
RSP	Revolutionary Socialist Party
SLFP	Sri Lanka Freedom Party
SLNSS	Sri Lanka Nidahas Sevaka Sangamaya
SSI	small-scale industry

TMC	Trinamool Congress
UF	United Front
UNP	United National Party
UPA	United Progressive Alliance
VRS	voluntary retirement scheme
WTO	World Trade Organization

MOBILIZING RESTRAINT

CHAPTER 1

Introduction

The Political Management of Industrial Conflict

How should developing countries manage the social and economic tensions inherent in periods of rapid economic change? Are democratic states handicapped in their efforts to promote rapid economic growth by the fact that they afford workers greater freedom to form unions and to strike? Or do the freedoms afforded to workers make protest more manageable over time?

These questions are hardly new. From the moment the Luddites began destroying looms in nineteenth-century Britain, states have struggled to manage the dislocation and unrest associated with modern factory production. Governments have employed a variety of strategies to curtail and institutionalize industrial conflict, ranging from the summary execution of union leaders to the enactment of legislation designed to promote collective bargaining and third-party mediation. For their part, trade unions have responded to the state in different ways. Some unions eschew politics altogether, while others develop close ties to political parties and invite government intervention in industrial disputes.

Today, the fiercest and most destabilizing industrial conflicts occur in low- and middle-income countries, where workers struggle to contend with the pressures and uncertainty associated with greater exposure to the global economy. Numerous examples illustrate how governments have endeavored to contain the damaging waves of economic protest related to market liberalization over the last two decades. Most prominently, China has grappled with the rising tide of headline-grabbing protest that has accompanied the phenomenal surge in foreign direct investment (FDI) and rapid industrial growth in that country (Gallagher 2005; Keidel 2005). Similarly, in the 1990s, Southeast Asian countries experienced a surge in violent worker protest associated with export-oriented development and greater exposure to trade (Kammen 1997). And over the last two decades, Latin American governments have sought to co-opt and undermine the organizational capacity of unions in order to push through neoliberal economic reforms (Kurtz 2004).

For many years, the conventional wisdom held that the repression and political exclusion of labor was necessary to promote industrial peace and economic growth. The continued policy relevance of this opinion is demonstrated by the fact that democratic ideals and institutions have spread through the developing world at a faster pace than commitments to labor rights. Despite the ubiquity of elections and parliaments, capitalism in most low- and middle-income countries continues to be characterized by despotic industrial relations as well as state exclusion and repression of organized labor. According to one source, labor rights are "severely restricted" in 41 percent of countries in Africa, Asia, and Latin America and "somewhat protected" in 58 percent of these countries. Out of the 135 countries listed in these three regions, labor rights are "fully protected" in just one (Japan).[1]

The available evidence, however, sheds doubt on the notion that labor repression constitutes a long-term viable strategy for managing industrial conflict in low- and middle-income countries. Findings in political science indicate that regime type does not correlate with developmental success, implicitly calling into question the argument that labor-repressive regimes grow faster than labor-permissive regimes (Geddes 1991; Przeworski et al. 2000). Studies in economics and sociology, which I discuss in greater depth below, have demonstrated that labor repression produces labor market distortions that hinder growth and lead to worker backlash, resulting in more disruptive patterns of industrial and political protest in later periods. Moreover, the debate over the extent to which the wholesale Soviet-style repression of labor benefits development has increasingly become less relevant as the rapid spread of democratic ideals induces even authoritarian and hybrid regimes to employ more subtle tactics to subdue organized labor (Kim and Gandhi 2010; Robertson 2011).

At the same time, previous studies leave a number of important gaps in our understanding of state-labor relations in the developing world.

While we know that brutal authoritarian tactics fail to achieve labor peace, we do not know enough about *why* these tactics fail or *how* democracies succeed in promoting industrial relations stability. This book aims to fill this gap through an examination of state-labor relations in South Asia. Specifically, the analysis points to the critical importance of two aspects of political democracy for managing industrial unrest—political competition and worker rights.

Political competition increases the reliance of parties on unions to mobilize votes for the party. In this way, a more competitive political system encourages parties to offer union leaders and workers material benefits and political representation of worker interests in exchange for their help in meeting party objectives. Over time, the ties between parties and unions that develop out of this exchange help to stabilize industrial conflict by linking workers to the broader societal interest in rapid industrial development. Major political parties are encompassing organizations that internalize the externalities associated with aggressive protest by their affiliated unions (such as unemployment and lost investment). Party leaders therefore endeavor to restrain the protest of affiliated unions and to encourage union members to pursue institutionalized forms of grievance resolution. In this way, the deepening of democracy helps to reduce worker protest in the context of greater economic openness.

Democracy is also associated with robust freedom of association and collective bargaining (FACB) rights, which are important for the institutionalization of industrial conflict. Robust worker freedoms are essential to the success of collective bargaining and labor institutions such as labor tribunals and labor courts. Policies and practices that compliment FACB rights may invite more worker protest by encouraging workers to air their grievances, but they also provide more sophisticated tools for managing worker protest. Workers in competitive democracies are permitted to go on strike, have the right to organize independent unions and negotiate legally binding collective bargaining agreements, and are represented by union officials or labor lawyers in arbitration and other legal proceedings. Because they are better represented and better prepared to defend their interests, workers in regions or sectors with more robust FACB rights are less likely to engage in highly disruptive forms of protest. They are also less likely to be exploited by employers, and the absence of such exploitation reduces turnover and boosts labor productivity. For these reasons, the provision of FACB rights translates directly into better economic outcomes. Regions that provide more opportunities for institutionalized grievance resolution and better protection of worker rights will enjoy higher productivity, higher industrial output, and more investment than regions that do not.

In contrast, nondemocratic states lack the organic ties to labor present in democratic countries and the political competition that might encourage governments to effectively utilize such ties to restrain worker protest. Consequently, authoritarian states use labor law and labor institutions more as means to co-opt, marginalize, and smash organized labor than to resolve worker grievances. This book demonstrates how the political exclusion and repression of organized labor is a highly ineffective strategy for managing industrial unrest. Repressive legislation erodes worker confidence in the state and collective bargaining, thereby making its institutions less effective at resolving the types of workplace tensions that lead to wildcat strikes and violent acts of desperation.

The Challenge: Managing Class Conflict in a Developing Democracy

The politics of class conflict have featured prominently in debates over how developing countries can accelerate industrial growth. The most clearly articulated argument about class politics in this literature is that successful late developers achieve rapid growth in part through the political exclusion and repression of organized labor. This argument is closely related to the view that governments must adopt a benign authoritarianism and cannot "afford" full-fledged democracy in the early stages of industrial development. The belief that labor repression facilitates growth has been highly influential in the policy world; and while it has been contested in academic circles, there has been no effort to develop an alternative framework illustrating how developing democracies can effectively manage tensions in the industrial relations arena.

The argument that labor repression promotes industrial development has a long intellectual lineage. As early as the 1950s, economists worried that the premature political mobilization of working-class interests would increase consumption at the expense of investment (de Schweinitz 1959; Galenson 1959; Mehta 1957; Sturmthal 1960). Subsequently, the argument that labor promotes economic growth was popular in the political science literature pertaining to "bureaucratic authoritarianism," which emerged from the developmental experiences of Latin American countries. According to the bureaucratic authoritarian view, the transition to a more capital-intensive stage of import substitution industrialization required heavy investments in technology and capital, a disciplined and efficient workforce, and a demobilization of working-class opposition to more disciplined economic policies—goals that many believed could not be achieved absent repression of organized labor (O'Donnell 1973; 1978).

More recently, the argument that repression compliments development found expression in the concept of the "developmental state," a theoretical enterprise that has sought to explain rapid economic growth in East Asian countries. One of the primary arguments in the developmental state literature is that rapid industrial growth becomes possible when a "plan-rational" state enjoys "autonomy" from society. Put simply, late developers must adopt some form of benevolent authoritarianism to catch up with the West. Elite politics and the exclusion of civil society are thus an inherent part of the developmental state narrative. In Japan, elite government officials, highly skilled bureaucrats, and owners of heavy industry achieved rapid industrialization through steadfast cooperation and shrewd economic planning (Johnson 1982). Similarly, states in other East Asian countries succeeded in promoting industrial development through the heavy regulation of medium- and large-scale industries, and by coercing firms to invest in sectors state planners believed would be the most viable (Wade 1990). For some observers, the authoritarian state-society relations useful for planning were also useful for producing the docile workforce that facilitated the East Asian "miracle" of decades of uninterrupted export-oriented growth (e.g., Deyo 1989; Haggard 1990).

As heavy industry took off in these newly industrialized countries (NICs), production of low-end manufactured products shifted to lower-wage venues. For many years, the vast majority of investment and jobs in low-end manufacturing went to China, which has been just as authoritarian in its handling of labor as the East Asian NICs. Nevertheless, labor shortages have recently fueled a wave of strikes as well as rapid wage growth in Chinese cities. In response, multinationals have begun shifting production—to rural areas in China but also to countries in South and Southeast Asia. Workers in many of these countries enjoy robust FACB rights and legal protections. Will employers encounter better or worse industrial relations conditions outside of the authoritarian contexts in which they are accustomed to operating?

By most accounts, South Asian countries have never emerged as successful developmental states. Herring, for example, characterizes India as "a state committed to planning, yet too democratic, soft and embedded to govern the market" (Herring 1999, 309). The highly pluralist and regionally fragmented political system has prevented the emergence of a coherent class-based politics at the center (Rudolph and Rudolph 1987, 20). Historically this absence of class cohesion prevented the owners of private capital from emerging as a dominant distributional coalition and allowed conservative factions of the Indian National Congress (INC) to agitate against planning (Chibber 2003, chap. 4). The lack of class cohesion on the part of industrialists has also meant that South Asian governments have been unable or unwilling to suppress organized labor, ensuring the continued vibrancy of the Indian labor movement in both the political and industrial relations arenas (Teitelbaum 2008). For most observers, the presence of a highly mobilized workforce and absence of class cohesion among elites put India at a disadvantage relative to East Asian countries, where the state could direct private investments to the most profitable sectors while holding wages at artificially low levels to squeeze productivity out of a docile workforce (e.g., Kohli 2004).

The notion that a cohesive state representing the interests of capitalists and planners must dominate a quiescent labor force as a prerequisite for industrial growth is pervasive, but it has not gone unchallenged. It is unclear, for example, whether unions in developing countries push up overall consumption enough to trade off with investment, or whether labor repression can push down consumption enough to boost economic growth (Freedman 1960; Fisher 1961). Even among the East Asian tigers, the link between repression and economic growth has not been demonstrated. On the contrary, a study of six East Asian countries showed that adherence to core labor standards had no effect on economic growth, and that East Asian growth rates did not result from labor repression (Freeman 1993). Moreover, in East Asian countries where the government was successful in repressing wages, the strategy backfired by generating artificial shortages (Fields 1994). In its study of the East Asian growth miracle, the World Bank suggests that, rather than being the result of labor repression, East Asian growth occurred because of substantial investments in infrastructure and human capital (World Bank 1993).

Additionally, repression can backfire in a number of ways. Cross-national comparisons suggest that labor-repressive countries experience more labor market distortions than nonrepressive countries (Banerji and Ghanem 1995), while a number of country studies show how repression generates more disruptive patterns of industrial protest. Freeman (1993) argues that the East Asian "crush strategy" of the 1970s led to a sudden burst of labor discontent and unionization in East Asian countries in later periods. Similarly, Evans (1995) suggests that repression in South Korea gave rise to a surge of industrial protest in the late 1980s and Seidman (1994) shows how the efforts of authoritarian states to deepen industrialization "manufactured militance" among industrial workers in Brazil and South Africa, ultimately placing workers at the forefront of democratic transitions in these countries.

While scholars have recognized that repression does not always work, the need to move beyond the discussion of whether repression succeeds or fails as a developmental strategy is apparent. With a handful of notable exceptions (e.g., Evans 1995; Heller 1999), existing studies fail to acknowledge that developing countries are capable of sophisticated strategies for engaging organized labor. Yet, as I discuss below, democracies have unique tools at their disposal for managing industrial conflict. Moreover, these tools tend to work very well in the pluralist settings prevalent in developing democracies, and are not dependent on a highly developed class politics or well-articulated corporatist political structures.

Economic Change and Industrial Conflict in South Asia

This book develops new arguments about the political management of industrial protest by drawing on data from the private manufacturing sector in South Asia where, over the course of the past three decades, economic reforms have increasingly placed the objectives of union leaders and party leaders at odds. Like their counterparts in other regions, policymakers in South Asia perceive industrial unrest as a major threat to investment and rapid economic growth.[2] By freeing investment and product markets from the grip of central government control, economic reforms have forced regional governments to compete with one another over private sector investment. This need to promote private sector investment has, in turn, increased the pressure on policymakers to restrain the protest of affiliated unions. At the same time, by exposing workers to market forces, reforms have made it more difficult for unions to win their demands, providing individual union leaders with incentives to ratchet up pressure against the management.

Within South Asia, the process of economic reform has been most robust in India and Sri Lanka, where national and regional governments have adopted economic policies that garnered broad support among voters and, with the exception of workers in the private manufacturing sector, presented very little challenge to traditional economic stakeholders.[3] In India the process of economic reform began in the 1980s as a halting, stealthy, and elite-led process, but then gained steam and wider support among the electorate during the 1990s.[4] Popular support for reforms came even earlier in Sri Lanka. In 1977 the center-right United National Party (UNP) came to power winning 83 percent of the seats in parliament on a platform of economic liberalization, a victory that was widely interpreted as a voter mandate for the UNP's proposed reforms.[5]

Despite their popularity among voters, the reforms presented a challenge to political parties by reducing the scope of public sector employment, which had historically served as a major source of political patronage (Chandra 2004). In the wake of the reforms, public sector job growth declined, particularly in manufacturing. During the 1980s and the early 1990s the Sri Lankan government began privatizing public sector industries in earnest as it simultaneously ramped up public investments designed to boost exports in low-end manufacturing. And while India has generally taken a gradualist approach to privatization, total employment in the public sector stalled at about 194 million jobs and began to trend downward toward the end of the 1990s as the government slowed investments in the public sector and began to privatize some of the larger public manufacturing companies (Kapur and Ramamurti 2002).[6]

In combination with the popularity of the reforms, this reduction in the availability of patronage resources put pressure on political leaders to stimulate investment and job growth in the private sector. Consequently political parties boosted their efforts to attract private sector investment, both domestic and foreign, to their regions through a variety of investor-friendly policies (Sinha 2005). Much of this effort focused on improving labor-market flexibility and industrial relations. Sri Lanka set up "export processing zones" (EPZs) where labor laws were not enforced and unions were prohibited from organizing, while states in India stopped enforcing some of its most stringent labor regulations. State governments turned a blind eye, for example, to provisions of the Industrial Disputes Act of 1947 (IDA) that require a company to seek government approval to retrench workers (section 25M) or to close a factory (section 25N) (Bardhan 1998).

The need to attract new investors also spurred major political parties to proactively moderate protest by affiliated unions. Such efforts involved drawing on ties with unions to mobilize worker restraint and putting to better use aspects of the IDA designed to institutionalize grievance resolution. This was true for all political parties, regardless of their political stripe. In the southwestern state of Kerala, leaders of the Communist Party of India (Marxist) (CPM) endeavored to forge class compromise as part of a broader effort to woo private investors back to the state (Heller 1999). Similarly, in West Bengal, Jyoti Basu, a CPM politburo member and chief minister from 1977 to 2000, traveled far and wide in the 1990s on a public relations campaign to overcome West Bengal's image as a "red state" and to attract international investment. Buddhadeb Bhattacharya, also a CPM politburo member, closely followed the example of his predecessor in the early and mid-2000s.

At the same time that regional governments in South Asia have struggled to promote investment and private sector job growth, greater economic openness has entailed increasing difficulties in the industrial relations arena. Workers in manufacturing began to contend with more competitive domestic product markets as early as the 1970s, when the bargaining power of unions was reduced by a dramatic increase in competition from rural and small-scale production units. These changes, along with the more recent neoliberal reforms that exposed the manufacturing sector to international competition, have put downward pressure on wages, made it difficult for unions to win their demands, and rendered routine strike tactics less effective.

Prevailing labor market conditions thereby put pressure on individual union leaders to mobilize resistance—to ratchet up militancy to overcome employer recalcitrance at the bargaining table. Fearing reputational damage from their inability to call out strikes and negotiate favorable contracts, some union leaders responded to new economic pressures by piling on demands and applying more aggressive and unorthodox protest tactics, including the strategic use of collective violence. The overall dynamic thus became one in which workers were reticent to go on strike, but those that did go on strike took a more aggressive and unorthodox approach to voicing their demands. In recent years, a number of high-profile strikes have called international attention to the increasingly tense and turbulent industrial relations environment in South Asia. In many of these strikes workers engage in acts of desperation like climbing to the top of high structures and threatening to jump or dousing themselves in kerosene. Others involve acts of vandalism, hostage takings, or violent confrontation between management and workers. In a small number of cases, such confrontations have even resulted in the deaths of workers or managers.

The Political Logic of Industrial Conflict

Despite the general trend toward a more tense industrial relations environment in South Asia, there has been substantial variation in patterns of industrial protest across regions and individual firms. This variation in the character of industrial protest gives rise to the central puzzle explored in this book: in the era of economic reforms, why do some labor union leaders restrain worker protest to facilitate social stability and long-term economic performance, while others use economic hardship to ratchet up militancy against employers and the state? My analysis points to two aspects of political democracy that are critical to the effective management of industrial conflict—political competition and the provision of FACB rights.

Political Competition

By engendering political competition and participation, democracy plays an important role in the effective management of industrial conflict. Enhanced electoral competition and voter turnout dramatically alter the relationship between political parties and the working class. On one hand, as was noted above, democracy magnifies pressures on politicians to promote private sector investment and industrial relations stability. The demands of voters for better-paying jobs become louder as voter turnout increases, and politicians come under greater pressure to respond to voters as winning margins in political contests become narrower. New platforms and positions unsettle economic debates as party systems become more dynamic and competitive, and new economic objectives can be antithetical to the interests of the working class.

On the other hand, competitive democracy requires parties to mobilize workers as a base of support, both as an important bloc of voters and as a key interest group capable of obstructing reform efforts. Consequently union-party ties have become an important tool for party leaders to mobilize worker support for party objectives. Union partisan ties have been shown to influence a variety of important outcomes, including the pace and success of democratic transitions (e.g., Collier and Collier 1991), the political viability of contentious economic reforms (Burgess 2004; Murillo 2001), and economic performance in advanced industrial democracies (e.g., Alvarez, Garrett, and Lange 1991; Garrett 1998). By serving as a conduit through which parties transmit their preferences about industrial relations outcomes, union partisan ties can have similarly important implications for the level and character of industrial conflict.

Democracy in South Asia, as in other regions, has been associated with strong union-party ties. In most parts of India, union partisan ties have been robust and enduring, with major parties such as INC and CPM relying on affiliated unions to mobilize votes and explain economic conditions and party objectives to the industrial workforce. Moreover, parties continually forge new alliances with workers. The Bharatiya Janata Party (BJP), for example, had a great deal of success in mobilizing workers during the 1990s and early 2000s with its affiliated union, the Bharatiya Mazdoor Sangh (BMS). In every case, however, the establishment of party-affiliated unions is a strategic choice on the part of party leaders designed to enhance the party's organizational capacity, its share of the vote and support for its polices. Union support for policies can manifest itself in a variety of ways, including in the industrial relations arena. Previous studies have provided good preliminary evidence of this link between union-party ties and class compromise in collective bargaining. In Kerala, left unions have helped to reduce wage militancy and forge productivity-linked wage agreements (Heller 1999), and in Mumbai politically affiliated unions have negotiated more modest wage agreements than nonaffiliated unions (Battacharjee 1987).

How do parties go about mobilizing restraint? In a democratic context, where unions are voluntary organizations competing against many other unions over members, party leaders are compelled to rely on inducements more than constraints in persuading union leaders and members of the value of party directives. While some unions may occasionally resort to force to ensure compliance with party directives, the frequent use of violence can diminish the reputation of union leaders and encourage workers to defect to competing union organizations. Union ties to political parties are typically comprised of overlapping leadership structures, meaning that powerful figures in the union movement are also powerful leaders in the political party. This organizational overlap provides the party with potential leverage over union leaders who are also party leaders, as well as union leaders who aspire to climb the ranks of party leadership. In this way, union-party ties provide a powerful alternative to labor repression in state efforts to curtail and institutionalize worker protest.

In authoritarian settings, by contrast, parties have been less inclined to develop strong ties with unions and lack the more subtle forms of control that emerge from stable relationships between parties and unions. In authoritarian Pakistan, for example, unions have been heavily repressed and the working class denied any meaningful role in politics (Candland 2001; 2007). In Bangladesh and Sri Lanka, the extent and quality of state-labor ties has varied tremendously over time, with governments facilitating union-party ties during democratic periods and eviscerating them during periods in which democracy has faltered.

The Logic of Political Encompassment

Even though democracy induces political parties to promote better labor-management relations, not all unions within a democracy mobilize restraint. My analysis reveals a political dynamic, *the logic of political encompassment,* which explains why unions affiliated to major political parties in particular are more likely to restrain union protest in adverse economic circumstances than leaders of small-party and political independent unions. The argument derives from the theory of organizational encompassment developed by Mancur Olson, which predicts that the behavior of encompassing organizations differs from that of individuals or narrow interest groups because encompassing organizations internalize the externalities associated with their actions (1982, 47–53).

In the political economy of wage bargaining in OECD countries, this argument is typically referred to as the "logic of encompassment" and has been broadly applied to explain wage restraint in the collective bargaining arena (e.g., Cameron 1984; Calmfors and Driffil 1988). The standard argument holds that large unions are more restrained in their negotiating tactics because their membership constitutes a substantial percentage of the population. It is therefore assumed that the union is the relevant encompassing organization that restrains the behavior of firm-level union leaders and workers.

But Olson's analysis has implications for the behavior of a variety of organizations, including political parties. It thus makes sense to ask whether the encompassment of political parties also matters for union behavior. This question is especially pertinent for developing countries, where even in highly fragmented systems political parties are frequently more encompassing than unions. In such situations, the preferences of party leaders may diverge from those of union leaders. This argument has implications for industrial relations that have thus far gone unexamined in studies of industrial relations and the political economy of wage bargaining. As long as political parties represent the interests of a broader constituency than unions, party leaders will advocate a more conservative approach to bargaining and protest than union leaders.

Crucially, however, I argue that the relationship between encompassment and worker restraint is nonmonotonic. In a competitive democracy major parties internalize externalities, but if a party becomes *too powerful* this tendency will decline. The absence of viable political opposition can render encompassing parties unresponsive to the concerns of voters and workers alike. Encompassment is therefore most likely to promote industrial peace when the fortunes of major political parties are likely to suffer as a result of the economic fallout associated with industrial conflict, such as unemployment and lost investment. Under such circumstances political leaders endeavor to restrain worker protest in the face of challenging market conditions and encourage union members to pursue institutionalized forms of grievance resolution. It is for this reason that we would expect the competitiveness of the party system to be associated with a party's increased emphasis on worker restraint, even though such competition may erode the vote share of major political parties.

In contrast to leaders of major party unions, individual union leaders are not constrained by the interests of a broader constituency. In fact, individual leaders have an incentive to adopt aggressive bargaining and protest tactics, because these more threatening forms of protest have the potential to bring about larger and more rapid settlements. A successful settlement and the spectacle of aggression and violence can bring greater notoriety to a union leader, thereby attracting new members to the union. Thus, in the absence of external constraints, union leaders may ratchet up militancy in pursuit of self-interested goals such as a reputation for toughness and increased union membership.

Three Union Types

In this book, I identify three types of unions based on the nature of their affiliations with external organizations, and make specific predictions regarding how each type of union will respond to the rapidly changing economic conditions of the postreform period. The first type of union is the major party union (MPU), that is, the type with ties to a major political party. Because political parties internalize the externalities associated with aggressive protest by their affiliated unions, MPU federation leaders restrain the protest of local leaders and members in the face of new market conditions and promote institutionalized forms of grievance resolution. In other words, when presented with evidence that the health of a firm or the broader economy would be substantially jeopardized as a result of industrial protest, MPUs eschew aggressive protest tactics and mobilize worker restraint.

Absent ties to major political parties, unions will likely be less constrained in their approach to bargaining and protest. Thus I identify a second type of union, the "narrow interest union" (NIU), which has an external leadership that is either politically independent or affiliated with a small (e.g., nonencompassing) political party. The term *narrow interest* is used to remind the reader of my hypothesis that nonaffiliated unions often become vehicles for achieving the parochial interests of a small group of leaders. For this reason, I argue that NIU leaders are more likely than leaders of MPUs to encourage greater militancy even when a strike is unlikely to secure union demands. Moreover, when negotiations become complicated, leaders of small-party and politically independent unions can up the ante by encouraging the use of extreme forms of protest such as hostage takings, damaging company property, and violent assault because they are unconstrained by a broader set of political or economic interests.

In addition to MPUs and NIUs, we can identify a third type of union, which is characterized by a leadership that is entirely "in house" as opposed to being recruited from outside the firm. Throughout the book, I refer to this type of union as an "enterprise union," because its leadership is confined to a particular enterprise. Although enterprise union leaders may have incentives to engage in aggressive protest behavior, they lack material and informational resources that external unions provide. These resource deficits tend to prevent enterprise unions from taking the same aggressive stance toward management that NIUs might take. Instead, enterprise unions are more likely to behave like MPUs, engaging in routine protest and subdued negotiations with management when more competitive labor and product markets make it difficult to win strikes.

Worker Rights

In addition to a more competitive political system, democratization entails greater political freedoms. Historically, workers have led the struggle for political freedoms in new democracies by demanding greater FACB rights. FACB rights are central to the management of industrial conflict because they provide workers with the organizational tools they need to engage in institutionalized grievance resolution. Metaphorically speaking, FACB rights are like the grease that ensures the smooth functioning of the industrial relations machinery. Without FACB rights, workers cannot effectively mobilize or articulate their grievances. Lacking effective voice, workers will be unable to engage in collective bargaining, and the effectiveness of industrial relations institutions such as labor courts and tribunals will be undermined because workers will view them with deep suspicion.

State and national governments in South Asia inherited and adopted very similar legal systems, but have used them to channel industrial conflict in very different ways. This variation in the implementation of industrial relations law has had implications for industrial protest and ultimately economic performance. In recent years, numerous studies have purported to show the adverse economic effects of labor legislation, many of which have focused on India's large body of protective labor law (e.g., Aghion et al. 2008; Besley and Burgess 2004; Fallon and Lucas 1991 and 1993; Hasan et al. 2007). However, these studies focus heavily on provisions of the IDA that restrict labor flexibility while largely ignoring the potential benefits of government intervention in the industrial relations arena that promote worker participation in various forms of institutionalized grievance resolution. One aim of this book is to show how the core elements of India's industrial disputes law have benefited economic performance by facilitating third-party mediation and providing workers with a more equal voice in the negotiating process.

Studies of advanced industrial democracies have established how unions boost worker satisfaction and labor productivity by allowing workers to air their grievances and by ensuring that workers perceive the resolution of industrial disputes as fair and just (e.g., Aidt and Tzannatos 2002; Freeman and Medoff 1984). In developing countries, where unions are less established and levels of worker education are lower than in the OECD, state intervention in industrial disputes can offset the imbalance between unions and employers, thus helping unions to actualize their "voice function" and yielding benefits for productivity.

In addition, greater worker voice also helps to thwart exploitation and employer reliance on sweated labor. Reducing exploitation has intrinsic merit from a human rights perspective, while mitigating the use of sweated labor benefits human development by increasing demand for healthier and more educated workers. At the same time, providing workers with robust FACB rights also benefits economic growth because reducing labor exploitation forces employers to make investments in capital and technology that in turn promote capital deepening and increase economies of scale.

For these reasons, India's established body of industrial disputes law has largely enhanced economic performance in India even as it has invited workers to mobilize in favor of their economic interests. However, there have been limits to the effectiveness of state intervention in the industrial relations arena. I identify two types of legislation that have had adverse effects on the Indian economy. The first, which have thus far received the most attention by scholars, are amendments to IDA that restrict the ability of employers to hire and fire workers. But in contrast to most previous studies, I note that the effects of this type of strict employment protection legislation are isolated to just a handful of Indian states.

Another area of industrial disputes law that has had adverse effects on Indian industry, but which has so far not been analyzed, is the legislation declaring particular industries (sectors) as a "public utility." Under the IDA, once an industry is declared a public utility, the government can impose severe restrictions on the ability of workers to call out strikes or employers to declare lockouts in that industry. Where it has been applied, this more heavy-handed form of state intervention in industrial disputes has shut down dialogue between workers and employers, and consequently has had exactly the opposite effect of legislation that promotes institutionalized grievance resolution and a more equal voice for workers. By reducing the space for negotiated settlement, public utilities legislation has generated more instability and worker alienation, thus diminishing investment, output, and productivity.

Case Selection, Data and Methods

South Asia boasts tremendous linguistic, cultural, economic, and political diversity that has been harnessed in numerous studies to explore an array of diverse questions, such as the determinants of human development (Drèze and Sen 1996), the effects of democratic politics on public spending (Saez and Sinha 2009), and the causes of agrarian insurgency (Urdal 2008). In a similar manner, this study uses variations in the level of democracy to examine how political competition and FACB rights relate to industrial conflict. Democracy varies both across and within South Asian countries. Within India the deepening of democracy has occurred in fits and starts, and unevenly across its great expanse. Until the late-1970s, democracy was characterized by the dominance of the INC. Following a brief suspension of democracy during the Emergency Period (1975–77), this one-party system unraveled as new regional and caste-based parties emerged to challenge Congress's dominance (Chhibber 1999). Meanwhile, India's neighbors have vacillated between democratic and authoritarian rule. Pakistan and Bangladesh have experienced extended periods of military dictatorship punctuated by periods of unstable democratic governance, while Nepal remained a monarchy until its very recent transition to a nascent democracy. While Sri Lanka has always enjoyed procedural democracy, the governments' respect for worker rights and other civil liberties has varied tremendously over time.

Regional Case Selection and Predictions

The core chapters of the book, which explore the effects of political competition and union-party ties on industrial relations, are based on original data from firm-level interviews and surveys conducted during eighteen months of field research in four regions in South Asia. The regional cases selected for this study include Sri Lanka and the Indian states of West Bengal, Kerala, and Maharashtra. These cases were selected based on the structure of the union movements and the extent of democratic deepening. The regional cases and the predicted industrial relations outcomes in each case are presented in the diagram in table 1.1

Kerala combines a union movement dominated by MPUs with very high levels of political competition and participation. In Kerala, two political union centers vie for control over the union movement—the Center for Indian Trade Unions (CITU), affiliated to the CPM or Communist Party of India (Marxist), and the INC-affiliated Indian National Trade Union Congress (INTUC). Propelled by the mobilization of working-class and lower-caste voters, Kerala's democracy is known as one of the most robust in the developing world (Heller 1999; 2000). Kerala's government is highly responsive to its citizens, and by almost any standard measure its political system is highly competitive. In the post-Emergency period parties have won elections in the state assembly (Vidhan Sabha) by an average margin of about 7 percent, whereas the average margin of victory across all major Indian states is 12 percent.[7] The party system is also more competitive than other states. For Kerala, the average "effective" number of parties competing in elections since the Emergency is 6.8 whereas the average across all states and years is 4.4.[8] The average number of parties holding power in the state assembly since 1977 is 5.3 and across all states the average is 2.8. Finally, voters in Kerala are highly mobilized. The average turnout for all post-Emergency elections in Kerala of 75 percent is higher than the all-state average of about 63 percent.

The theory developed in this book predicts highly favorable industrial relations outcomes in Kerala. Strong union-party ties provide the mechanism for parties to restrain and institutionalize protest, while competitive elections and voter participation produce the impetus to do so. Kerala will thus experience low overall levels of industrial conflict, and when conflict does occur it will be highly institutionalized.

TABLE 1.1
Regional cases

Regional case	Structure of union movement	Level of democracy	Predicted militancy
Kerala	**MPU Dominance:** Union movement controlled by two political union centers—the Center for Indian Trade Unions (CITU), affiliated to the Marxist CPM and the Congress-affiliated Indian National Trade Union Congress (INTUC).	**High:** Highly responsive and competitive democracy. Narrow winning margins, competitive party system and high voter turnout.	**Very Low:** MPUs very successful in restraining affiliated unions. Low levels of industrial conflict; highly institutionalized industrial relations.
West Bengal	**MPU Dominance:** Union movement controlled by two political union centers—CITU and INTUC, with CITU being the more dominant force.	**Moderate:** Competitive two-party system. Low party turnover but very narrow margins of victory and higher-than-average turnout.	**Low:** MPUs mostly successful in restraining affiliated unions. Moderate levels of industrial conflict; fairly institutionalized industrial relations.
Maharashtra	**Mixed:** Highly competitive union movement with equal presence of MPUs, NIUs, and enterprise unions.	**Moderate:** Competitive party system, but relatively high margins of victory and average turnout.	**Moderate:** MPUs restrain protest and enterprise unions quiescent, but NIUs engage in aggressive protest. Moderate levels of industrial conflict, but less institutionalized industrial relations.
Sri Lanka	**NIU Dominance:** NIUs dominate union movement; large presence of small-party and politically independent parent union organizations.	**Low:** Functions as a hybrid regime or "anocracy" in 1980s; legacy of labor repression has long-term implications for industrial relations.	**High:** MPUs unsuccessful in restraining protest while NIUs engage in aggressive protest. High levels of industrial conflict; extremely chaotic industrial relations.

Like Kerala, West Bengal's trade union movement is also mostly dominated by MPUs. In West Bengal, the CITU organizes a majority of workers in the manufacturing sector and competes with INTUC and, in more recent years, the Indian Trinamool Trade Union Congress (INTTUC)—an offshoot of the INTUC affiliated to the Trinamool Congress Party. At the same time, West Bengal's political system is slightly less competitive than Kerala's. By some measures West Bengal's democracy is highly developed. The average margin of victory for parties winning assembly elections has been about 4.5 percent since Independence (much lower than the national average) and voter turnout has been as high as in Kerala. However, West Bengal's party system has been less competitive and arguably less representative than many others. Since 1977, the party system in West Bengal has approximated a two-party system. The average effective number of parties competing in elections in West Bengal has been 3.7 and the average effect number of parties holding seats has been 2.7. The CPM, which is dominated by high-caste Hindus, recently celebrated thirty-three years of continuous rule.

The theory developed in this book therefore predicts that West Bengal will experience moderate levels of protest, and that protest will be fairly institutionalized when it occurs. Strong union-party ties provide the requisite tools for mobilizing restraint, but less intense political competition means that there is less impetus to restrain and institutionalize protest than in Kerala.

In contrast to the union movements of Kerala and West Bengal, the union movement in Maharashtra is much more diverse in its composition. In Maharashtra, a number of MPUs and NIUs vie for the allegiance of the working class and a large percentage of manufacturing firms have in-house unions. Maharashtra's party system is more dynamic and representative of lower-caste voters than West Bengal's. Since 1977, the average effective number of parties competing in elections has been 5.3 and the average effective number of parties holding seats has been 3.8. But turnout is at about the national average and winning margins in state assembly elections are much higher than the national average.[9] Since 1977, the average margin of victory in Maharashtra has been about 17 percent.

Consequently, my proposed theoretical framework predicts that like West Bengal, Maharashtra will experience mixed industrial relations outcomes, but for slightly different reasons. A moderately competitive political system compels political leaders to reduce industrial conflict in favor of investment and job growth and some workers are organized by MPUs who endeavor to restrain their protest. Enterprise unions are also quiescent. However, the mixed composition of the labor movement also entails a large number of NIUs that are more aggressive in terms of the protest tactics they employ. Thus I predict that Maharashtra will encounter moderate levels of protest due to the restraint of MPUs and the quiescence of enterprise unions, but that when protest does occur it will be less institutionalized than in Kerala or West Bengal.

Sri Lanka serves as the illustration of how the evisceration of union-party ties and a relatively fragile democracy give rise to very poor industrial relations outcomes. A long period of labor repression in Sri Lanka served to decimate legitimate ties between parties and unions. Thus politically independent parent unions and parent unions affiliated to small political parties dominate the Sri Lankan union movement. The theory outlined in this book predicts that the dominance of NIUs along with shaky democracy will make Sri Lankan industrial relations uniquely unstable.

Sri Lanka is a nation-state and therefore differs from the other three cases, which are states within the Indian federation. Selecting a case from outside of India for this study was in some sense unavoidable. India has been a relatively stable democracy in the post-Independence period, so it is difficult to illustrate the deleterious effects of labor repression solely relying on evidence from India. Moreover, it is difficult to identify a region with both a low density of major party unions *and* low levels of political competition since a large percentage of workers in most regions in India are organized by MPUs. Nevertheless, it is important to acknowledge that Sri Lanka is different from the other cases and to account for this difference in the subsequent analysis of industrial conflict.

Interviews and Surveys

Within each regional case, I randomly selected senior managers from individual manufacturing firms as well as federation union leaders for participation in surveys and interviews. First, in order to establish the frequency of violent, nonroutine, and routine protest events in each regional case, I randomly selected approximately a hundred firms from directories of manufacturers for participation in a brief telephone survey. In these surveys, I asked senior managers questions about recent industrial protest and the affiliations of any unions in manufacturing units owned by the firm. The data from these surveys help to show how industrial conflict in each regional case relates to levels of political competition and the structure of union movement.

Subsequently, I randomly selected a subsample of approximately forty firms for participation in a structured in-depth interview from the list of a hundred firms participating in the telephone survey. In each interview, I asked respondents more in-depth questions about protest events experienced by the union and the relationship between the company's workers and external unions. These in-depth interviews yielded fine-grained data on hundreds of protest events that could be used in a firm-level statistical analysis of industrial protest. The in-depth company interviews also yielded valuable narratives regarding how the external affiliations of unions affect union protest behavior.

Finally, I conducted interviews with the leaders of union federations that organized workers in the manufacturing companies selected for in-depth interviews. These interviews provided a check against senior managers' accounts of the motivations and behavior of workers. Interviews with union leaders also yielded valuable insights regarding the motivations of union leaders in encouraging workers to engage in protest or refrain from it. In the case of politically affiliated unions, union leaders provided information regarding the origins and trajectory of the union's relationship with the political party.

Other Data Sources

In addition to original survey data, this study draws on data from secondary sources, including data on labor protest, elections, and economic performance for fifteen major Indian states. These data permit a broader test of the argument that electoral competition reduces industrial conflict in a cross-section time-series framework. They are also used to examine the effects of industrial disputes legislation on industrial protest and economic performance. Finally, I draw on sector-level data for a more fine-grained analysis of how "public utilities" laws, which are designed to limit union activity and restrict strikes, affect economic performance.

Structure of the Book

The remaining chapters of this book elaborate on the major themes developed in this introduction. The book divides into two parts. The first part, composed of chapters 2 and 3, presents in greater detail the puzzle and the argument of the book. In chapter 2, I outline the dynamics of industrial protest during the 1980s and 1990s, when most national and regional governments in South Asia undertook major economic reforms. The common trend across all regions was a decline in the frequency of routine strike protest and a simultaneous rise in nonroutine and violent forms of industrial protest. Economic reforms generated more product and labor market competition that made employers less likely to give in to union demands. In response to employer recalcitrance, some unions began to ratchet up pressure on management by resorting to more aggressive tactics, whereas others simply engaged in less protest. These basic protest dynamics constitute the puzzle that is addressed by the remainder of the chapters in the book: why do some union leaders respond to hardship by ratcheting up pressure on the management, whereas others encourage their members to exercise restraint?

In chapter 3, I develop the central argument of the book—that union response to economic conditions is the product of political competition and FACB rights. The chapter draws on evidence from interviews with employers and union leaders to illustrate the differing motivations of major party and narrow interest union leaders. I also discuss the interests motivating the behavior of enterprise unions and unorganized workers, and explain why these types of unions are likely to be quiescent.

The second part of the book presents empirical evidence to support the arguments developed in chapter 3. In chapter 4, I test the argument about political competition using a mix of secondary source data from fifteen Indian states and original survey and in-depth interview data gathered in four regions of South Asia (Sri Lanka and the Indian states of Kerala, Maharashtra, and West Bengal). Data from the fifteen Indian states demonstrate a negative relationship between political competition and industrial protest while original survey data help to establish the causal mechanism at work, namely the strength of union-party ties. The results of a telephone survey show that regions with democracy and a high presence of MPUs experience less protest than regions with less democracy and union movements that are dominated by NIUs. An analysis of data from in-depth surveys shows that unions controlled by major political parties are less likely to go on strike and less likely to engage in violence than workers controlled by narrow interest unions.

In chapter 5, I examine the impact of the provision of worker rights on economic performance through an analysis of labor legislation enacted in the Indian states. The analysis in this chapter demonstrates how legislation that promotes third-party mediation and worker rights is correlated with better economic performance and, conversely, how legislation that inhibits freedom of association hinders growth. The first part of this analysis demonstrates the beneficial effects of legislation that promotes worker access to industrial relations institutions such as industrial tribunals, labor courts, and conciliation proceedings. The second part of the analysis shows the deleterious effects of legal provisions that are used to prohibit strikes in particular economic sectors.

In chapter 6, I explore the effects of labor repression in Sri Lanka, where labor repression has served to disrupt the link between federations affiliated to major left parties and their local leaders and members. This disruption of ties set up a two-part dynamic. First, encompassing left parties, which had a political interest in restraining and institutionalizing worker protest, became unable to defend workers effectively and thereby lost control over local union leaders and members. Thus members of unions affiliated to left parties took matters into their own hands by engaging in more aggressive protest behavior. Second, some workers became so discouraged with the traditional left leadership that they joined smaller, more aggressive unions whose leaders had little political interest in mobilizing restraint. During the 1990s, many of these unions engaged in extreme and violent protest that chased away much-needed foreign direct investment.

In the concluding chapter, I summarize the arguments made in the preceding chapters and outline the implications of the analysis for broader theoretical and policy debates. Specifically, I discuss the implications of the findings for the study of democracy and development. I also look at the implications of the findings for state investment promotion strategies, for workers' rights and freedoms, and finally for labor market reforms in South Asia.

PART I

A PUZZLE AND AN ARGUMENT

In recent years, workers in South Asia have been more heavily exposed to market forces than in the past. For many workers in the formal industrial sector, this exposure was associated with economic reforms that undercut their bargaining power. This section of the book looks in detail at how economic liberalization has affected workers and develops an argument about why some workers respond to their declining bargaining power differently than others.

In chapter 2, I show how competitive product and labor markets have made it more difficult for workers to go on strike in India. Some workers have responded to this fact by becoming quiescent, other workers by engaging in higher levels of militancy to force the employer's hand, and still others by redoubling their efforts to negotiate favorable settlements with management, frequently offering productivity increases in exchange for better wages. Why do workers respond so differently to the same economic challenges?

In chapter 3 I argue that these differences in worker protest behavior are attributable to variations in levels of democracy. Two aspects of democracy are relevant for explaining the frequency and character of industrial protest: political competition and FACB rights. Political competition forces political parties to forge ties with unions in order to win elections. These ties benefit unions but also constrain union behavior because electoral pressures compel major political parties to provide a favorable investment climate. At the same time, democracy and strong ties to labor mean that parties can no longer rely on repression to quell protest. Instead, parties grant FACB rights, which make it possible for workers to engage in institutionalized grievance resolution and for political leaders to moderate union protest behavior without resorting to repressive tactics.

CHAPTER 2

Industrial Relations in the Context of Economic Change

Battle lines are being drawn in labor actions across India. Factory managers, amid the global economic downturn, want to pare labor costs and remove defiant workers. Unions are attempting to stop them, with slowdowns and strikes that have led at times to bloodshed.

—*Wall Street Journal,* 2009

In January 1982, Datta Samant, president of the Maharashtra Girni Kamgar Union (MGKU), led a quarter of a million textile workers on a sectorwide strike in Mumbai. Samant's demands included a wage increase of between 25 and 50 percent (depending on the factory), a bonus increase of 20 percent, and guaranteed permanent employment for all textile workers (Lakha 2002, 236). Lasting for more than eighteen months, the strike was the largest in India's history by almost any measure.[1] Samant drove a hard bargain, but employers refused to budge. Ultimately, rather than meeting the union's demands, owners of dozens of firms decided to instead outsource production to suppliers in the small-scale sector, to shift production to rural areas, or to simply close their mills altogether. For the more than 150,000 textile workers who lost their jobs, the consequences of the strike were disastrous. Many former strikers fell into abject poverty. Some workers were driven by their desperation to sell family members into prostitution or to commit suicide.[2] For decades former strikers continued to agitate for government takeover of the mill lands and against their redevelopment by private companies.[3]

The Bombay textile strike represented a turning point in the history of Indian industrial relations. It signaled a dramatic loss of bargaining power of workers in industry and the beginning of an era in which protracted struggle would be required to win even the simplest demand. In the quarter century following Independence, organized labor had benefitted from the protections afforded by pervasive state intervention in private manufacturing. Individual manufacturing companies were profitable, if inefficient, and unions could win large demands with short strikes. But new economic policies began to undermine the strength of medium- and large-scale manufacturers as early as the 1970s, and by the 1980s industries in many sectors (including textiles) were ailing. Employers contested each and every union demand as markets became more competitive.

In response to employer recalcitrance, some union leaders began to consider more aggressive protest and bargaining tactics. In using the frustration bred by economic recession to ratchet up militancy toward management, the MGKU was at the vanguard of this trend. The strategy inevitably led not only to protracted struggles, but to industrial violence as well. For example, four MGKU members were involved in the January 1979 stabbing of industrialist N. P. Godrej, his mother-in-law, and his pregnant daughter-in-law in relation to a long-standing dispute at Godrej and Boyce Manufacturing Company.[4] In January of the following year, MGKU members were involved in a strike in Taloja that began with a march and ended with several workers being shot (one fatally) and the factory being burned to the ground.[5]

Even more violent unions and leaders were to emerge as new economic policies took hold and more industries fell on hard times. A number of well-known union leaders in Mumbai during the 1980s and 1990s were essentially mafia dons who grew powerful by settling property and labor disputes in the dying mill sector.[6] But the tendency to utilize more aggressive protest and negotiating tactics has spread well beyond the boundaries of Mumbai's mills to affect companies in many sectors across South Asia. In just the last few years, continuing violence in Indian factories has attracted significant attention in the media at home and abroad. A recent front-page article in the *Wall Street Journal*, for example, reported on a dispute over contract labor in Coimbatore that ended with workers beating the human resources manager to death in his office.[7] The CEO of an Italian transmission company based in Noida was killed in a similar manner following a meeting with two hundred workers that had recently been dismissed by the company.[8] A prolonged strike at Rico Auto Industries, a major auto parts supplier in Haryana, attracted attention after it affected production in North American factories owned by GM and Ford.[9] The Rico strike also turned violent after thugs hired by management killed one employee and injured forty others.[10]

As I emphasize in later chapters, a myopic focus on these violent anecdotes distracts from important variations in union response to the challenges of a more open economy. Nevertheless, it is important to understand how economic circumstances force union leaders to choose between mobilizing greater restraint and ratcheting up militancy against the management. This chapter analyzes the relationship between market reforms and the bargaining power of unions in India. While other countries in South Asia have undertaken similar policies, India's stable democracy, long history of reform, and its readily available data make it the ideal case for demonstrating how market forces link up with trends in industrial relations.

By increasing the competitiveness of labor and product markets, two sets of policies have enhanced the challenge of maintaining industrial relations stability in India. The first are well-known neoliberal reforms, which dismantled India's infamous "license-quota raj" and opened the economy to foreign investment and trade. This type of neoliberal reform is fairly common across South Asia. In 1978, Sri Lanka attracted the attention of the international development community as one of the first developing countries to commit to a neoliberal program of economic reforms and has greatly expanded the scope of private investment in manufacturing over the course of the last three decades.[11] Similarly, Bangladesh began reforming input markets in its agrarian sector in the late 1970s, which it followed with industrial deregulation in the 1980s and trade reform in the 1990s (World Bank 2003). Even Pakistan, which has been slower than other South Asian countries to commit to structural adjustment, embarked on a more comprehensive program of reform in 1999 (World Bank 2006).

A second set of economic policies that are fairly unique to India relate to the political rise of the agrarian sector. These policies have had a substantial impact on manufacturing that has largely been ignored by experts on Indian political economy. Specifically, the political mobilization of rural constituencies in the late 1970s and 1980s precipitated agricultural procurement policies that shifted the agriculture-industry terms of trade in favor of agriculture. Moreover, as the rural sector grew in political importance, legislators became increasingly concerned with generating employment in rural areas and consequently instituted a series of tax incentives designed to stimulate production in small-scale, rural units.

Together, these two sets of policies undermined union bargaining power, thereby altering the character of industrial relations. Neoliberal reforms exposed Indian manufacturers to greater competition from abroad, while rural bias in agricultural development policy brought higher product wages and competition from the small-scale sector. These developments diminished the pricing power of manufacturing. Increasingly, instead of meeting union wage demands, employers responded to the challenges of economic openness by substituting capital for labor in an effort to enhance efficiency, yielding a large pool of unemployed workers in manufacturing.

The resulting decline in bargaining power has made it more risky for unions to call out strikes and harder for union leaders to win demands. These circumstances serve as a source of frustration for workers and provide union leaders with greater incentive to engage in extreme and violent forms of protest. Consequently, industrial relations have grown increasingly more turbulent even as the overall frequency of strikes declined.

Neoliberal Reforms

Unions and left parties in India are known for their strident opposition to neoliberal reforms that most directly threaten the interests of workers in organized manufacturing. Yet despite their success in opposing key policies, such as the privatization of public sector industries and the wholesale dismantling of India's body of protective labor law, trade unions have been weakened by policies that have exposed Indian industry to market forces.

In 1991, the Indian National Congress (INC) adopted a series of reform measures that marked an emphatic break from the closed, state-led strategy of economic development that India had followed in the decades immediately after Independence. The 1991 reforms emerged out of a balance-of-payments crisis, for which the short-term causes were a global spike in oil prices following the Gulf War, and a decline in exports resulting from the collapse of the Soviet Union (Rakshit 2004, 89–91).

The crisis was caused more fundamentally, however, by the long-term lackluster performance of India's state-led strategy of industrialization. Rooted in Jawaharlal Nehru's economic vision of industrial development, India's prereform economic policy reflected the deep distrust of the private sector and markets, and great faith in public sector industry that was common among development economists and policymakers of Nehru's era (e.g., Nurkse 1953). Nehruvian industrial policy restricted growth in the private manufacturing sector through an industrial licensing system commonly referred to as the "license-quota raj" and protected both private and public sector industry form international competition with high tariffs and subsidies. With hindsight the results of protectionism and regulation were perhaps predictable. Shielded from significant competition in its large domestic product market, Indian industry became increasingly uncompetitive. Exports suffered, contributing to the 1991 balance of payments crisis, while shortages and chronically slow growth shifted elite sentiment in favor of a dramatic change in economic policy.[12]

Following the template of the standard neoliberal package advocated by the World Bank and International Monetary Fund (IMF), India's 1991 reforms occurred in two stages—stabilization and structural adjustment. The stabilization program included a series of macroeconomic reforms designed to alleviate the balance of payments crisis and establish long-term budgetary viability. These included an 18 percent devaluation of the rupee in two stages, a reduction of state expenditures to bring down the fiscal deficit, and giving the Reserve Bank of India (RBI) greater autonomy to maintain the balance of payments. The government also opened the country to foreign investment and liberalized the financial sector through the partial privatization of state banks and financial institutions, and permitted the entry of private-sector banks (Rakshit 2004, 84–85).

The structural reforms, which were aimed at promoting growth and long-term economic viability, marked the definitive and official abandonment of traditional state-led industrialization and development planning (Byres 1998). The primary focus of these reforms was to inject dynamism into the industrial sector. To this end, the government liberalized trade and investment at the same time that it eased restrictions on industry. During the 1990s, import quotas were removed and import tariffs were drastically reduced. Between 1990 and 1997, the government lowered maximum tariff levels from 300 percent to 40 percent, while the weighted average of nominal import tariffs declined from 87 percent to 20 percent (Jenkins 1999, 16). To facilitate foreign investment, the government relaxed the provisions of the Federal Exchange Regulation Act (FERA) that prohibited foreign control of Indian companies. The new regulations permitted foreign firms to hold up to a 51 percent stake in companies in thirty-four industries (Jenkins 1999, 20). Changes to industrial policy were equally dramatic. The government abolished the system of industrial licensing except in a handful of defense-related and "strategic" sectors. It substantially relaxed the Monopolies and Restrictive Trade Policies (MRTP) Act, which had inhibited the growth of large-scale manufacturing, and it opened many industries that were previously reserved for state-owned enterprises to private investors.

While the reforms of the early 1990s represented a definitive break from the post-Independence legacy of state-led industrialization and planning, it is important to recognize their roots in previous reform efforts, particularly those of the 1980s. As Kohli (2006) notes, the Indian government began to move gradually away from a Nehruvian state-led import substitution model of development under the leadership of Indira Gandhi in the 1980s and continued to do so under Rajiv Gandhi through the late-1990s. Leaders of the Congress Party thus began to prioritize economic growth over redistribution and aligned themselves with business as a political ally. Indira Gandhi set up powerful committees to recommend a long-term plan of action for promoting growth and made a number of immediate changes to economic policy. These included amending the MRTP to allow expansion of large enterprises in core industries, tax relief to big business, and regulatory changes that made it easier for business to raise capital from private equity markets (Kohli 2006, 1256). Further, much of the increased growth and dynamism that is typically associated with the watershed 1991 reforms actually began in the 1980s. As many authors have noted, industrial and overall economic growth rates were relatively steady through the 1980s and 1990s, although much higher than the lost decade of the 1970s (e.g., De Long 2003; Nagaraj 2000; Rodrik and Subramanium 2004).

Implications of Neoliberal Reforms for Indian Industry

Economic reforms were a mixed blessing for Indian industry and their effects varied across industrial sectors. Overall, the reform measures of the 1980s and 1990s can be said to have led to a resurgence of industrial

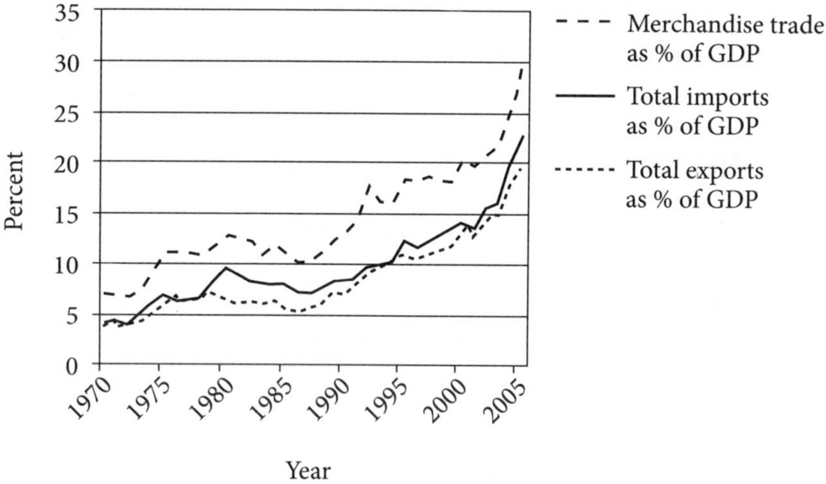

Figure 2.1: India's exposure to international trade
Notes: Figures taken from the World Bank's World Development Indicators (WDI).

growth. It is clear that the reforms of the 1980s and 1990s have been associated with a recovery from the anemic growth of the 1970s, when formal (or "registered") manufacturing grew at an average annual growth rate of just under 2.8 percent.[13] In the 1980s, growth in registered manufacturing recovered to 7.3 percent. It then fell to 5.8 percent as a result of the economic crisis in the early 1990s, but surged to over 9.5 percent during the first half of the last decade. Further, regardless of how the "postreform" period is defined (as the post-1980 or post-1991 period), the growth rates for registered manufacturing are virtually identical for the two periods—7.3 percent for the post-1980 and 7.45 percent for the post-1991 period.

While they contributed to growth, reforms also exposed Indian manufacturers to the competitive forces of international markets. Figure 2.1 displays trends in trade in merchandise, total imports, and total exports for the period 1970–2006. As these figures demonstrate, trade began to surge in the late-1980s as the government started eliminating quotas and tariffs. Prior to 1987, total trade in merchandise had hovered around 10 percent of GDP. By 2000, trade in merchandise had doubled to 20 percent of GDP and then increased again by more than half to 32 percent of GDP in 2006. Similarly, the total volume of imports rose from 7 percent of GDP in 1987 to 25 percent in 2006, while the total volume of exports rose from 6 percent to 22 percent of GDP.

Rural Development Policy

Although the reforms in the 1980s and 1990s had a substantial impact on industry, they did not occur early enough to fully explain changes in industrial relations, which as I will show, date back to the early 1970s. It is thus important to consider a second major set of changes in economic policy, associated with the rising influence of rural constituencies in Indian politics, to explain these earlier trends in industrial relations.

Immediately following Independence in 1947, the logic of urban bias dominated India's policymaking process (Varshney 1998b). This was due to Nehru's emphasis on growth in the industrial sector. The rapid industrial development advocated by Nehru required heavy state investments in industry and infrastructure that traded off with spending in the agricultural sector. Nehru thus championed tenure reform to increase agricultural productivity in place of the types of expensive agricultural inputs and price subsidies that would eventually bring about India's Green Revolution.[14] At the same time, the government directed the vast majority of industrial investment towards medium- and large-scale units in urban areas, meaning that it effectively reserved high-paying jobs in industry for urban dwellers.

Later, however, agricultural and industrial development policies underwent substantial shifts. From the 1960s onward, agricultural development policy shifted toward stimulation of agricultural growth through higher procurement prices and agricultural subsidies. Meanwhile, industrial policy shifted away from Nehruvian principles and toward countervailing Gandhian ideals, which involved a more democratic distribution of investment through support for labor-intensive small-scale sector industry in the countryside at the expense of medium and large-scale urban production. These shifts in development policy were accelerated by the subsequent political mobilization of the agrarian sector, and they had a substantial impact on workers and producers in medium- and large-scale industries for decades to come. Pricing policy affected the pricing power of manufacturing, while the rise of small-sector units challenged the dominance of medium- and large-scale producers.

Food Procurement Policy and the Pricing Power of Manufacturing

Following Nehru's death, C. Subramaniam, India's powerful food and agricultural minister between 1964 and 1966, pushed India's new prime minister, Lal Bahadur Shastri, to implement policies that would stimulate growth in the agrarian sector, including the procurement of food grains at above-market prices by the Food Corporation of India (FCI) for the public distribution system. Since the FCI purchases approximately 10 percent of food grains every year (Mooij 1999), FCI purchases at above-market rates constituted an artificial stimulus for food grain prices and a production incentive for farmers. Combined with subsidies for fertilizers, these price incentives are credited for India's Green Revolution during the late 1960s.

This initial shift in food price policy was largely at the bureaucratic level and involved debates among technocrats. Producer prices eventually faded as a bureaucratic imperative in the early 1970s, but subsequently Indira Gandhi championed the agrarian cause in a much more politicized manner in the mid- and late 1970s.[15] Indira's rural populism was followed by the even more potent mobilization of Chowdhry Charan Singh's Janata Party. Singh's mobilization made the producer price issue a fixed part of the political landscape that no party could ignore. Although the dominance of the Janata Party in the national parliament was brief, food grains were consistently procured at above market rates from the 1980s onward because producer prices became an irrevocable political privilege for farmers. The extent of this privilege is now such that even "deficit states," which take more food from the central distribution system than they contribute (and so have an interest in low food prices), demand price increases for their agricultural products (Varshney 1998b, 85).

Absent a similar stimulus for manufactured products, one would expect the artificial stimulus to food prices over two decades to substantially influence the rural-urban terms of trade. The best measure of the terms of trade for time-series analysis is the gross terms of trade, which is calculated as the ratio of agriculture and manufacturing price deflators:[16]

$$TT = \frac{\dfrac{GDPag\,(CURRENT)}{GDPag\,(CONSTANT)}}{\dfrac{GDPmfg\,(CURRENT)}{GDPmfg\,(CONSTANT)}}$$

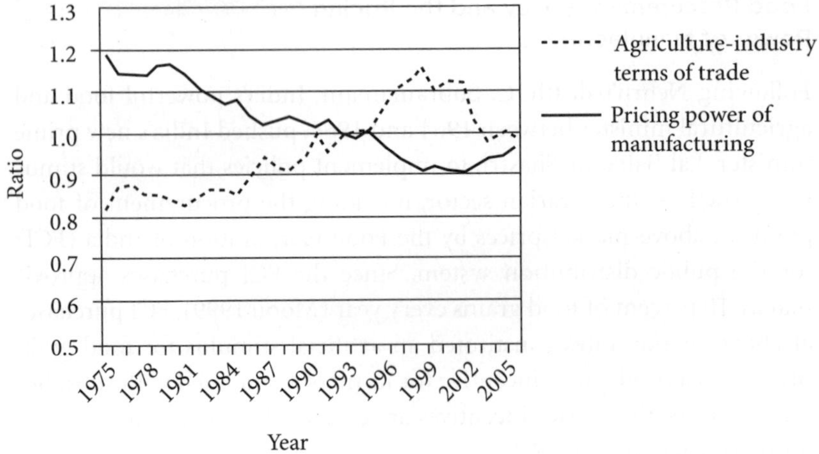

Figure 2.2: Agriculture-industry terms of trade and pricing power of manufacturing
Notes: Agriculture-industry terms of trade is measured as the ratio of agriculture and manufacturing GDP price deflators. The pricing power of manufacturing is measured as the GDP price deflator for manufacturing relative to the GDP price deflator for all other sectors. See the text for a more detailed discussion. The current and constant output figures used to construct each index are taken from National Accounts Statistics, Ministry of Planning and Programme Implementation (MOSPI), Government of India.

Figure 2.2 displays the gross terms of trade as well as the overall pricing power of manufacturing, measured as the ratio of manufacturing prices to prices for all other sectors, from 1975 to 2006. Not surprisingly, from the mid-1980s through the early 2000s, the gross terms of trade trended toward agriculture. And because agriculture constitutes approximately 60 percent of gross domestic product during this period, the shift in the agriculture-industry terms of trade also caused a substantial decline in the overall pricing power of manufacturing.

Industrial Policy and the Rise of the Small-Scale Sector

A second major implication of the political mobilization of the rural sector was the rise of small-scale industry, which provided a new source of competition for medium- and large-scale manufacturers where most unions have their members. The effects of rural mobilization on industrial policy were reflected in the Fourth Five-Year Plan (1969–74), which marked a watershed in Indian industrial policy. In it, the Planning Commission stressed the "competitive rather than complementary aspects

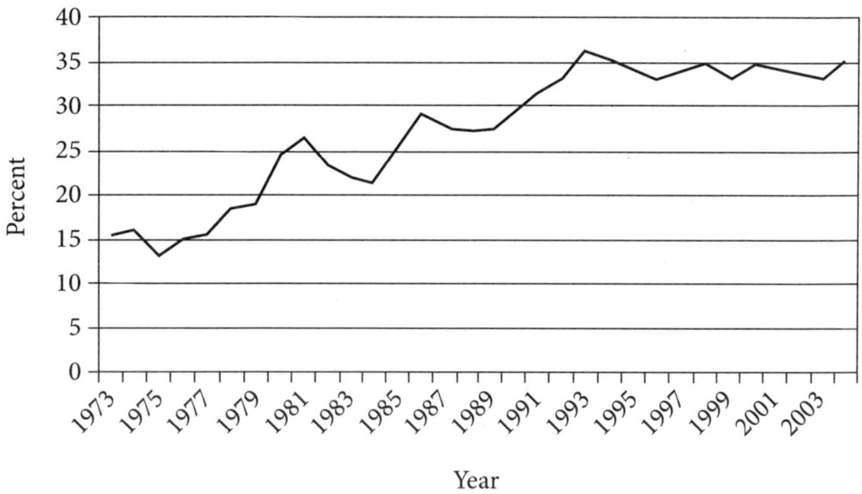

Figure 2.3: Small-scale industry share of total exports
Notes: Data on SSI output comes from Small Scale Industries in India, Office of the Development Commissioner, Ministry of Small Scale Industries, Government of India. Data on exports come from the World Bank's World Development Indicators (WDI).

of the development of the small-scale and the large-scale sectors" and advocated a set of financial incentives and protections for small-scale and rural industries designed to increase the regional dispersal of labor-intensive economic growth (Ahluwalia 1998, 265). Members of the planning commission believed that targeting the small-scale sector would boost industrial development in rural areas because the average rural entrepreneur has only a very small amount of resources to invest. Thus the planning commission viewed the goals of dispersing growth across rural and urban regions and the growth of the small-scale sector as one-and-the-same.[17]

Important incentives provided to small-scale sector industries included subsidized loans, reduced sales and excise taxes, and the reservation of certain items for exclusive production by small-scale sector units. Starting with a handful of items in the late 1960s, the number of reservations grew to almost nine hundred by the 1990s (Joshi and Little 1996, 200). Additionally, to ensure the growth of small-scale industries in rural areas, the Indian government began using the industrial licensing system to restrict the expansion of large- and medium-scale production units in urban areas while making it easy to start medium- and large-scale units in industrially "backward" districts. The national government also offered tax exemptions for companies setting up production units (including medium- and large-scale units) in "backward," or "no-industry," districts and invested in special economic zones in rural areas (Ahluwalia 1998).

These incentives were highly successful in transforming the structure of production in India's manufacturing sector. Over the last three decades, small-scale units have provided a rapidly growing source of competition for medium- and large-scale producers, particularly in export-oriented industries. Figure 2.3 presents the value of small-scale sector exports as a percentage of the total value of exports. In 1973, small-scale industry produced just 15 percent of total exports. This figure had climbed to 24 percent in 1980, to 27 percent in 1990 and leveled off at 35 percent in the mid-1990s.

Declining Bargaining Power and Industrial Conflict

The two sets of economic policies discussed above—liberalization and rural development policy—led to important changes in Indian industry and industrial relations. Liberalization exposed Indian manufacturers to competition from abroad, while rural development policy undermined the pricing power of industry and spurred competition from small-scale producers. In turn, declining pricing power and more competitive product markets had two major implications for the bargaining power of workers.

First, declining producer prices and competitive product markets put downward pressure on wages, which made it more difficult for workers to demand wage increases. This pressure is reflected in the "product wage," or wages in manufacturing deflated by producer prices. Despite stagnation in nominal wages, the fall in producer prices has effectively made wages more expensive for employers, while more competitive product markets have made it difficult to pass on the cost of wage increases to consumers.

Second, in response to adverse economic conditions, manufacturers undertook a process of capital deepening that involved both the more efficient use of labor and the introduction of labor-saving technology. Capital deepening has thus resulted in a higher jobless rate among manufacturing workers and India's oft-noted "jobless growth" as employers shed labor in favor of increased investments in capital. The increasing prospects of job loss and unemployment associated with this trend have substantially eroded the bargaining position of workers who manage to remain employed in medium- and large-scale production units.

Declining bargaining power has had dramatic effects on the character of industrial relations. Adverse economic conditions have made it difficult for union leaders to call out strikes and have forced them to strike for a longer period of time in order to win demands. For obvious reasons, the inability to go on strike creates frustration among workers. Industrial relations have consequently become more turbulent as workers resort to extreme and violent protest tactics to ratchet up militancy and to resist the strikebreaking tactics of employers.

Pricing Power of Manufacturing and the Product Wage

During the 1980s and 1990s, increasing competition in product markets and a shift in the terms of trade toward agriculture had major implications for the pricing power of manufacturing (see figure 2.2). This decline in pricing power meant that many inputs became more expensive for industry and also had important implications for wages. The impact of pricing power on wages is captured by trends in the "product wage," which measures the movement of wages relative to producer prices. The product wage is defined as the total wage bill divided by the number of workers deflated by the sectoral producer price. A rising product wage indicates that producer prices are not keeping pace with the rising costs of labor. Conversely, a declining product wage indicates that producer prices are rising faster than the cost of labor.

The link between rural-urban terms of trade and wages is relatively straightforward. If the terms of trade are going in favor of agriculture, then wages, in tandem with food prices, will grow faster than the prices of manufactured goods and the product wage will rise. On the other hand, if the terms of trade are going in favor of industry then the prices of manufactured goods will grow faster than wages, and the product wage will fall (Anant and Sundaram 1996, chap. 2).

In India, the relationship between the terms of trade and the product wage has been magnified by two factors. First, in the 1980s and 1990s, the wages of many workers in medium and large-scale firms were tied to the Consumer Price Index (CPI) through cost of living adjustments

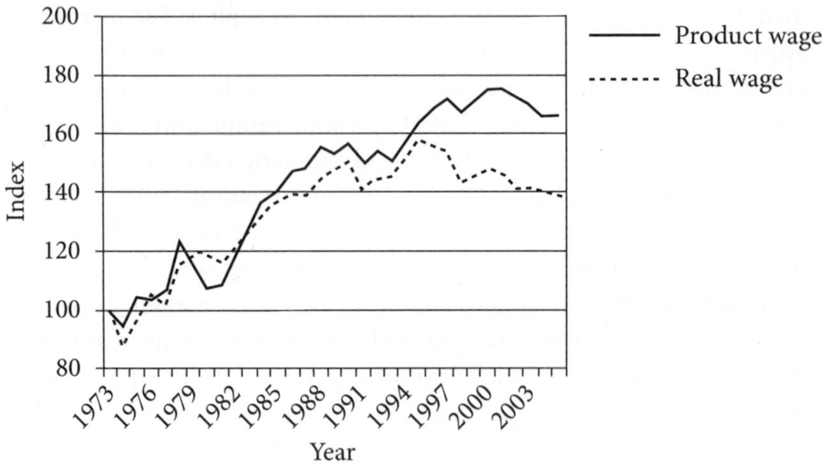

Figure 2.4: Trends in the product wage and real wages
Notes: The product wage is measured as wages per worker deflated by the wholesale price index (WPI). The real wage is measured as wages per worker deflated by the consumer price index for industrial workers (CPI-IW). Data on wages and workers comes from the Annual Survey of Industries, Ministry of Statistics and Programme Implementation, Government of India.

(COLAs). While there has been a trend away from COLAs in recent years, their earlier prevalence helped drive up the product wage in tandem with rising food prices. Additionally, as in most developing countries, food items constitute a large portion of the basket of goods used to calculate the CPI. This means that food prices have a very large effect on inflation and thus on wages.

It is important to note that changes in the product wage can differ from those in the real wage, which deflates wages by a cost of living index. The product wage can rise as real wages fall if inflation of consumer prices outpaces inflation of producer prices and vice versa. Previous studies have noted that real wages have remained stagnant in India, reflecting the weak bargaining position of unions (Nagaraj 1994). Further, from the 1960s through the late 1990s, productivity growth outstripped wage growth (Kannan 1994; Goldar and Banga 2005; Papola 1994; Sundaram 2007).

In contrast to the downward trend in real wages, the product wage has been on the rise in India. Figure 2.4 shows trends in the product wage and real wages from 1973 to 2006. The dark line represents an index of product wage growth and the dotted line an index of real wage growth. As the figure suggests, the product wage rose in tandem with the gross agriculture-industry terms of trade throughout the 1980s and 1990s. Closer scrutiny confirms the correspondence between the product wage and the gross terms of trade. The turning points for the product wage and terms of trade are similar and the correlation coefficient between the two variables is 0.8. Real wages, by contrast, leveled off in the mid-1980s as union bargaining power waned and employers became reluctant to pay increasingly higher wages in a more competitive economic environment.

These trends in the product wage and real wages paint a very clear picture of declining union bargaining power in the 1980s and 1990s. Real wages stagnated as the product wage continued to rise, suggesting that wages were worth less to workers but were becoming more expensive to employers. This dynamic alone made it very difficult for workers to achieve significant wage gains; but in combination with the effects of job loss described below the situation was quite dire for organized labor.

Capital Deepening and Unemployment

One of the most remarked-on features of postreform India is the phenomenon of "jobless growth." From 1980 to 2004, the value of gross valued added in manufacturing grew at an annual rate of 7.44 percent, while employment grew at an average rate of just 0.78 percent (Kannan and Raveendran 2009, 84). In one sense, this trend is surprising since productivity growth was quite substantial during the 1980s relative to earlier periods. According to one set of calculations, the average annual increase in labor productivity was 6.3 percent during the period 1979–90—approximately three times higher than the growth rate of labor productivity in the 1960s and 1970s (Unel 2003). Additionally, the growth rate of the capital-output ratio was lower in the 1980s (1 percent) than in the 1960s and 1970s (2.3 percent), implying a higher growth rate in capital efficiency. Total factor productivity growth ranged between 1.8 and 3.2 percent in the 1980s—much better than in the 1970s, when on average total factor productivity growth was slightly negative.

Many expected that these gains in productivity would offset the rise in the product wage, thereby leading to faster job growth. The causes of persistently slow job growth in the presence of increased productivity have been debated at length. One commonly cited explanation for jobless growth relates to overemployment in manufacturing caused by an industrial slowdown in the 1970s (Nagaraj 1994; Papola 1994). When demand for manufactured products increased in the 1980s, firms used existing labor more intensively rather than hiring on new workers, decisions that were, in turn, influenced by deregulatory policies and increased public investment (Bhalotra 1998). Other scholars have focused more closely on the nature of consumer demand. One such theory is the Fordist argument that the majority of India's workers, who toil in the low-wage informal sector, cannot afford to purchase a high volume of manufactured products (Kannan 1994). A related argument is that the demand among middle-class and international consumers is for high-end products that require a high degree of capital intensity to produce, as opposed to the low-end manufactured goods that would generate substantial employment growth in India's manufacturing sector (Kannan and Raveendran 2009).

Another possible explanation for jobless growth relates to the effects of the policy changes outlined in this chapter. Productivity gains and labor shedding may have been due to an overall restructuring of industry prompted by more competitive product markets and a loss of pricing power that were in turn brought about by neoliberal economic reforms and an increasing rural bias in development policy. The restructuring of industry entailed both a higher level of investment in capital and technology *and* the shedding of labor, explaining the simultaneous gains in productivity and stagnation in manufacturing sector employment growth.

Indeed this interpretation is supported by the fact that capital deepening was associated with substantial job loss in manufacturing. From 1979 to 1990, the capital-labor ratio increased at an average annual rate of 7.3 percent, one percentage point faster than the growth rate of labor productivity during the same period (Unel 2003). This trend in capital deepening accelerated throughout the 1980s and 1990s. The capital-labor ratio doubled from 13.4 in 1980 to 28.7 in 1990 and then increased another 50 percent to 42.8 in 2000.[18] During the same period, the jobless rate in manufacturing was also rising. According to ILO figures, the number of unemployed production workers increased from 1.4 million in 1980 to 2.1 million in 1990. Joblessness in manufacturing reached a high of almost 9 million workers in 1999 before settling around the 4.5 million mark in the early 2000s.[19]

Neither the argument about an industrial slowdown in the 1970s nor arguments about consumer demand do a very good job of explaining these trends. If it were simply the case that there was an oversupply of labor following the recessionary period of the 1970s, or that there was not enough consumer demand for manufactured goods, then we would expect to see stagnation in employment. The accelerated shedding of labor seen in the unemployment data suggests a fundamental shift in how manufacturing companies utilize labor that is more likely the result of structural transformations brought about by changes in policy than of short-term fluctuations in the supply of and demand for labor.

Labor's Share of Value Added

Data on value added help to shed further light on the restructuring process that occurred in the manufacturing sector and its impacts on organized labor. Labor's and capital's shares of value added in manufacturing are depicted in figure 2.5. Because productivity has grown while wages have stagnated, labor's share of value added has steadily declined during the postreform period while capital's share of value added has steadily increased.

In 1980 labor's share of value added was 50 percent and capital's share was just 20 percent. During the first half of the 1980s, labor's share of value added remained steady and capital's share decreased as employers made investments in labor-saving technology (Teitelbaum 2007). After 1987, however, labor's share of value added fell precipitously while capital's share shot upward, suggesting that employers were taking greater profits. Labor's and capital's shares of value added then held steady at 30 percent following the 1991 balance of payments crisis. The shares in valued added of labor and capital began to diverge again a decade later, but this time in capital's favor. By 2005, the respective shares of labor and capital were completely the inverse of a decade earlier, with capital obtaining 60 percent of value added and labor just 23 percent.

The value-added data thus show a struggle between capital and labor in the 1990s as neoliberal reforms took hold, with capital emerging as the clear victor as the manufacturing sector returned to profitability. Other economic data help to confirm the health of Indian industry. Growth rates in manufacturing jumped from 5.8 percent in the 1990s to 9.5 percent in the first half of the 2000s (see figure 2.1). The pricing power of manufacturing improved as the terms of trade began to trend back in favor of manufacturing (see figure 2.2) and the product wage leveled off (see figure 2.4). Finally, as was noted earlier, although the jobless rate in manufacturing remained high in the early 2000s, there were half as many jobless in 2005 than in 1999.

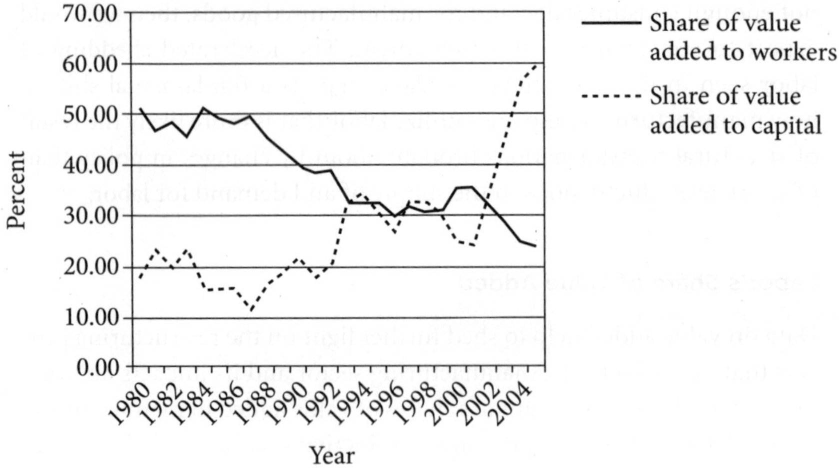

Figure 2.5: Share of value added to labor and capital
Notes: Author's own calculations using data from Annual Survey of Industries, Ministry of Statistics and Programme Implementation, Government of India.

Despite the health of industry and employers' ability to take profits, employees did not see an increase in their share of value added. The stickiness of manufacturing wages suggests the enduring effects of increased product market competition on the bargaining power of workers. As well, the remaining pool of unemployed continued to hamper the ability of union leaders to mobilize workers. Although manufacturing firms were now highly profitable and had begun hiring again, the large reserve of highly skilled workers who lost jobs in the 1980s and 1990s continued to discourage workers from agitating in favor of a greater share of value added.

The Transformation of Industrial Relations

The declining bargaining power of unions had a predictable yet dramatic effect on industrial relations. Previous studies on strikes find a consistent relationship between business cycles and strike activity.[20] Strike frequency (the number of strikes per thousand workers) is generally found to be procyclical, while average strike duration (the number of workdays lost to strikes per striker) is countercyclical. Put simply, workers tend to strike more often when labor market conditions are good, but strike less and fight longer for their demands when labor market conditions are poor.

The same has been true in India. Figure 2.6 presents trends in the frequency and duration of industrial disputes. Since the early 1970s, the frequency of industrial disputes has declined dramatically, indicating the hesitation among union leaders to call out strikes. In light of the previous discussion, the reasons for this hesitation are obvious. Declining bargaining power has meant that workers need to fight longer in support of their demands. At the same time, victory is much less certain and the fears of lockouts and job loss are greater. In the early 1970s, average dispute duration was around twenty days per striking or locked-out worker, reflecting the relative ease with which workers could win demands. In 1982, the year of the Bombay textile strike, average dispute duration spiked to one hundred days and remained high thereafter. Throughout the 1980s and 1990s, average duration fluctuated between forty and sixty days per striking or locked-out worker, and in the early 2000s lengthy lockouts pushed average dispute duration above eighty days.

Further disaggregation of industrial disputes data provides additional evidence of the declining leverage of workers in the industrial relations arena. Disputes data are comprised of strikes (disputes initiated by workers) and lockouts (disputes initiated by employers). Since the mid-1980s, the overall volume of strikes has declined markedly while the volume of lockouts has remained constant, indicating that although workers are unable to mount a credible threat to go on strike, employers continue to use lockouts to bring organized labor to heel. Not surprisingly, analysts have interpreted these dual trends in strike and lockout activity as indicative of the increasing dominance of employers in the collective bargaining arena (Dutt 2003; Sundar 2004).

Needless to say, these trends have been worrisome from the perspective of union leaders, while the inability to voice demands has engendered deep frustration among workers. The ironic result has been that organized labor has become increasingly quiescent at the same time that industrial relations have become more tense and turbulent. Union leaders are aware of new economic realities and the need for greater compromise, but union members whose wages are falling are understandably resistant to taking a more cooperative stance toward management. Further, as I argue later in the book, there is a great deal of variation in the degree to which union leaders emphasize new economic realities and

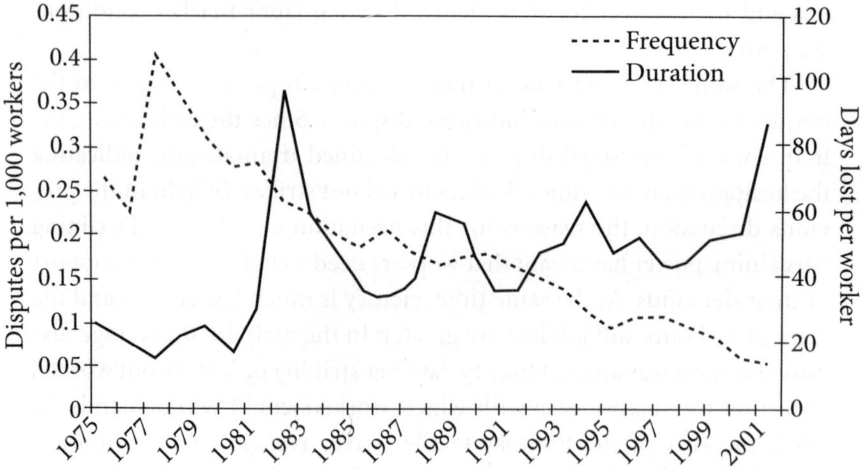

Figure 2.6: Frequency and duration of industrial disputes in India's manufacturing sector
Notes: Dispute frequency is the number of industrial disputes per 1,000 workers. Dispute duration is the number of workdays lost per striking (or locked-out) worker. National-level data on the annual number of disputes, workdays lost, and number of workers involved in disputes in the manufacturing sector are available in the Laborsta database, published online by the International Labor Organization. National-level data on the number of workers in manufacturing are taken from the Annual Survey of Industries, Central Statistical Organisation, Department of Statistics, Ministry of Planning and Programme Implementation, Government of India.

encourage workers to reduce militancy; and even union leaders who seek to encourage worker restraint cannot always exert enough control over union members to prevent wildcat strikes.

Consequently, industrial relations have been characterized by two opposing trends. First, workers exhibit a decreased propensity to go on strike to demand wage increases or job security and an increased propensity to sign productivity-linked wage agreements. Such agreements have not only helped to spur labor productivity but have included clauses that permit employers to rationalize the production process, make new investments in technology or even reduce the size of the workforce to maintain the profitability of the production unit (Venkata Ratnam 2001). At the same time, industrial relations have become more violent. In some cases, militant union leaders have utilized worker frustration and encouraged worker violence in order to ratchet up pressure on the management. In other cases, violence occurs when workers who are frustrated with their declining bargaining power take matters into their own hands.

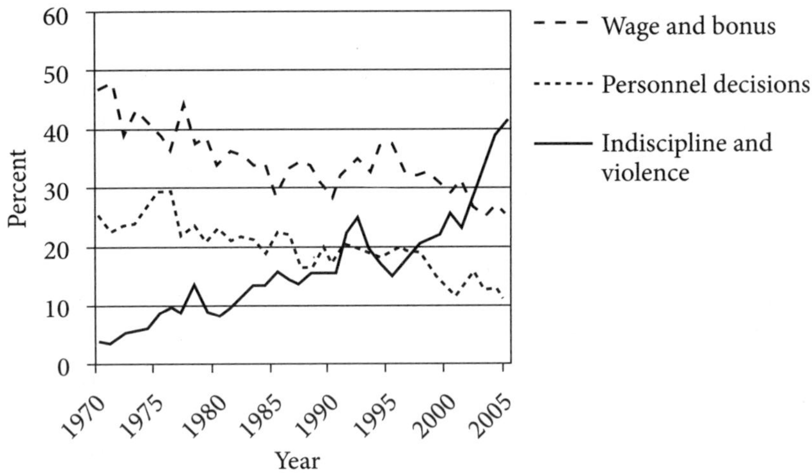

Figure 2.7: Causes of industrial disputes in India
Notes: The dotted lines represent the percentage of industrial disputes in which wages and personnel decisions were reported as a primary cause. The solid line represents the percentage of disputes that were precipitated by worker indiscipline or violence. These data are from the India Labour Yearbook, Ministry of Labour, Government of India.

This overall dynamic is depicted in figure 2.7, which shows trends in three primary causes of industrial disputes in India: wages and bonus, personnel decisions, and "worker indiscipline and violence."[21] Demands for higher wages and bonuses have never been the only major cause of disputes in India, but for a long time they were the biggest cause. In the early 1970s wage demands precipitated between 39 and 47 percent of industrial disputes. The second biggest cause of industrial disputes was decisions regarding personnel, namely the hiring and firing of individual workers. In the early 1970s, the percentage of disputes due to personnel decisions ranged between 23 and 30 percent. A dispute precipitated by worker indiscipline and violence is usually a lockout that occurs following an act of insubordination or a violent confrontation between managers and workers. Such disputes signal a complete breakdown of negotiations and a failure of collective bargaining as well as the failure of state institutions to channel conflict. In the 1970s, fewer than 4 percent of disputes were attributable to indiscipline or violence.

Since the early 1970s, industrial disputes attributable to bread-and-butter issues like wages and job security dropped steadily while strikes precipitated by acts of frustration and violent behavior climbed until the relative importance of the two sets of causes was completely reversed. By 2005, wage and bonus issues caused about 25 percent of disputes, while personnel decisions caused just 10 percent. In the same year 41 percent of disputes were caused by worker indiscipline and violence—the single biggest cause of disputes that year.

Conclusion

The statistics presented in this chapter portray a remarkable transformation of the character of industrial protest over the course of three and a half decades. Changes in economic policy substantially undermined the bargaining power of workers in manufacturing. Neoliberal reforms transformed domestic product markets and exposed the manufacturing sector to trade. Rural development policy undermined the pricing power of manufacturers and introduced competition from small-scale production units. These changes put downward pressure on wages and led to a process of capital deepening that increased joblessness in manufacturing.

Under these precarious economic circumstances workers in organized manufacturing found it increasingly difficult to voice their demands. Demands were no longer easy to win through routine strikes, and an increasing number of employers have responded to worker demands with retaliatory lockouts. As a result, many workers simply stopped voicing grievances through normal channels and instead took matters into their own hands. Consequently employers and workers have engaged in fewer negotiations over wages and job security, and the industrial relations environment has become increasingly chaotic and violent as workers confront managers outside of the normal channels of institutionalized grievance resolution. These trends present a major challenge for employers, union leaders, and the government. How this challenge can be met in a developing democracy while maintaining robust civil liberties constitutes the focus of the remainder of this book.

CHAPTER 3

A Political Theory of Industrial Protest

In chapter 2, we saw how economic liberalization, globalization, and the shift of production to small-scale units and rural areas decreased the bargaining power of unions. Instead of meeting union demands in a rush to resume production, employers increasingly responded to routine strike actions by locking workers out of factories, shifting operations, or closing down factories altogether. These economic trends made it more difficult for workers to call out strikes and at the same time increased tensions between workers and managers, thereby giving rise to more turbulent industrial relations.

At the same time, not all unions in South Asia responded to competitive markets in the same way. In some companies workers responded to the new economic environment by resorting to extreme and violent protest. For example, in January 1995, workers at Ansell Lanka (Pvt) Ltd. in Katunayake, Sri Lanka, went on strike under the banner of the Ceylon Federation of Trade Unions (CFTU) with one demand: "Please recognize our union." When the management refused to extend recognition, the workers took drastic steps. One group of workers climbed to the top of the factory's water tower and began a "fast until death." A second group removed the management staff from their offices and led them to a storage area at gunpoint. A third group surrounded the factory with flammable chemicals. All would die, they threatened, unless the management met their simple demand for recognition.

In other companies, however, union response to openness and competitive markets was quite different. Many union leaders encouraged workers to sign productivity-linked collective bargaining agreements and to refrain from striking if doing so were to entail violent or extreme protest behavior. For instance, in 1995 leaders of two unions—Center for Indian Trade Unions (CITU) and the Indian National Trade Union Congress (INTUC)—led fifteen hundred workers on strike at a tire manufacturing facility in Kerala, India. The strike was a rare occurrence of conflict in a factory where management and the unions continuously broker three-year collective bargaining agreements. No violence occurred during the strike and the matter was resolved in a few hours. Despite the strike, the management had high praise for the unions, which they said helped to increase productivity and contain costs in an increasingly competitive global market. In an interview, one senior manager from the company said this about the unions:

> Of late I have seen a positive attitude from both of the outside [union] leaders.... They advise their ranks, "Look, you have to understand the reality. Times are changing.... You have to get along with the management to run the business. Otherwise, managements can just close down and walk away. So you have to produce a conducive atmosphere to run the industry in a profitable manner."... That was the advice given by the union leader, even though, some of the local [members]... grumble.[1]

As this quote indicates, the advice of the union leaders was as much a response to "changing times" and "new economic realities" as it was a response to management. Rather than using difficult economic circumstances to raise the ire of workers and foment dissention, union leaders in the Kerala tire factory were working hard to explain changes in the economic environment to workers and redirect their energies toward negotiating the types of agreements that could still result in a salary increase despite tough economic times.

What explains variation in unions' repertoires of contention (Tarrow 1998)? Why do some labor union leaders respond to adverse economic conditions by restraining worker protest to facilitate social stability and long-term economic performance while other union leaders play on economic hardship to ratchet up militancy against employers and the state?

In recent years this question has been increasingly important for developing countries, where policymakers have been concerned with obtaining union support for economic policies that may impose severe short-term hardships on workers and where union leaders have had to decide whether to facilitate or oppose market reforms sought by their governments.

Building on insights from previous studies, this chapter presents a new theory of union behavior that helps to explain the motivations of union leaders in restraining worker protest. I argue that democracy influences industrial relations in two ways. First, political competition has compelled major parties to deepen union-party ties because historically parties have relied on union organizational capacity and the vote of the industrial working class to win elections. Although leaders of politically affiliated unions benefit from these ties, they are also constrained by the interests of the political party. Specifically, I argue that because they are encompassing organizations, political parties internalize the effects of worker militancy. Political parties thus encourage leaders of affiliated unions to privilege broader societal development goals over the short-term interests of union members.

In addition to political competition, democracy facilitates industrial peace by encouraging institutionalized grievance resolution through the promotion of freedom of association and collective bargaining (FACB) rights. These include the right to form unions, the right to engage in union activities, the right to engage in collective bargaining, and the right to strike. Because parties rely on workers for votes, democracies cannot crush dissent in the way that authoritarian regimes can. Instead, democracies must empower workers to resolve their grievances through adjudication, arbitration, and routine bargaining. Ultimately the development of robust labor institutions and the protection of worker rights is a more successful strategy for managing industrial conflict than the political exclusion and repression of organized labor.

In this chapter, I elaborate these arguments in the following way. I begin with a discussion of the incentives for individual union leaders to engage in militant protest and aggressive bargaining. I then discuss in very broad terms the role of democracy in reducing industrial conflict. This is followed by an in-depth discussion of the mechanisms at work. I show how partisan ties encourage union leaders to restrain worker protest and show how this impetus is common across the ideological spectrum. I then discuss how labor legislation promotes economic performance by enhancing third-party mediation and promoting worker rights, and I end with a discussion of expectations to be tested empirically in the remaining chapters. My analytical approach in this chapter is primarily inductive: I draw on numerous anecdotes as well as interview data to generate hypotheses and motivate broader theoretical insights.

Union Incentives for Militancy: Muscle Power, Membership, and Money

The question of why workers go on strike has been the subject of many social-scientific studies. Following Hicks (1948), many scholars have characterized strikes as "mistakes" that occur as a result of imperfect information. Since strikes result in economic loss for both sides, both parties have an incentive to avoid the strike if it has a predicted outcome. The fact that strikes occur, when under conditions of complete information they should not, is known as the "Hicks Paradox."

But Hicks, ostensibly in an effort to escape his own paradox, was perhaps the first to raise the possibility that unions use strikes more as a demonstration of muscle power than a tool for extracting higher wages from employers. For unions, aggressive bargaining and protest serves at least three useful purposes. The first is that it translates into increased bargaining leverage that can then be used to secure a greater share of the value added produced by a firm for union members. The second motivation is to maximize union membership. In this way, an aggressive bargaining posture helps unions to achieve their core mission, which is to "create or capture monopoly rents available in an industry" (Farber 1986, 1044). Unions can capture rents by exploiting existing product market imperfections or regulations in an industry, but just as commonly unions create rents by monopolizing the sale of labor when they are able to organize a significant portion of the labor force. Strikes are thus frequently directed at the retention of key union members when firms cut the size of the workforce during economic downturns (Golden 1997). Similarly, a show of force can help to attract new members who may be impressed by a union's reputation for toughness. Third, a demonstration of muscle power can help some unscrupulous union leaders to extract rents from management. While such practices do not characterize the behavior of all union leaders, of whom many are quite principled, racketeering is not an uncommon practice in South Asia or indeed any other part of the world.

The intuition that strikes are intentional displays of force, rather than mistakes, is supported by a wealth of econometric evidence. Almost every study on the political economy of industrial conflict shows a procyclical rise in strike frequency (e.g., Griffin 1939; Kennan 1986; Rees 1952; Weintraub 1966; Yoder 1938). There is also some evidence of a countercyclical rise in strike duration (Kennan 1986; Teitelbaum 2007). The fact that workers go on shorter but more frequent strikes when the economy is good suggests that in an upturn workers are striking as a demonstration of their bargaining power. Unions are most likely to win substantial demands when the demand for a firm's products is high and when the firm will settle quickly to avoid losing valuable orders and market share. But we would also expect employers to give in to worker demands more frequently *to avert a strike* in good times because strikes are more expensive to the firm. Thus the fact that strikes become more frequent in upturns suggests that workers are going on strike to reap reputational or membership benefits of a successful strike, even when they do not need to strike in order to win their demands.

The same incentives that give rise to union protest in upturns may give rise to more violent protest in economic downturns. In a situation of declining bargaining power, going on strike results in embarrassing losses, not quick victories. For this reason, individual union leaders may feel inclined to compensate for their declining bargaining power by engaging in more aggressive forms of protest, such as the use of violence or threats against the management. As was discussed in chapter 2, for example, violence became a much more common feature of industrial relations in India following the Great Bombay Textile Strike of 1982.

Another way in which unions may compensate for a lack of bargaining power is through unorthodox forms of occupation, obstruction, and hostage taking. Such actions became quite common throughout Asia in the 1980s and 1990s and were developed into something of an art form in Sri Lanka. The Ansell Lanka strike that was mentioned at the beginning of the chapter was probably one of the most spectacular examples of this phenomenon, but there are many others like it. During this period climbing to the tops of high structures to attract broad attention to worker grievances became a staple of the Sri Lankan strike. To take one example, members of the Ceylon Industrial Workers' Union (CIWU) at a coir factory in Sri Lanka attracted media attention when they protested by climbing to the top of the company's water tower and staging a "fast unto death."[2] Similarly, the Inter-Companies Employees Union (ICEU) attracted attention when its members occupied and later attempted to set fire to the rooftop of the manufacturing facility of the shoe company that employed them.[3]

Closely related to these protest tactics are the aggressive bargaining tactics union leaders employ. Frequently unions will place demands well beyond the level at which worker representatives expect the management to negotiate. For example, workers at a company I visited producing high-precision metal components in West Bengal demanded that the company double their wages but in the end settled for a relatively modest wage increase.[4] A related tactic is to present multiple demands for negotiation. Realistically, unions bargain over one or a very small handful of issues. Of the hundreds of disputes I discussed with employers, only one dispute at a rolling mill in Calcutta was over a full "charter," or list, of demands.[5] Another dispute, at a paint factory in Kerala, was over three demands—a bonus increase, transfer policy, and changes in production norms.[6] The vast majority of disputes were over one or at most two issues. Typically, these were wage disputes, although sometimes they were over disciplinary actions taken against union members or over job security. Yet unions in South Asia frequently begin negotiations with a full charter of demands, even though many of these demands are ancillary or superfluous, and force the management to discern which are the core demands.

Unions set demands well above the level the company can afford and generate confusion over their core demands for reputational and bargaining reasons. Frequently unions inflate demands to demonstrate toughness to the employer but in some instances unions seek to impress their own members by matching the demands made by unions at other factories. Unions also inflate demands in the hope that the employer will overshoot and provide a larger settlement than if the leadership had presented complete and perfect information about the union leadership's expectations. Unions present multiple demands to generate more bargaining leverage that they can use to secure their actual demands. For example, workers may strategically concede demands regarding workplace conditions in order to secure a higher wage increase, or concede demands regarding workplace amenities in favor of greater job security.

Ratcheting Up Militancy for Personal Financial Gain

While some may find the argument controversial, it is generally thought that some union leaders utilize their bargaining leverage mainly to enhance their personal wealth as opposed to bargaining purely on behalf of their members. In fact, the charge is not very outlandish as this type of brokerage role is to some extent institutionalized in Indian industrial relations. The extreme case is Maharashtra, where the law permits the union to take up to 10 percent of any wage increase they negotiate, giving union leaders incentive to bargain for wages that may not be sustainable for the firm over the long term.

However, a second avenue through which union leaders have enriched themselves is a classic labor racketeering scenario—employers make direct payments to union leaders to prevent strikes. Such practices were widely reported in interviews with employers in Maharashtra, perhaps explaining the aforementioned attempt to institutionalize the practice through legislation. For example, the production manager of a small manufacturing company in Pune referred to the company's payments to union leaders as a form of "internal conciliation," a satiric comparison to official conciliation proceedings presided over by officials from the Ministry of Labour.[7] The director of a welding equipment company just outside of Bombay described his interaction with a NIU leader who, after threatening him with violence, demanded money for the purchase of a new vehicle.[8]

Complaints about racketeering are not limited to employers, however. Union leaders also expressed their frustration with the corrupt behavior of other union leaders. One senior union leader in Maharashtra characterized a famously aggressive peer as a "chain snatcher" who views his union as a lucrative business and whose "primary aim is to take money from workers and management."[9] He questioned how such leaders, who began their careers as "paying guests" now own property in some of the most expensive neighborhoods of Mumbai. Part of the explanation, he argued, is the payoffs these leaders take from employers to force workers to sign unfavorable voluntary retirement scheme (VRS) agreements that then allow employers to outsource production to the informal and small-scale sectors. This view was widely shared by other union leaders and employers, who noted the tendency of certain leaders to use violence against workers to force them to sign onto VRS agreements they would otherwise not accept.

At the same time, it is important to note that racketeering is not a common practice for all or even a majority of South Asia's union leaders. Only a few union leaders have earned a reputation as outright criminals, and militancy is just as often associated with idealism as with racketeering. Bala Tampoe, leader of the Ceylon Mercantile Union (CMU), is one example of a leader whose tough idealism has earned him respect among employers as well as workers. The secretary-general of the Employers' Federation of Ceylon (EFC) has praised the degree of institutionalization achieved in collective bargaining between the EFC and CMU.[10] Over six decades of leadership, Tampoe has driven a hard bargain but has effectively negotiated agreements with hundreds of EFC firms. Many leaders have developed similar reputations for their honest and effective mediation of disputes, and in a democratic context where workers can hold union leaders accountable for their actions such a strategy is more likely to pay long-term dividends.

Employer Response to Worker Militancy

Employers are generally conservative in their approach to industrial relations and refrain from initiating industrial disputes for one basic reason: a day's profits are greater than a day's wage. For a company operating in the black, the loss of a day's production is substantially more costly to the employer than to any individual worker. Additionally, the economic pain of an industrial dispute lingers for an employer in a way that it does not for the employee. For workers, industrial disputes result in the loss of a few days' pay. For employers, industrial disputes result in the loss of current production and profits *plus* orders for future production. Thus an employer running a profitable business has very little incentive to call a lockout.

Nevertheless, worker militancy can increase the tendency of employers to instigate lockouts, especially in a difficult economic climate. For many years lockouts became more frequent than strikes throughout South Asia. For the most part, this trend was not due a rise in bona fide industrial disputes but represented the attempts of employers to close their factories. Lockouts provide an opportunity for unprofitable companies to circumvent chapter V-B of India's Industrial Disputes Act, which requires that employers obtain permission from the government to close their factories. Employers sometimes find it possible to receive approval for closure if they can demonstrate a substantial problem, such as an "intransigent" workforce or, in lieu of such permission, to use a lockout as a de facto form of closure. Thus lockouts in India have by and large not been the attempts of profitable employers to resolve longstanding issues with unions, but the attempts of unprofitable companies to close their factories.

Violent strikes are especially likely to provoke a lockout and speed the closure of a firm because protest has a uniquely poisonous effect on the character of industrial relations. As the manager at a food processing company in Sri Lanka put it, employers want to have a nonviolent union because "you won't risk your life for business."[11] The majority of employers I talked to said they preferred routine to violent protest even if routine protest meant a long and costly strike. Employers also voiced concern regarding the long-term negative effects of violence on managerial authority and labor productivity. This concern is illustrated by the experience of a production facility manufacturing railway cars in West Bengal, where violence that led to the hospitalization of one manager and the closure of one of its factories. When asked about why the strike resulted in the closure of the factory, a manager at the company stated that it was in part attributable to violence, which "demoralizes supervisory and managerial personnel on whom you have to depend for your production."[12] Generally speaking, such concerns make employers less inclined to engage in negotiations that could keep a company in business and more likely to lock workers out in an effort to close the factory when they are confronted by worker violence.

The Role of Democracy in the Management of Industrial Conflict

While individual union leaders have incentives to engage in militancy, party leaders seek more effective ways to manage industrial conflict as democracies become more inclusive and more responsive to voters. The process of "democratic deepening" can occur along a number of dimensions, all of which have important implications for how parties manage the behavior of affiliated unions. The positions and platforms of new parties can unsettle economic debates while increased voter turnout amplifies the demands of voters for a better economy and better jobs. More competitive elections put politicians under greater pressure to respond to voters, forcing them to draw on available resources to reign in worker militancy. At the same time democratization also brings with it more civil liberties, the struggle for which is frequently led by workers who are demanding greater FACB rights. Such rights may make it easier for workers to protest but at the same time provide workers with the organizational tools they need to engage in institutionalized grievance resolution.

Democracy and the Development of Union-Party Ties

Scholars of industrial and labor relations have noted two distinct effects of political competition on the strength and character of union-party ties. Scholars focusing on developing countries have by and large emphasized how partisan competition over union members undermines worker support for contentious economic reforms. Studies based on evidence from nascent democracies in Latin America show how partisan competition undermines state control over organized labor by enabling workers to play one political party off of another (Murillo 2001). Political competition can also fragment the union movement, providing workers with exit options that force parties to be more responsive to worker demands (Burgess 2004; Tafel and Boniface 2003).

On the other hand, as scholars of industrial and labor relations in the OECD have noted, competition in the electoral arena can facilitate the political mobilization of the working class, the development of union-party ties, and a "political exchange" between workers and the state (Swenson 1989). This exchange effectively shifts the locus of class politics from the industrial relations to the political arena, dramatically altering the character of strike protest. Across Western countries, industrial strikes have become shorter but more frequent and larger as they are used more as a tool for political than economic protest (Shorter and Tilly 1974). In Nordic countries and Austria, where labor-based social-democratic parties prevailed, even the overall volume and size of strikes declined as the dominance of the working-class, the growth of the public sector, and redistributive social welfare policies rendered contention in labor markets superfluous (Hibbs 1978; Korpi and Shalev 1980).

In South Asia, ties between parties and unions have been cultivated over more than a century of political struggle and have resulted in union-party dynamics similar to those seen elsewhere. The first political mobilization of workers dates to the late nineteenth century, when *Swadeshi* leaders attempted to integrate mill workers into India's nascent nationalist movement (Basu 2004, 131–37). These early attempts were followed by more successful efforts by INC and a variety of socialist leaders to organize party-affiliated unions (see Basu 2004, chaps. 5 and 6). One can trace the lineage of many of the major unions in India, including the All India Trade Union Congress (AITUC), CITU, and INTUC, to these early political struggles.

Having been forged through struggles led by nationalist elites prior to the emergence of an industrial economy or the emergence of an educated workforce, union-party ties have entailed an exchange that is likely more favorable to parties than workers. But while South Asian unions may not dominate public policy to the extent Nordic *Landsorganisationen* (LOs) do, their members derive two significant benefits from their close ties to political parties. First, overlapping leadership structures ensure that union representatives have seats in the state assemblies and in parliament. This voice in politics has enabled workers to obtain significant legal protections, which I discuss in greater detail below. Further, a strong voice in the political arena has enabled organized labor to slow the pace of economic reforms that present the biggest burdens for organized labor (Candland 2007, chap. 3).

Second, workers also derive sound industrial relations advice and effective voice in the industrial relations arena through their ties to political parties. The additional organizational capacity stemming from union political ties is a crucially important benefit that is frequently overlooked by scholars of industrial relations. Because they head national organizations, leaders of party-affiliated confederations have much more organizational know-how, much better negotiating skills, and a much broader and deeper understanding of labor markets than local union leaders and members. These skills are essential to knowing when to go on strike and how long to stay on strike, in negotiating settlements at the bargaining table, in resolving disputes in arbitration, and in arguing matters before labor tribunals and labor courts. It could be argued that these skills are counterbalanced by the cost of an outsider's agenda. Indeed, there is some truth to this argument, but as was noted earlier, all outsiders, including politically independent union leaders, have an agenda. As we shall see below, the most important distinction is whether that agenda is parochial or one that is motivated by the goals of a larger organization.

Democracy and FACB Rights

In addition to strong union-party ties, democracy endows workers with robust freedom of association and collective bargaining (FACB) rights, which include such rights as the right to establish and join worker organizations, the right to collectively bargain, the right to strike, and the right to freely engage in other union-related activities. There is tremendous cross-national variation in the protection of FACB rights that has implications for important economic outcomes (Kucera and Sarna 2006). The degree to which governments protect FACB rights varies systematically with regime type. Not surprisingly, countries that score high on civil liberties and democracy indexes tend to do a better job of providing FACB rights (Kucera 2001, appen. A.2).

The provision of FACB rights provides democracies with an advantage over authoritarian and hybrid regimes in the management of industrial conflict. The robust protection of FACB rights gives workers independence from employers and the state that is critical to the organization of effective trade unions and negotiation of legally binding collective bargaining agreements (Kucera 2007). For the same reason, FACB rights facilitate the functioning of labor institutions and enhance the benefits of union-party ties. Without independence from the state, institutions such as labor courts, tribunals, and arbitration proceedings merely become mechanisms for the imposition of employers' interests on workers and consequently grievances cannot be adequately resolved. Similarly, in the absence of FACB rights, state-labor ties are little more than a mechanism for cooptation.

Because of these institutional advantages, we would expect more democratic regions to be better equipped to handle the dislocations associated with economic liberalization and increased exposure to competitive markets than authoritarian regimes. There is wide variation across South Asia in terms of government respect for FACB rights. Although there has been some slippage in enforcement in recent years, India is generally recognized as having some of the strictest legal protections for organized sector workers anywhere in the world (World Bank 2000, chap. 6; Sachs et al.

1999; Stern 2001). A complex web of regulations govern Indian industrial relations, with forty-nine central government acts alone governing various aspects of the employment relationship (Malik 2005). Thirty-three of these acts govern the organized industrial sector. Twenty-one of them apply to the industrial sector as a whole, while twelve provide sector-specific worker protections. Further, state legislatures have enacted many proworker amendments to these central acts, some of which place stringent restrictions on the employment relationship.[13]

Other countries in South Asia have poorer reputations when it comes to the provision of labor rights. In the immediate post-Independence period, Pakistan had quite a robust union movement following on that country's rapid industrial development; but as early as 1952 "the bureaucracy and industrialists began to collude to repress the industrial working classes" (Candland 2007, 38). Despite the enactment of the Industrial Relations Ordinance (IRO) of 1969, which was designed to meet union demands for basic FACB rights, things only got worse for workers as military dictators and authoritarian populists failed to provide these rights in practice (Candland 2007, 40–50). Similarly, Bangladesh is the frequent target of criticism by the International Confederation of Free Trade Unions (ICFTU) for facilitating employer discrimination against unions. Finally as I demonstrate in chapter 6, Sri Lanka underwent a dramatic transition from a labor-friendly to a labor-repressive state in the early 1980s.

Democratic Deepening and the Growing Impetus for Restraint

The reforms undertaken by India and Sri Lanka in the 1980s and 1990s garnered wide support among voters without challenging powerful economic stakeholders (Bardhan 1998, 123–32). In India, economic reform began as a stealthy and elite-led process in the 1980s (Jenkins 1999) but drew broader support from the electorate beginning in the 1990s. The electoral dominance of the Bharatiya Janata Party (BJP) during the 1990s resulted in part from the support from high-caste and middle- and upper-class voters encouraged by the BJP's promises to expand and accelerate the reform process (Chhibber 1999). Moreover, the desire to portray India as a modern nation on the ascent led to the universal acceptance of economic liberalization among Hindu nationalists, for whom surpassing the infamous "Hindu rate of growth" became the path to national redemption (Rajagopal 2001). In Sri Lanka, widespread support for reforms came very early. In 1977, the center-right United National Party (UNP) came to power winning 83 percent of the seats in parliament on a platform of economic liberalization, which was widely interpreted as a broad mandate in support of the UNP's proposed reforms.

At the same time, reforms did present a challenge to political parties by reducing the scope of public sector employment (Chandra 2004), thus putting pressure on political leaders to stimulate investment and job growth in the private sector. Consequently, political parties boosted their efforts to attract private sector investment to their regions through a variety of investor-friendly policies and practices, including attempts to improve labor market flexibility and the quality of industrial relations. These efforts entailed drawing more heavily on ties with affiliated unions to restrain worker militancy.

Such pressure to reign in protest is likely to increase as democracy deepens and voters exert greater influence on elected representatives. For many years, Indian politics has been characterized by a patronage system in which the Indian National Congress (INC) relied on upper-caste intermediaries, such as local landlords and business elites, to exercise their clout over local communities at election time (e.g., Kothari 1964; Weiner 1967). Over the last three decades, however, India's political system has been radically transformed from a highly centralized system dominated by the INC, into a "cleavage-based" system structured largely along caste lines with multiple parties competing for votes (Chhibber 1999). Initially, these parties mimicked the behavior of the Congress by doling out patronage to local elites in exchange for the votes of their communities. More recently, however, there have been signs that Indian politics might be moving away from the traditional patronage system and in a programmatic direction, as over time the rising costs of providing selective benefits to an ever-expanding number of local elites forces parties away from clientelistic behavior (Wilkinson 2006). As programmatic modes of campaigning replace traditional patronage politics, politicians are under increasing pressure to deliver economic growth and private sector jobs to their constituents.

It is important to note however that democratic deepening has not been experienced uniformly across India. The competitiveness of the party system has increased in some states more than others. In the literature on party systems, the primary measure of party fragmentation is the "effective number of parties" approach devised by Laakso and Taagepera (1979).[14] In 1980, the average effective number of parties at the state level was 4.42, which had increased to 5.25 by 1990; but across states this figure ranged from 2.64 in Orissa to 7.42 in Kerala. A closely related phenomenon is the uneven mobilization of working-class and lower-caste voters, which results in wide variation in the quality of democratic governance across India (Heller 2000). It is likely that the electoral impetus for parties to restrain unions as well as to protect FACB rights will vary in relation to the extent of party competition and voter participation in elections.

The Role of External Leadership in Producing and Reducing Worker Militancy

Standard collective action theory tells us that although workers have strong incentives to engage in protest for higher wages, better working conditions, and so on, they face significant impediments in do doing so (Olson 1971). Even if workers are successful in overcoming the free-rider problem through cultural norms of cooperation or the strategic use of selective incentives, they face an uphill battle against employers with superior resources and better access to information about labor and product markets. These material and informational deficits make it very unlikely that nonunionized workers will engage in protest against the management.

A similar logic applies to the behavior of workers who are organized by Japanese-style enterprise unions, which are characterized by a leadership that is entirely "in house," as opposed to being recruited from outside the firm. On the one hand, it may seem logical to expect enterprise unions to behave aggressively, because such unions are free from external constraints. Yet economists and industrial relations experts have noted that enterprise unions are generally less contentious than those affiliated with external federations.[15] This is because federations provide access to resources that help workers to overcome collective action problems that most enterprise unions cannot; these resources include strike funds, enforcement of picket lines, negotiating skills, and information about product and labor market conditions that make it easier to sustain a strike. So while their incentives to engage in militant protest seem clear, enterprise-level leaders frequently lack the capacity to mobilize on their own in the face of the superior resources and capabilities of the employer. At the same time, some form of internal organization should enable enterprise unions to protest more than nonunionized workers.

By contrast, workers affiliated with external federations are much more likely to have the organizational capacity necessary to bargain as well as protest. In the foregoing discussion, we saw that individual union leaders have incentives to ratchet up pressure on management while political parties are under increasing pressure to restrain the protest of workers. This leads us to consider how worker affiliations to different types of union federations may condition the nature of worker response to economic adversity. External leadership can potentially increase both the likelihood of worker protest and the aggressiveness with which unions present their demands; but external leaders will be much less likely to engage in militant protest behavior if they also hold key leadership posts in a major political party.

Two Types of External Federations

External federations provide workers with substantial informational and material resources that nonunionized workers and workers organized by enterprise unions are lacking, but the way these resources are employed is likely to be influenced by the type of external federation union with which the workers are affiliated. Specifically, I distinguish between two types of external federations. I refer to the first type of federation as "narrow interest unions" (NIUs), meaning those unions with an external leadership that is not constrained by the interests of an encompassing political party. This term is used mainly for convenience but is also intended to remind the reader of my hypothesis that nonaffiliated unions can become vehicles for pursuing the parochial interests of a small group of federation leaders. NIUs include federations affiliated with small political parties, that is, those having only limited success in the electoral arena, as well as politically independent union federations. Leaders of nonaffiliated unions are more likely to pursue their parochial interests because they are not constrained by the interests of any affiliated organizations.

I refer to the second type of federation as "major party unions" (MPUs), defined as those unions affiliated with political parties that are highly competitive in the electoral arena and have a stake in the success of development policy at the national or state levels. In the following discussion, I argue that major political parties encourage federation leaders, who would otherwise ratchet up militancy, to show restraint because the leaders of political parties internalize the externalities associated with militant union behavior. In other words, leaders of MPUs have the necessary informational and monetary resources to overcome collective action problems but opt to rein in protest and instead support broader developmental objectives.

Political Parties as Encompassing Organizations

The argument in this book about why partisan unions mobilize restraint in the collective bargaining arena builds on Mancur Olson's theory of organizational encompassment. In this theory, frequently applied to explain union behavior in the OECD, Olson observes that the larger an organization becomes, the more likely its members are to benefit from sacrifices for the common good or to suffer the consequences of socially disruptive behavior. Thus, he argues, leaders of organizations will work harder to curb the socially costly behavior of members as the organization comes to encompass a larger percentage of the population.

In line with this hypothesis, studies of wage bargaining in the OECD have emphasized the role of encompassing unions and centralized labor markets in facilitating union wage restraint.[16] However, as Olson notes, the logic of encompassment also applies to the outlook of political parties, to which large unions are frequently affiliated:

> One sometimes sees labor or socialist parties that emerged from trade unions, but with leaders that sometimes take a less parochial view than the parent unions, presumably because the party leader has a more encompassing constituency. There are also parallel cases of conservative parties that draw their core support from business and professional associations, yet sometimes withhold certain favors from these lobbies in the interest of a thriving national constituency.[17]

Due to a myopic focus on the organizational encompassment of unions, the interests of political parties in worker restraint and the potential influence of political parties over union behavior have largely been overlooked in subsequent studies of union bargaining behavior in the OECD. But if the logic of encompassment is correct, then the leaders of an encompassing political party are just as motivated to restrain the behavior of affiliated unions as the leaders of a large union.

Because the percentage of workers organized by unions in developing countries is typically much lower than in the OECD, the logic of political encompassment is likely to be more relevant for analyzing union behavior in developing countries than is the standard logic of union encompassment. In high-labor-union-density countries in Western Europe, individual union federations constitute highly encompassing organizations. In Nordic countries and Austria union-controlled unemployment (the Ghent system) and other institutional incentives have resulted in union density figures as high as 80 percent—levels that have persisted even in the context of economic globalization and exposure to intense competition in international product markets (Western 1997). Moreover, the union movement in countries with the most centralized labor markets tends to be organized by either a single or a handful of union federations. The dominance of the LOs in Nordic countries presents the most prominent example of this phenomenon.

In developing democracies, levels of union density never reach those of the most organized countries in the OECD. This is partly because the industrial sector, where unions have historically found it easier to organize workers, plays a much smaller role in the economies of low- and middle-income countries. Just as important, however, a larger percentage of industrial output in developing countries is concentrated in the informal (unregulated) sector of the economy. One study estimates that the informal sector constitutes 41 percent of economic output in developing countries and 38 percent in transition countries, but only 18 percent in OECD countries (Schneider 2002). In India informal sector workers constitute 38 percent of the nonagricultural labor force, whereas formal sector workers constitute just 18 percent (Agarwala 2008). Informal sector workers are notoriously difficult to organize, both because workers are dispersed across small enterprises and because FACB rights are not enforced in the informal sector.

As in other developing areas, low levels of industrialization and large informal sectors in South Asia tend to dilute the organizational encompassment of unions. Although union density approaches 80 percent in the industrial sector of some regions of India, unionized workers constitute 33 percent of employees in the entire formal sector and just 6 percent of all nonagricultural workers.[18] But even where union density is high, the organizational encompassment of unions is undermined by the fact that union movements are typically much more competitive and less centralized than in the OECD. The union movement in the Indian state of West Bengal, where more than three-quarters of the industrial workforce is organized by the Center for Indian Trade Unions (CITU), stands out as an exceptionally unified movement, but as I demonstrate in chapter 4 it is much more common to see unions of a variety of political stripes, as well as independent unions, vie for the support of the working class.

In contrast to unions, major political parties are highly encompassing organizations in low- and middle-income countries. From an organizational perspective, they have a larger "membership base" than even the largest unions. They are also encompassing from a representational perspective because they are beholden to the demands of the median voter. As Przeworski notes in his discussion of unions and social democratic parties, "there is a permanent tension between the narrower interests of unions and the broader interests represented by parties" (Przeworski 1986, 14).

Because major parties are broad-based organizations that vie for the political support of a large constituency, we would expect their leaders to prefer a more conservative approach to industrial relations than the leaders of affiliated unions. This conservative orientation applies to initiating disputes with management as well as to the types of protest strategies employed. Specifically, political leaders should encourage routine protest as opposed to high-pressure tactics, such as the destruction of company property, the use of threats, or violence against management.

At the same time, we should not expect a one-to-one correspondence in the relationship between a party's degree of encompassment and a reduction in the militancy of affiliated unions. While party encompassment is an important component of the explanation for why MPUs restrain worker protest, major parties must at the same time be accountable to electoral pressures. In other words, the logic of political encompassment is predicated on a competitive electoral system. In a one-party system, encompassment is reflective of a lack of political competition and the party, although encompassing, will be less responsive to the concerns of voters than a major party in a more competitive system. Thus while a major political party will typically have a different orientation toward worker unrest than a small political party, the effects of encompassment on worker protest may level off or even reverse if the party becomes so dominant as to make the political system uncompetitive. For this reason, we would expect political encompassment to be relevant even in a fragmented party system and measures of party competition to positively correlate with worker restraint.

The Importance of Overlapping Leadership Structures

Although restraint by workers may serve the interests of the party, political leaders cannot simply impose their will on federation leaders or union members. In order to convince workers to refrain from aggressive union behavior, the directives of party leaders must filter down through the ranks. Parties, in other words, must counterbalance the interest that shop-floor leaders and the rank and file have in a more aggressive bargaining and protest posture. While the development of a model of federation control over firm-level leaders and members is beyond the scope of this study, it is important to consider how political parties and their affiliated unions mobilize restraint and how party success in coordinating class compromise may vary across firms.

Recent studies point to a number of factors that govern both the strength of the relationship between political parties and union federations and the ability of party leaders to secure the cooperation of union leaders and members. As Collier and Collier point out in their seminal article, parties have typically achieved control over unions through the strategic deployment of inducements (such as providing the union with organizational and financial support) and constraints (such as direct interference in the internal governance of unions) (Collier and Collier 1979). Burgess identifies the distribution of leadership positions within the party and the government as a uniquely important set of inducements available to party bosses and repressive legal measures as an important set of constraints (Burgess 2004). Levitsky and Way (1998) provide a slightly different characterization of variation in the strength of union-party ties. They emphasize the sociological factors, such as "social linkages, shared identities and networks of close personal ties," that bind union and party leaders. According to this view, it is the extent of organizational overlap more than the strategic use of incentives and constraints that determines whether unions follow party directives.

In South Asia governments have relied on a similar mix of inducements, constraints, and overlapping leadership structures to control the behavior of affiliated unions. Not surprisingly, national and regional governments with less robust democratic traditions have relied more on repressive legislation and direct interference in collective bargaining to exert their control. During the 1980s, for example, the UNP in Sri Lanka utilized a variety of repressive mechanisms, including emergency regulations and the establishment of special economic zones, to dismantle opposition unions and push through its program of neoliberal economic reforms.[19] Similarly, in Pakistan unions have experienced severe repression, enjoy little influence over economic policy, and have little power in the collective bargaining arena (Candland 2001).

In democratic contexts governments have relied more on inducements and overlapping leadership structures than on repressive labor legislation. In India the legal framework governing industrial relations was designed by conservative elements of the Congress Party and was intended to be highly interventionist; but this effort to subdue organized labor ultimately failed, and the type of state corporatism intended by some members of the Congress never materialized (Teitelbaum 2008). Similarly, in Sri Lanka the climate of labor repression that prevailed in the 1980s gave way to the resurgence of democratic state-labor relations in the mid-1990s. Parties in India and Sri Lanka have thus tended to rely on inducements, such as concessions on economic policy, to sway union leaders in recent years.

Arguably, however, the most important factor influencing the behavior of union leaders is the social linkages between parties and unions and related opportunities for political advancement. Leaders of politically affiliated federations frequently aspire to be or currently serve as members of parliament or members of the state legislative assemblies. For example, one of the leaders of a striking tire factory I visited in Kerala was Ooman Chandy, who was the ruling party convener in the Kerala Legislative Assembly. Similarly, Ganesh Naik, leader of the Maharashtra-based Sharmik Sena, belonged to the Shiv Sena from 1995 to 1999, during which time his union was affiliated to the Bharatiya Kamgar Sena (BKS), and when I interviewed him was a member of the legislative assembly (MLA) for the Nationalist Congress Party (NCP). Jitendra Joshi was vice president of the Maharashtra branch of the INTUC and also the secretary of the Rashtrawadi Congress Party (RCP).

Many other union leaders who are not already powerful politicians aspire to use their union post as a platform for a political career. The manager at a small packaging company in Kerala described to me how union leaders are selected and groomed for a political career in his factory.[20] Leaders are either appointed by the party or are elected by workers from a very narrow pool of candidates selected by the party. This relatively undemocratic method of selection prevents union leaders from developing a personal power base in the union, making them dependent on the central political organization for both their union *and* future political careers. Once a union leader develops status in the party, the party replaces him with a new aspiring politician.

If union leaders are aspiring politicians, they have every incentive to adopt the preferences of party leadership, and if union leaders are also party leaders, then there is no real distinction between the preferences of union leaders and those of party leaders. In my interviews, I found substantial evidence that the preferences of MPU leaders regarding choice of bargaining and protest tactics were in line with those of the party. Employers and trade union leaders repeatedly suggested that MPUs have responded to changing economic circumstances in a conservative manner. Rather than playing on worker frustrations or whipping up antiglobalization sentiment, MPUs have generally responded to the ineffectiveness of routine strike protest by attempting to restrain demands, institutionalize industrial relations, encourage productivity-linked wage agreements, and educate workers regarding the prevailing conditions in product markets.

This is not to say, however, that local leaders and members always buy into the priorities of federation and party leaders. The vigorously competitive nature of South Asia's union movement is likely to have a negative impact on the ability of parties and federations to control shop-floor leaders and members. Other factors, such as local economic conditions, the level of internal democracy within shop-floor unions, or the responses of management toward a union may also influence a union's ability to satisfy workers' demands and exert control over their behavior. It is important to account for this variation in federation control over the rank and file in any quantitative model of industrial protest.

A Shared Emphasis on Restraint across Ideological Boundaries

A common suspicion is that the political restraint of industrial protest is influenced by political ideology. There are a number of variations of this argument. One is that conservative parties are more likely to restrain wage demands and strike protest because of a free market ideology or an antilabor political stance. The opposite perspective holds that left parties are more likely to succeed in restraining affiliated unions because they are better at gaining the trust of workers. A final argument, which finds some support in the OECD, is that parties mobilize restraint according to who is in power (Alvarez, Garrett, and Lange 1991). Parties restrain wage demands and protest when they are in power and call out strikes to embarrass the incumbent party when they are in the opposition.

In India, at least, the response of political parties to industrial unrest has been less partisan. Anecdotal evidence suggests that the popularity of reforms and the competition over private sector investment has led to a shared emphasis by MPU leaders on restraint in the industrial relations arena. In Maharashtra, where MPUs are primarily affiliated to right and center-right parties, employers emphasized the continuation of a positive synergy between the management and the union that has existed since at least the 1980s. The personnel manager of a major automobile manufacturer echoed the prevailing sentiment among managers in Maharashtra when he stated that relative to the enterprise union in the company's Pune-based factory, the Shiv Sena-affiliated BKS, was better able to "take charge" of workers and did a better job of "selling agreements" and ensuring their implementation.[21] Managers in Maharashtra viewed MPUs as helpful in negotiating even the most difficult agreements. For instance, the management at a plastics factory in Bombay indicated that the BKS was helpful in negotiating and implementing a voluntary retirement scheme, which required navigating the heavy restrictions placed on layoffs and closures by firms in the organized sector in chapter V-B of the Industrial Disputes Act.[22]

Beyond implementing agreements, managers reported that MPU leaders were helpful in providing an environment conducive to investment. For example, the managing director at a lubricants factory based in the Thane-Belapur industrial belt outside of Bombay discussed the efforts made by the leadership of the MPU in his company—the INTUC-affiliated Association of Chemical Workers (ACW)—to moderate worker demands and to restrain worker protest. According to the manager, the secretary-general of the union, K. H. Dastoor, considers the company's economic position and makes an effort to convince workers of the importance of competitive pricing and savings in operating costs.[23]

The lubricant factory manager contrasted Dastoor's stance with that of the late Datta Samant, the renowned union leader of the MGKU (an NIU), who organized workers in many of Thane-Belapur's factories prior to Dastoor's dominance. Whereas Samant was indifferent to the fact that his militant trade union actions had led to the closure of dozens of units in Thane-Belapur industrial belt, Dastoor has taken a great interest in the well-being of establishments. Dastoor has taken the initiative to organize joint conferences with industrialists in the region to determine whether his union might have contributed to the exit of factories from the Thane-Belapur industrial belt and to encourage companies to refrain from moving their production facilities elsewhere. In an interview, Dastoor confirmed this impression by comparing his own style of unionism with that of Bai Jagtap, the leader of the Bharatiya Kamgar Karmachari Mahasangh (BKKM), an aggressive independent union known for its heavy use of violent tactics. Dastoor was adamant that his union does not "compete on that level," stating that he eschews violence and "thinks ten times before taking action."[24]

Other MPU leaders in Maharashtra echoed this philosophy. Ganesh Naik, leader of the Sharmik Sena union articulated the conservative philosophy to which many BKS and INTUC leaders adhere. Naik argued that the purpose of trade unionism is just as much to get the worker to "understand his responsibilities" and the financial position of the company as it is to get the management to agree to higher wages and benefits. Naik likened trade unionism to horse racing, saying that "if you want to go the distance, you have to be patient."[25] Using violent and aggressive protests are shortsighted tactics that destroy opportunities for negotiated settlements and leads to factory closures, which is ultimately counter to the interests of workers.

Jitendra Joshi, leader of the INTUC-affiliated Kamgar Utkarsh Sabha (KUS), stressed that rather than threatening to withhold labor, INTUC's basic strategy is to achieve wage gains by using productivity as a bargaining chip:

> We control the productivity. Our basic approach is this. First, the company should survive. If the company survives, then there is continued employment. The government lays down laws regarding the minimum wage. If you want more than the minimum wage, then you have to support the company. You have to allow the company to rationalize the deployment of persons, to modernize technology, and to increase productivity.[26]

In Joshi's view, the union plays a crucial role in convincing workers of the need for mutually beneficial productivity increases. The management is unable to convince workers themselves, because a large percentage of workers are illiterate: "To convince the worker, they require a really strong person who can deliver the goods.... They cannot negotiate with every person because our people are not that much educated."[27]

The stories of cooperative behavior by MPU leaders were no less striking in Kerala and West Bengal, where the union movement is more heavily dominated by left unions, and in particular, the CPM-affiliated CITU. The strike at a Kerala tire factory led by CITU and INTUC that was described at the beginning of this chapter is one example, and there are many others like it. The managing director at a packaging company in West Bengal, for example, expressed a common sentiment when he said that his relationship with the CITU is so good that the CITU leader tries to drum up business for the firm when sales are low.[28] While most companies set their sights on three- or four-year agreements, this company signs agreements lasting as long as seven years with the union.

A further consequence of the softer bargaining stance of MPUs noted by several employers in Kerala and West Bengal is their increased willingness to sign productivity-linked wage agreements. The director of an engineering firm in West Bengal stated that his workers signed a productivity-linked agreement because the central leadership helps them to "understand the meaning of liberalization and globalization."[29] These agreements are well adhered to and are renegotiated every four to five years.

At the same time, the cooperative behavior of left MPU leaders was said to be a more recent development in West Bengal and Kerala. In these two states, employers emphasized the radical transformation of the left's stance toward management, which only occurred after the 1991 economic reforms. The human resources manager at an electronics factory in Kerala described the transformation of union behavior as being linked to the recognition of the need to face the challenges of a more open economy:

> The unions have become more practicable, more pliable. They are willing to listen to what management says. They are willing to learn about the issues related to productivity, issues related to marketing, issues related to finance, et cetera. They are now willing to study how the business runs, what are the difficulties faced by business. They are also willing to give their part, to play their part to help this organization survive and face the globalization.[30]

Many employers in Kerala conveyed a similar sentiment, including the director of a company in the cashew sector—traditionally a stronghold of radical left unions. The employer stated his opinion that Kerala's "period of radicalism is over" and that a new generation of union leaders and workers was more likely to consider the economic constraints faced by management.[31]

The same opinion was expressed even more forcefully by employers in West Bengal, who emphasized the radical transformation of union leaders' attitudes with respect to employer constraints and the character of union demands and protest tactics since liberalization. The managing director of a steel company stated that in the 1970s and 1980s, CITU was a "nightmare, but today it is the easiest union to handle."[32] He attributed this turnabout in the CITU's behavior to the CPMs policy of avoiding confrontation and violence in the factories and indicated that the CPM government is willing to help managers deal with violent workers by removing them from the factory.

Other employers also emphasized the helpfulness of central CITU and CPM leadership in resolving disputes with local leaders and workers. The general manager of human resources at a company that manufactures industrial clothing suggested a divergence between the union's public statements to workers, which often rail against employers' efforts to introduce laborsaving technology or to outsource production, and its actions, which are employer friendly. He emphasized the ease with which he could seek the help of CITU central leadership, or even the assistance of the chief minister, to prevent disagreements from becoming full-fledged industrial disputes.[33] The director of a company that manufactures cooling towers stated that he was so enthusiastic about the professionalism of the central CITU leadership and the control they exerted over workers that he *invited* CITU leaders to organize his factory to prevent the entry of a more aggressive, politically independent union.[34]

Labor Legislation, FACB Rights, and Economic Performance

The final mechanism through which states can influence the industrial relations climate is through labor legislation and the provision of FACB rights. Some laws, such as those that improve workers' ability to engage in collective bargaining or workers' access to labor courts and arbitration proceedings, can facilitate institutionalized grievance resolution and mitigate the deleterious effects of greater exposure to market forces. Other laws, such as those that restrict workers' ability to exercise FACB rights, may have exactly the opposite effect.

In recent years, scholars have generated a tremendous amount of research on the effects of labor laws on economic performance in low- and middle-income countries.[35] A number of prominent studies have focused on India, touching off a fierce debate regarding the economic impact of its thick web of protective labor law. Most of the debate has centered on the effects of employment protection law (EPL) that imposes limits on the ability of managers of medium- and large-scale firms to hire and fire workers at will. Guided by neoliberal economic theory, econometric studies have purported to show that EPL designed to help workers has instead given rise to rigidities that hamper job creation in labor-intensive manufacturing. Further, it is argued that strict EPL pushes production into the informal sector as employers seek to evade regulations in the formal sector, which in turn results in higher inequality and poverty. Ultimately, these dynamics produce an unfair dualism in the labor market: a "privileged" class of industrial workers is awarded high wages and job security at the expense of insecure low-wage workers in the informal sector.

No set of employment protection provisions has drawn as much fire for its potential impact on labor markets, however, as those in chapter V-B of the IDA. Chapter V-B was inserted in the IDA in 1976 during the height of the Emergency period. It initially required that any industrial establishment employing three hundred or more workers seek the government's permission in order to lay off or fire workers, or in order to close down a factory. In 1982, an amendment was introduced to lower the threshold to one hundred workers, substantially expanding the number of industrial establishments covered by its provisions.[36]

The timing of the introduction of chapter V-B, as well as its subsequent expansion and strengthening at the national and state levels, contributed to a widespread suspicion that India's strong EPL was responsible for jobless growth in manufacturing in the 1980s and early-1990s. The first econometric studies by Fallon and Lucas (1991; 1993) analyzed the effects of the new restrictions at the national level.[37] However, it was with the publication of a study in the *Quarterly Journal of Economics* a decade later that the debate over the relationship between India's labor regulation and economic performance began to gain momentum and an international audience (Besley and Burgess 2004). This article led to a flurry of studies in development economics that analyze the economic impact of state-level amendments to the IDA (e.g., Aghion et al. 2008; Hasan et al. 2007; Topolova 2004).

Unfortunately, state-level legislation amendments to the IDA have been grossly mischaracterized in the economics literature. Standard econometric analyses of Indian labor law purport to distinguish between "proworker" and "proemployer" amendments to the IDA, and to show that so-called "proworker" legislation has generated rigidities in labor markets that hamper economic performance. In fact, most provisions of the IDA are written to facilitate neutral third-party mediation of industrial disputes, and it is very difficult to characterize its provisions as inherently biased in favor of either employers or workers (Bhattacharjea 2006; 2009).

The IDA originated in the struggle between conservative elements of the Congress Party and the left over control of India's labor movement. It is a strong act that, among other things, provides the government with the authority to refer disputes to courts, tribunals, or specially constituted boards for compulsory arbitration.[38] In the years immediately following its enactment, the state leaned on the IDA quite heavily to intervene in industrial disputes and thereby prevented the resolution of disputes through bipartite collective bargaining. As Chibber notes, "Matters that were usually settled through collective bargaining were now dealt with through detailed regulations within labor law and the number of industrial disputes rapidly declined. Congress had, at least momentarily, achieved labor peace" (Chibber 2003, 105).

Over time, however, there has been substantial variation in how the IDA has been applied at the state level. Since Independence, the authority of labor courts, tribunals, and ministries of labor has been in some cases augmented and in others undermined by state-level amendments to the IDA. While some state-level amendments introduced restrictions on hiring and firing of workers, and thus have a proworker bent, strict employment protection law constitutes a minority of state-level amendments. In fact, most state amendments to the IDA relate to the ability of state government to intervene in industrial disputes and are fairly neutral in terms of their impact on employers and workers. Examples include amendments that expand the jurisdiction of labor courts and tribunals to hear specific types of cases, that provide the government with greater authority to enforce the awards of labor courts and tribunals, or that enhance the power of the government to compel attendance at conciliation proceedings.

Like the strategy of mobilizing restraint through union-party ties, these state-level amendments to the IDA represent states' attempts to deal with the increasingly volatile industrial relations situation described in chapter 2. During the 1980s and 1990s, workers were squeezed by increasingly competitive product markets, which put downward pressure on wages and increased unemployment in manufacturing. In these adverse economic conditions, unions were unable to press their demands through routine strike protest and began engaging in more unconventional and violent forms of protest. Viewed in this context, it is easy to see how many of the state-level amendments adopted in the 1980s were designed to promote greater stability through government intervention in industrial disputes.

Such amendments are difficult to characterize as "proworker" or "proemployer" since it is not clear a priori which party in a dispute will benefit from greater state intervention in industrial disputes. Moreover, if we assume that the state intervenes as a neutral arbiter, there are good reasons to expect state intervention in industrial disputes to have a positive impact on the Indian economy. First, labor legislation promotes a stable investment climate by enhancing the role of third-party mediation. Realizing that industrial conflict is costly to both employers and workers and can negatively affect growth, governments have put considerable effort into developing institutional solutions to address the informational asymmetries that lead to bargaining failures and strikes (Hicks 1948). Institutions like labor courts, conciliation proceedings, and the legal framework supporting collective agreements help to facilitate bargaining and promote industrial peace (Card 1988).

The state can also boost productivity through the provision of associational rights. In legitimating and amplifying the voice of workers, state involvement in industrial relations helps to maximize the "participatory benefits" of unions such as improved efficiency of communication between managers and workers (Aidt and Tzannatos 2002). By protecting associational rights, the state amplifies the role of unions, which have been shown to save management time in the negotiating process, reduce disputes over work rules and seniority provisions, and reduce turnover by boosting worker morale (Freeman and Medoff 1979; 1984).

Finally, by giving workers greater access to labor courts and privileging the formal resolution of disputes, industrial disputes legislation can reduce the tendency of employers to rely on highly vulnerable and easily exploitable workers. The relationship between workers and employers in the informal sector is largely despotic and precapitalist (Heller 1999), and entails a heavy reliance on low-wage and child labor that deters investment in new technology (Weiner 1991). Laws and institutions that force employers to recognize unions as legitimate bargaining partners, and which establish procedures for worker grievances, make it very difficult for employers to engage in the type of autocratic and demeaning treatment of workers that is so common outside of the organized sector. Higher labor standards force employers to pay higher wages and benefits, thus providing incentive to invest in new technology and improve human resource practices (Schrank 2007). The end result is to promote capital deepening and greater economies of scale in the formal sector—exactly the opposite of what neoliberal theory would predict.

At the same time, not all labor law in India has been beneficial for industrial development. In chapter 5, I show how the large body of legislation declaring particular industries (sectors) as "public utilities," which has so far been overlooked in the literature, has negative effects on economic performance. Under the IDA, once an industry is declared a public utility, the government can impose severe restrictions on the ability of workers to call out strikes or employers to declare lockouts in that industry. By reducing the space for negotiated settlement, public utilities legislation has produced greater instability and worker alienation, thus diminishing investment, output, and productivity.

Summary of Expectations

This chapter began with two anecdotes—one about a violent strike at a rubber products manufacturing facility in Sri Lanka and the other about routine protest and collective bargaining at a tire factory in Kerala, India. Just as they helped to frame the issues that this chapter aimed to address, these anecdotes help to illustrate the theory developed in this chapter. Sri Lanka and Kerala are at opposite ends of the spectrum with respect to the development of union-party ties as well as their level of respect for democratic rights and freedoms since Independence.

The strike in Sri Lanka occurred at Ansell Lanka, a factory inside of an Export Processing Zone (EPZ). As I elaborate in chapter 6, such zones are designed to keep out unions, and workers within them are afforded with no FACB rights. The inability of the workers' parent union, the Ceylon Federation of Trade Unions (CFTU)—a union with a very moderate approach to industrial relations—to manage the local union had a great deal to do with the violence that occurred in this strike. An embarrassed and bewildered CFTU leadership only learned of the extreme actions of its members well after the strike had begun. The Ansell Lanka strike is therefore a clear example of how state repression of organized labor encourages violent protest by preventing the development of union-party ties and by preventing workers from exercising FACB rights.

In contrast, the strike at the Kerala tire factory illustrates how MPUs in a fully democratic context moderate the protest behavior of workers. Bound by the interests of a broader constituency, CITU and INTUC leaders avoided aggressive bargaining tactics and eschewed violence, and instead encouraged workers to secure wage increases through productivity-linked agreements. Through the analysis of a broad range of data, the remaining chapters of this book will test the arguments developed in this chapter. The following are the core set of expectations developed in the preceding analysis.

The first argument of the chapter was that in the era of economic reforms, democratic competition increases the impetus for political parties to mobilize restraint. This is because political competition forces unions to be responsive to a broader constituency and not just the interest of core supporters like union members. In order to win elections in a competitive democracy, parties must deliver economic benefits to a broad swath of voters. Thus political competition should result in decreased strikes overall.

In addition to its competitive dimension, democracy has a rights-granting dimension. Democracies typically afford workers better protection of FACB rights and better access to labor institutions. These protections provide workers with more opportunities to organize in favor of their interests and to air their grievances. Yet they also help to institutionalize protest by improving the reach and effectiveness of the state's industrial relations machinery. The rights-granting aspect of democracy will therefore correlate with more protest, but will improve productivity by reducing turnover and by reducing exploitation of sweated labor. Better provision of worker rights also improves the investment climate by reducing the propensity of workers to engage in highly disruptive forms of protest. Overall then, FACB rights increase worker protest but have positive effects on productivity, investment, and growth.

The foregoing discussion also yielded predictions regarding the behavior of specific types of unions. We saw that shop-floor leaders and members have incentives to ratchet up pressure on management and thus to engage in militant protest behavior. Yet we also noted that nonunionized workers and workers without any support from an external federation are not likely to protest very much at all. Workers have strong incentives to engage in protest but may find it difficult to overcome collective action problems in order to do so. Even if workers are successful in surmounting the free-rider problem, they are confronted with the superior material and informational resources that employers possess. Nonunionized workers will thus be quite unlikely to engage in protest against management.

A similar logic applies to the behavior of enterprise, or "in-house," unions. Although enterprise unions are free from the constraints that govern leaders of unions affiliated with major political parties, they are quiescent because they lack the resources that external federations provide. While members of enterprise unions have incentives for militancy, they face many of the same barriers to collective action as workers in nonunionized firms. On the other hand, enterprise unions have a higher level of internal organization than nonunionized workers that may enable them to engage in some protest.

External federations provide workers with the informational and material resources lacked by nonunionized workers and workers organized by enterprise unions, but the type of external affiliation influences the way these resources are employed. Narrow interest unions are likely to engage in aggressive protest because NIU leaders are free from the constraints of a more encompassing organization. Thus we should expect NIU members to engage in more aggressive protest as NIU leaders exert greater control over firm-level leaders and members.

By contrast, major political parties encourage federation leaders, who would otherwise ratchet up militancy, to show restraint because the leaders of political parties internalize the externalities associated with militant union behavior. In other words, leaders of MPUs have the necessary informational and monetary resources to overcome collective action problems but opt to rein in protest and instead support broader developmental objectives. Thus we should expect that the more control an MPU is able to exert over firm-level leaders and members, the more likely it is to prevent workers from calling wildcat strikes or employing violent or extreme protest tactics.

PART II

THE EVIDENCE

Part I of the book explored differences in how workers in the organized industrial sector respond to increased exposure to market forces. It argued that democracy helps to explain why some workers continue to engage in routine protest and institutionalized grievance resolution despite declining bargaining power, while others engage in more militant protest to achieve their demands. This section of the book tests this argument in three ways. In chapter 4, I look at the relationship between political competition and industrial protest. I use state-level data to test the argument that more competitive party systems, elections, and higher levels of voter turnout help to reduce worker protest. I then draw on original firm-level survey data to demonstrate the primary mechanism linking political competition with better industrial relations outcomes—union-party ties. In chapter 5, I turn to the relationship between labor legislation and economic performance in the Indian states. If the arguments about state-labor relations advanced in chapter 3 are correct, then legislation that facilitates third-party mediation and worker voice should produce better economic performance, whereas legislation that violates FACB rights should produce worse outcomes. Finally, in chapter 6, I illustrate my argument about the corrosive effects of labor repression through an examination of state-labor relations in Sri Lanka. In an historical and a quantitative framework, I show how the United National Party's repressive stance towards unions in the 1980s led to worse industrial relations and economic outcomes in the two decades that followed.

CHAPTER 4

Democracy, Union-Party Ties, and Industrial Conflict

The analysis in the last chapter generated a set of specific predictions regarding how democracy and the organizational structure of the union movement relate to the protest behavior of workers. We saw that political competition encourages the development of union-party ties as party leaders rely more heavily on unions to establish political support among working-class voters. At the same time, union-party ties help to moderate worker protest. Because they are constrained by the interests of a broader political constituency, major party unions (MPUs) will mobilize restraint, eschewing aggressive bargaining and protest tactics and refraining from strikes when they are unlikely to win their demands. In contrast, narrow interest unions (NIUs) are likely to engage in more aggressive bargaining and protest to boost their chances of winning their demands. Finally, while enterprise union leaders have incentives to protest aggressively, they lack the external leadership necessary for collective action and therefore engage only in subdued forms of protest.

In this chapter, I test these predictions in three distinct ways. Since Independence, Indian states have varied a great deal in the extent and quality of their democratization (Heller 2000; Kohli 1990). In my first test, I harness this variation to analyze the relationship between democracy and worker protest in fifteen major Indian states in the post-Emergency period.[1] Specifically, I analyze how variations in the party system, winning margins, and voter turnout relate to levels of industrial conflict. If the deepening of democracy promotes synergistic union-party ties and induces parties to mobilize worker restraint, then we should see a negative correlation between measures of political competition and participation on the one hand, and levels of industrial conflict on the other.

Second, I analyze telephone survey data from four regional cases to explore how democracy and the presence of major party unions relate not just to the level but the nature of industrial conflict. To do this, I examine how variations in worker militancy correspond to MPU dominance in the industrial relations arena in Sri Lanka and three Indian States—Kerala, Maharashtra, and West Bengal. If the hypothesis that party encompassment engenders union restraint is correct, we should see more routine protest and bargaining and lower levels of worker militancy in more democratic regions where MPUs dominate the union movement.

Third, I use fine-grained data from an in-depth employer survey to more rigorously test the relationship between external federation control and the protest behavior of workers. These data are used to model both the frequency and nature of industrial conflict in union-management dyads. The models show how the protest behavior of workers organized by NIUs differs from both MPUs and enterprise unions as the external federation tightens its control over firm-level leaders and members. The survey data also permit me to test a number of competing explanations for union behavior and verify the cross-regional robustness of the relationship between union type and worker militancy.

Analysis of Industrial Conflict in Fifteen Indian States

As the most general test of the argument that democratic deepening promotes better industrial relations, I analyze strike data from fifteen major Indian states from 1978 to 2005. This period was selected for analysis because it is the period during which economic reforms began to take hold and the period after which major changes in the structure of India's political system took place.

The end of the Emergency in 1977 marked both the dénouement of a political crisis and the rebirth of Indian democracy. Following the restoration of democracy, dramatic changes in the party system were accompanied by more competitive elections and an increasingly issue-based politics. At the root of India's political transformation was the decline of the INC. Indira Gandhi's draconian behavior during the Emergency led to a decline in the party's popularity and the eventual loss of power in 1979. Subsequently, caste-based reservations (quotas) for university seats and government jobs emerged as a contentious issue in Indian politics that rent asunder the cross-caste coalitions on which INC hegemony had previously depended (Chhibber 1999). Consequently, throughout the 1980s and 1990s, India's party system was transformed from a single party system to one that was fragmented along regional and ethnic lines. The process was accelerated in the mid-1980s by the passage of the Anti-Defection Law (ADL), under which members of parliament can be disqualified for switching parties or for voting against their parties' policies (Nikolenyi 2009). While the ADL was designed to impose party unity and discipline, it had exactly the opposite effect because it created incentives for politicians to create new parties to advocate in favor of their preferred platforms and policies.

While it is still difficult to characterize Indian politics as fully programmatic, these changes in the party system arguably unleashed the power of the median voter by making politics less vertically structured and more issue-based (Wilkinson 2006). It is crucial to note, however, that the transformation of Indian politics was spatially and temporally uneven. States such as Maharashtra and Tamil Nadu saw a very steep rise in the number of parties competing in elections whereas in states such as Andhra Pradesh levels of party fragmentation were much lower (Chhibber and Nooruddin 2004). Moreover, party competition is not the only aspect of democracy that has made India's political system more competitive. The erosion of INC dominance was also accompanied by narrower winning margins and higher turnout in many states. All of these changes made India's political system more dynamic and more representative of the policy positions held by its political leaders as well as voter preferences.

Dependent Variable

The dependent variable in the first analysis is the count of strikes in a given state/year. The data come from various issues of the Indian Labour Yearbook (ILY), an annual publication of the Ministry of Labour, Government of India (GOI). The strikes in the ILY are those reported to the government by employers or workers as required by the Industrial Disputes Act. I model strikes using fixed effects negative binomial regressions. This approach is preferred for this analysis because it accounts for the nonnegative discrete nature of the variable and directly models overdispersion (contagion) in the observed counts (Hausman et al. 1984).

Independent Variables

I regress the number of strikes on four measures of the competitiveness of the political system: (1) the effective number of parties in terms of vote share (ENPV); (2) the effective number of parties in terms of seats won (ENPS); (3) winning margins; and (4) voter turnout. The effective number of parties measure is $1/\sum x_i 2$ where x_i refers to the percentage of votes (or seats) captured by the ith party (Laakso and Taagepera 1979). ENPV reflects the number of parties competing in elections whereas ENPS reflects the number of parties that actually wield power in government. I clean these two measures of outliers by removing observations that are more than three standard deviations above or below their mean values.[2] My theory about the relationship between the competitiveness of the party system and strikes suggests that these variables should be negatively correlated with strikes.

The winning margin is the difference in the percentage of seats won by the leading party minus the percentage of seats won by the party with the second largest number of seats. It reflects the closeness of elections and therefore measures the effort a party must expend to win an election. Since increased winning margins are indicative of a less competitive election, this variable should positively correlate with strike protest.

Finally, the analysis includes voter turnout, measured as the percentage of voters who participate in an election and reflects the level of citizen involvement in the political process. If the median voter is in favor of economic reforms and increased private sector investment, this variable should correlate negatively with strikes.

Each of these variables is lagged one year in the analysis to account for the time it takes for new political realities to affect industrial relations outcomes. The data for all four variables are from election reports for Vidhan Sabha (state assembly) elections published by the Election Commission of India, GOI.

Controls

In chapter 2, I discussed a number of economic factors that have reduced the propensity of workers to go on strike since the late-1970s, the most proximate of which are the product wage and unemployment. The product wage is measured as wages divided by producer prices in manufacturing and, as per the discussion in chapter 2, is predicted to have a dampening effect on strikes because it represents the cost of labor to employers. India does not regularly publish unemployment figures from surveys, so instead I include the number of factory workers in formal sector industry. I also include real wages in the analysis. Both of these variables are predicted to correlate positively with strikes because they are the most direct measures of the bargaining power of workers. The data on wages and number of workers come from the Annual Survey of Industries published by the Ministry of Statistics and Programme Implementation, GOI. Data on producer prices are from the wholesale price index for manufactured items. Data on consumer prices are from the consumer price index for industrial workers. I take the natural log of these three variables to account for outliers and nonnormality.

The models include a lagged dependent variable for two reasons. The first is to account for the influence of past events on workers' propensity to strike in the current year. The second is to account for the possibility that a strike recorded in a given year is a continuation of a strike that began in the previous year.

Results

The results of the models, shown in table 4.1, provide a good deal of support for the argument that deeper democracy reduces the likelihood of strikes. As predicted, increased fragmentation of the party system and voter turnout correlate negatively with strike protest, while winning margins correlate positively with strikes. In a negative binomial model, we can interpret the coefficients as factor changes by first multiplying them by the quantity of interest and then exponentiating the result. Thus, according to model 1, a one standard deviation change in ENPV decreases the probability of a strike by 6 percent.[3] From model 2 we see that a one standard deviation change in ENPS decreases the probability

TABLE 4.1
Determinants of strikes in fifteen Indian states

DV = Count of Strikes	(1) Party System 1 (ENPV)	(2) Party System 2 (ENPS)	(3) Electoral Competition	(4) Participation
Effective number	–0.046**			
of parties (votes)$_{t-1}$	(0.023)			
Effective number		–0.077**		
of parties (seats)$_{t-1}$		(0.036)		
Winning margins$_{t-1}$			0.006**	
			(0.002)	
Voter turnout$_{t-1}$				–0.011***
				(0.003)
Number of strikes$_{t-1}$	0.004***	0.004***	0.003***	0.004***
	(0.000)	(0.000)	(0.000)	(0.000)
Log product wage	–1.801***	–1.862***	–1.799***	–1.703***
	(0.293)	(0.301)	(0.292)	(0.284)
Log number of	0.612***	0.562***	0.668***	0.679***
factory workers	(0.174)	(0.178)	(0.170)	(0.169)
Log real wages	1.142***	1.203***	1.118***	1.043***
	(0.364)	(0.369)	(0.358)	(0.349)
Constant	5.063***	5.269***	4.822***	5.356***
	(1.532)	(1.562)	(1.482)	(1.510)
Observations	317	315	328	327
Number of states	15	15	15	15
Log-likelihood	–1384	–1372	–1426	–1420
χ^2	735.37	730.25	736.97	722.21

Notes: Fixed effects negative binomial regressions. Dependent variable is the count of strikes. Standard errors in parentheses. *** p < 0.01, ** p < 0.05, * p < 0.1.

of a strike by 8 percent.[4] A one standard deviation change in winning margins (model 3) increases the probability of a strike by 8 percent, and a one standard deviation change in voter turnout (model 4) decreases the probability of a strike by 11 percent.[5]

The analysis also reveals the importance of economic determinants of strikes discussed in chapter 2. In fact the substantive significance of economic determinants of strikes is uniformly greater than the political factors. Based on the results of model 1, a one standard deviation change in the product wage decreases the probability of a strike by 40 percent.[6] Conversely, a one standard deviation change in real wages increases the probability of strikes by 52 percent, and a one standard deviation change in the number of factory workers increases the probability of strikes by 18 percent.[7] Considering the discussion in chapter 2 and the findings of previous studies reviewed in chapter 3, it is not surprising that economic factors are of great significance in shaping protest behavior.

Overall, this analysis provides fairly convincing evidence that political factors influence the propensity of workers to go on strike. At the same time, the specific argument developed in this book relates to how union-party ties structure worker response to hard times, and this analysis can only serve as a preliminary test of that argument. In the remainder of this chapter I analyze data from surveys of employers in four regions to more thoroughly explore the relationship between union-party ties and worker protest. These data not only allow us to directly test how politics matters for the propensity of worker protest; they also permit an exploration of the relationship between union-party ties and the character of worker protest.

Survey Data from Four Regional Cases

To test predictions regarding the divergent preferences of MPUs and NIUs over industrial relations outcomes, I conducted a series of interviews and surveys between 2002 and 2004 in Sri Lanka and three Indian States—Kerala, Maharashtra, and West Bengal. As was explained in the introductory chapter, these regions were selected for analysis based on variations in the relative dominance of MPUs versus NIUs in the trade union movement as well as variations in the level of democracy. Preliminary field research and secondary source literature suggested regional variations in the dominance of MPUs, with MPUs being more prevalent in Kerala and West Bengal and other types of unions being more prevalent in Maharashtra and Sri Lanka. The cases also range along a continuum from most to least democratic, with Kerala having the most competitive and representative democracy and Sri Lanka being the least democratic (see figure 1.1).

Field research yielded two sources of information—a telephone survey of approximately one hundred companies in each region and an in-depth survey of approximately thirty-five companies in each region. Results of the telephone survey help to confirm the hypothesis that union movements that are dominated by MPUs are less likely to experience extreme and violent protest than those dominated by NIUs, while results of the in-depth surveys provide data for more fine-grained quantitative tests of the arguments advanced in chapter 3.

Approximately one hundred manufacturing companies were selected from local directories of manufacturers for participation in the telephone survey. The selection process resulted in 416 completed surveys, 385 of which yielded useful information.[8] The telephone survey included questions about the recent history of union activity at individual production facilities since 1991. These included questions about which unions had operated in a given facility and questions about the nature of union protest events, such as whether worker protest was violent and extreme or routine in nature. The year 1991 was selected as the frame of reference, both because it is the point at which India began to accelerate its reforms and because it seemed reasonable to expect that managers would be able to recall events that occurred within an approximate twelve-year span of time.

Subsequently, 35 to 40 companies were selected from the 100 companies participating in the telephone survey for an in-depth survey. These companies were selected through a stratified random sample, in which the strata were whether the company reported experiencing worker protest in the telephone survey.[9] Ultimately 149 companies across the four regional cases participated in the in-depth survey and 148 of these surveys yielded usable data.

The in-depth survey included questions designed to get at the external affiliations of various unions operating in the company as well as the degree of influence of external leaders. An important question for the analysis that follows was about the level of control external union federation leaders had over shop-floor leaders and members. Specifically, company managers were asked to assess, based on their interactions with the union during negotiations, whether the parent union "always," "sometimes," or "never" had control of the actions and behavior of the local union. Finally, the in-depth survey asked managers to identify characteristics about individual production units, such as the number of workers employed, the gender composition of the workforce, estimated revenue, and labor cost as a percentage of revenue.

Reliability of the Survey Data

The fact that much of the data used in this chapter are derived from original surveys may raise legitimate questions regarding their quality.

One question relates to the quality of survey data relative to other potential sources, like press reports or government records. Survey data have tremendous advantages over such sources. Press reports have obvious biases. Journalists tend to cover the most spectacular events and those in the largest and most visible companies. Government data, at least in the South Asia context, are dependent on self-reporting of industrial disputes by the company or union, or reporting by a third party. While the Industrial Disputes Act requires companies and unions to report strikes, there is no penalty for failing to do so. Further, government strike data include only information on the frequency, volume, and duration of strikes—not the character of industrial protest.

The firms contacted for this study, by contrast, were randomly selected from a directory of manufacturers, eliminating the types of biases found in datasets based on press reports and government data. Moreover, the response rates for the surveys were high—ranging between 42 and 76 percent. Most of the nonresponse was due to a failure to contact the respondent, as opposed to the potential respondent explicitly declining to be interviewed. For example, the highest number of explicit refusals was for the telephone survey in West Bengal, where 226 calls yielded 92 completed surveys and 15 explicit refusals.[10] In Kerala, Maharashtra, and Sri Lanka, the number of explicit refusals averaged fewer than 7. The high willingness of managers to participate in the survey, combined with the large percentage of these companies that reported experiencing industrial protest (see table 4.4) should mitigate concerns regarding biases in the responses to the survey.

Another legitimate question relates to whether managers (as opposed to unions) are the best source of information regarding industrial protest. This study began in Sri Lanka, where I hired translators to accompany me to speak with shop-floor union leaders and members in addition to management. In these interviews, I found the union accounts of protest events to be very similar to those of management with respect to reasons for the protest and the nature of the protest that occurred. But accounts differed regarding the issue of external federation control of shop-floor leaders and members. Whereas employer responses to questions regarding the degree of external control varied a great deal, shop-floor union leaders seemed shy about answering the question, as though they may be challenging the authority of the federation leadership by suggesting that the federation did not control their actions. Thus shop-floor union leaders and members almost always said that the external federation "always" controlled their protest behavior. It is possible that in a different context (in their living rooms for example), shop-floor leaders and members would have been more forthcoming in response to my questions about their relationship to external leaders. However, lacking the resources or time to shift the venue of the interview, or to build the type of trust with union leaders required to elicit more truthful responses, I decided instead to rely on information regarding union-party ties from the management, who appeared to be more objective in their responses.[11]

Finally, it should be acknowledged that some of the questions in the survey produced more, and better, data than others. For example, there was very little variation in the gender composition among unionized manufacturing companies, as most unionized workers are men. Figures relating to the finances of the company, such as labor cost, revenue, and wages were largely "guesstimates" since very few managers consulted their books before answering, and not all firms were able to provide this information. Consequently, much of these data, which were intended to serve as controls in the quantitative analysis, were not included because they were incomplete or of low quality.

Identifying MPUs and NIUs

For the purposes of this analysis it is necessary to clearly distinguish between union types. The theory of party encompassment developed in the previous section suggests that major political parties are more restrained because they incorporate the interests of a broader constituency than the union itself. In operationalizing the concept of "major party union," it is thus important to identify unions affiliated with parties that garner a large enough share of the votes to encompass a diversity of interests and not simply those of organized labor or the working class. Unions are therefore classified as MPUs if the parent union is affiliated with a major political party, where "major party" is defined as a party that was a major coalition partner or the leading opposition party in a state or national assembly anytime since 1991. A "major coalition partner" is in turn defined as having either the first or second most number of seats of any party in a state or national assembly and having at least 25 percent of the required number of seats to form a majority coalition. Unions are classified as NIUs if the parent union is affiliated with a political party that does not fit the definition of a "major party" or if the parent union is politically independent. Enterprise unions are those that are not affiliated with any external union federation.

Identification of MPUs

Based on the criteria outlined above, eight unions affiliated with as many major political parties in the four regions qualify as MPUs. Table 4.2 lists these MPUs, the geographic regions in which they operate, and the political orientation and strength of their affiliated parties since 1991. The four regions include national and regional MPUs affiliated with parties espousing a variety of political ideologies. The Center for Indian Trade Unions (CITU) and the All India Trade Union Congress (AITUC) are affiliated with regionally dominant left political parties. The CITU is affiliated with the Communist Party of India (Marxist), or CPM, a powerful force in the politics of West Bengal and Kerala. The CPM has alternated as Kerala's ruling or opposition party since it broke from the Communist Party of India (CPI) and won a plurality (30 percent) of the seats in Kerala's 1965 state assembly elections.[12] In West Bengal, the CPM has instituted a de facto one-party rule by maintaining its position as the state's ruling party since 1977. The CPI has been a less dominant force than the CPM, but often wins a substantial number of the seats needed to establish a left front coalition in Kerala's highly fractured and competitive political landscape. In 1996 for example, the CPI won 18 seats in Kerala's state assembly elections—almost exactly 25 percent of the 71 seats needed to form a ruling coalition in Kerala's 140-member legislative assembly.[13]

In stark contrast to the left regionalist parties in Kerala and West Bengal, Maharashtra-based Bharatiya Kamgar Sena (BKS), or the "Indian Worker's Army," is affiliated with the right wing Shiv Sena whose leader, Bal Thackeray, has famously referred to himself as the "Hitler of India." The Shiv Sena is a Hindu nationalist party with a strong Maratha identity and has enjoyed regional dominance in the state of Maharashtra. The Shiv Sena was the opposition party in the State Assembly from 1990 to 1995 and from 1999 to the present. It was the leading coalition partner when it governed in coalition with the Bharatiya Janata Party

TABLE 4.2
Political affiliations and ideological orientations of major party unions

Political Party	Affiliated Union	Geographic Region(s)	Electoral Performance Since 1991	Political Orientation
Communist Party of India, Marxist (CPM)	Center for Indian Trade Unions (CITU)	Kerala & West Bengal	*Kerala Assembly*: leading opposition party, 1991–1996; leading ruling coalition partner, 1996–2001; leading opposition party 2001–present *W. Bengal Assembly*: leading ruling coalition partner, 1991–present	Left
Communist Party of India (CPI)	All India Trade Union Congress (AITUC)	Kerala	*Kerala Assembly*: major ruling coalition partner, 1996–2001	Left
Congress	Indian National Trade Union Congress (INTUC)	National (India)	*National Assembly*: leading ruling coalition partner 1991–1996; opposition party 1996; leading ruling coalition partner 1996–98; opposition party 1998–2004 *Kerala Assembly*: leading ruling coalition partner, 1991–1996; opposition party, 1996–2001; leading ruling coalition partner 2001–present *W. Bengal Assembly*: opposition party, 1991–2001 *Maharashtra Assembly*: leading ruling coalition partner, 1990–1995; opposition party, 1995–1999, leading ruling coalition partner, 1999–present	Centrist
Trinamool Congress (TMC)	Indian Trinamool Trade Union Congress (INTTUC)	West Bengal	*W. Bengal Assembly*: opposition party, 2001–present	Centrist
Bharatiya Janata Party (BJP)	Bharatiya Mazdoor Sangh (BMS)	National (India)	*National Assembly*: opposition party, 1991–1996; leading ruling coalition partner, 1996; opposition party 1996–1998; leading ruling coalition partner 1998–2004 *Maharashtra Assembly*: major ruling coalition partner, 1995–1999	Right
Shiv Sena	Bharatiya Kamgar Sena (BKS)	Maharashtra	*Maharashtra Assembly*: opposition party, 1990–1995; leading ruling coalition partner, 1995–1999; opposition party, 1999–present	Right
Sri Lanka Freedom Party (SLFP)	Sri Lanka Nidahas Sevaka Sangamaya (SLNSS)	National (Sri Lanka)	*Parliament*: opposition party, 1978–1994 and 2001–2004; leading ruling coalition partner, 1994–2001	Center-Left
United National Party (UNP)	Jathika Sevaka Sangamaya (JSS)	National (Sri Lanka)	*Parliament*: leading ruling coalition partner, 1978–1994 and 2001–2004; opposition party, 1994–2001;	Center-Right

(BJP) from 1995 to 1999. The Shiv Sena has had some limited success in national politics. For example, Shivsainik Manohar Joshi was the speaker of the Lok Sabha from 2002 to 2004.

The Bharatiya Mazdoor Sangh (BMS) is affiliated with the Hindu nationalist Bharatiya Janata Party (BJP), a conservative, right-leaning party with a clear middle- and upper-caste/class support base. The BJP was highly successful at the national level during the 1990s, serving as the opposition party from 1991 to 1996 and from 1996 to 1998. The BJP came to power as the ruling coalition partner for a brief period in 1996 and was the dominant party in the Lok Sabha from 1998 to 2004.

The Indian National Trade Union Congress (INTUC) and the Indian Trinamool Trade Union Congress (INTTUC) are unions affiliated with what are most easily described as centrist political parties. The INTUC is affiliated with the Indian National Congress (INC) (also known as the Congress Party, Indira's Congress, Congress (I), or simply "Congress"). The INTTUC is affiliated with the Trinamool Congress (TMC), an offshoot of the Congress in West Bengal.[14]

The policies of the INC have sometimes made it difficult to place it on a left-right spectrum. Nehruvian development policy was clearly based on the socialist model of state-led development implemented by the Soviet Union, but a closed economy clearly benefited some capitalists whose interests sometimes dominated policy formation (Chibber 2003). Indira Gandhi split the party in response to a challenge by its right wing in 1967 and won the 1971 elections with a populist platform and guarantees to eradicate poverty ("giribi hatao"), but subsequently ruled the country in an authoritarian fashion during the 1975–77 Emergency period—jailing union leaders, clearing slums by force, thrusting the homeless into forced labor camps, and orchestrating a campaign of forced sterilization of the poor. Since the 1980s, the party has continued to campaign on a populist agenda but has also become a staunch advocate of economic reform. Manmohan Singh, the current prime minister in the Congress-led government is an Oxford trained economist who, as finance minister, was one of the primary architects of India's 1991 economic reforms.

Both the TMC and the INC qualify as "major political parties" according to the definition provided above. In 2001, the TMC became the leading opposition party in West Bengal, winning 20 percent (60) of the 294 seats in the legislative assembly. The INC has long been one of the most powerful national parties in India. In 2004, the INC surprised political analysts predicting its permanent decline when the party and its allies won enough seats in the fourteenth Lok Sabha to form the ruling United Progressive Alliance (UPA) coalition.[15] The Congress was also the leading ruling coalition partner in the tenth (1991–96) and twelfth (1996–98) Lok Sabhas and was the leading opposition party in the eleventh (1996) and thirteenth (1998–2004) Lok Sabhas. Additionally, the Congress has been substantially influential in state assembly elections. In Kerala and Maharashtra, the Congress has acted as the leading ruling coalition partner or leading opposition party in every assembly since 1991. In West Bengal, the INC was the leading opposition party until it lost this place to the TMC in 2001.

The Sri Lanka Nidhas Sevaka Sangamaya (SLNSS) and the Jathika Sevaka Sangamaya (JSS) are MPUs affiliated with national parties in Sri Lanka. The SLNSS is affiliated with the Sri Lankan center-left Sri Lankan Freedom Party (SLFP), and the JSS is affiliated with the center-right United National Party (UNP). These two parties have traditionally alternated as the party in power and the leading opposition party. The UNP was the majority party from 1978 to 1994 and the leading ruling coalition partner from 2001 to 2004. The SLFP was the leading ruling coalition partner from 1994 to 2001.

Identification of NIUs

As I demonstrate below, within the four regions, the vast majority of NIUs operate in Maharashtra and Sri Lanka. The largest and best-known NIU federations are the two formerly headed by Datta Samant—the Association of Engineering Workers (AEW) and the Maharashtra General Kamgar Union (MGKU). Since Datta Samant's violent demise in January 1997, the unions have been led by his younger brother, P. N. "Dada" Samant.[16]

Although not substantial in terms of membership, the Bharatiya Kamgar Utkarsh Sabha (National Workers' Progress Union), has garnered increasing attention in Maharashtra in recent years. The union is led by Bai Jagtap, who once led the union under the banner of the INTUC but was expelled for his use of violence to break existing unions and compel workers to join his union and sign unfavorable agreements.[17] According to one set of reports, Jagtap stabbed workers at Pfizer Inc. in order to force them into a voluntary retirement scheme, taking ample payment for his "services."

In Sri Lanka, the majority of NIUs are small-party unions. The largest and most active of the small-party unions are the Intercompany Employees' Union (ICEU) and the Ceylon Industrial Workers' Union (CIWU). The ICEU is headed by S. Amerasinghe and is affiliated with the Jathika Vimukthi Peramuna (JVP), or "People's Liberation Front," a socialist party that is currently a member of the ruling coalition.[18] The CIWU is led by Linus Jayathilaka and affiliated with the Nawa Sama Samaja Party (NSSP), or "New Socialist Party," a minor left party unique in its outspoken opposition to Sri Lanka's civil conflict and its advocacy of a Tamil homeland.

A large percentage of workers also belong to the Ceylon Mercantile Union (CMU), led by Bala Tampoe. While the CMU once had close ties to the Lanka Sama Samaja Party (LSSP), or "Lanka Socialist Party," it has maintained strict political neutrality since it refused to join other left-affiliated unions in Sri Lanka's 1980 general strike. A much smaller percentage of workers belong to the Ceylon Federation of Labor (CFL), which maintains a strong affiliation with the LSSP, and the Ceylon Federation of Trade Unions (CFTU), affiliated with the Communist Party (CP).

Results of the Telephone Survey

Table 4.3 displays the percentage of companies in the survey that reported having active MPUs and/or NIUs in each regional case. Results from the telephone survey confirmed the supposed regional variations in the structure of the trade union movement in the four cases, indicating a clear dominance of MPUs in Kerala and West Bengal and a greater presence of NIUs in Maharashtra and Sri Lanka. Among manufacturing companies surveyed in West Bengal, 76 percent reported having one or more MPUs, and in Kerala the figure was 50 percent. In contrast, only 32 percent of companies in Maharashtra and 11 percent of manufacturing companies in Sri Lanka reported the presence of MPUs in their production units.

In both West Bengal and Kerala, the dominant union is the CPM-affiliated CITU. Sixty-six percent of companies surveyed in West Bengal

TABLE 4.3
Political structure of the union movement in four regional cases

Type of Union	Percentage of Companies Surveyed				
	Sri Lanka	Maharashtra	Kerala	West Bengal	All Regions
Major party unions	**11**	**32**	**50**	**76**	**40**
CITU	–	4	35	66	–
AITUC	–	1	8	8	–
INTUC	–	19	27	42	–
INTTUC	–	–	–	15	–
BKS	–	14	–	0	–
BMS	–	4	18	11	–
SLNSS	6	–	–	–	–
JSS	9	–	–	–	–
Narrow interest unions	**34**	**26**	**8**	**11**	**18**
External leadership affiliated to small party	28	8	5	7	10
External leadership politically independent	12	19	4	5	11
Enterprise unions	**0**	**30**	**1**	**5**	**9**
Any union	**38**	**71**	**50**	**79**	**60**

Source: Telephone survey of 385 managers and directors conducted between November 2002 and May 2004. Figures do not add up to 100 as companies surveyed may have more than one union.

and 35 percent of manufacturing companies in Kerala reported the presence of a CITU union. The major competitor to CITU in West Bengal and Kerala was the INC-affiliated INTUC, which had a presence in about 42 percent of manufacturing companies in West Bengal and in about 27 percent of companies in Kerala. Fifteen percent of companies in West Bengal reported the presence of the recently formed Indian National Trinamool Trade Union Congress (INTTUC), a breakaway faction of the INTUC. Eight percent of companies in Kerala and West Bengal reported the presence of the CPI-affiliated All India Trade Union Congress (AITUC). The survey also shows that the Bharatiya Mazdoor Sangh (BMS), affiliated with the Hindu-nationalist Bharatiya Janata Party (BJP), has a relatively strong presence in Kerala, where 18 percent of companies reported the presence of a BMS union, and a moderately strong presence in West Bengal.[19]

The survey results also confirm the initial perception that NIUs are rare in West Bengal and Kerala but represent the dominant form of worker representation in Maharashtra and Sri Lanka. NIUs were present in 11 percent of manufacturing companies surveyed in West Bengal and in only 8 percent of companies in Kerala. In Maharashtra, by contrast, 26 percent of surveyed companies reported the presence of at least one NIU and in Sri Lanka the figure was 34 percent.

The major difference between Maharashtra and Sri Lanka is the higher presence of small-party unions in Sri Lanka, and a higher presence of enterprise unions in Maharashtra. In Sri Lanka, 28 percent of companies reported the presence of a union affiliated with a small political party and 12 percent reported the presence of a union affiliated with a politically independent union center. No companies in Sri Lanka reported an enterprise-level leadership free from parent union control or management interference.[20] However, the enterprise-level union constituted a dominant form of worker representation in Maharashtra. Thirty percent of manufacturing companies in Maharashtra reported the presence of internal unions. Nineteen percent of manufacturing companies in Maharashtra reported having a union controlled by a politically independent federation and 8 percent reported the presence of a small-party union.[21]

These regional variations in the structure of the union movement correspond closely with regional variations in industrial protest. Table 4.4 displays the percentage of manufacturing companies experiencing various forms of union protest in each regional case. These forms of protest fall into four categories: work stoppage; violent or extreme protest; obstruction or occupation of company premises; and routine protest. A work stoppage can take the form of a strike, in which members of the union refuse to work, or a lockout, in which the employer refuses to allow union members to work. Violent or extreme forms of protest include assaults by union members on managers or other workers, damage to company property, or threats to managers. Forms of obstruction or occupation of company premises include climbing and occupying high structures (such as water towers, antennas, or buildings), public fasting, sit-ins, blocking company gates, and a unique form of protest in South Asia—the *gherao. Gherao* translates to "encirclement" in Hindi and occurs when workers surround a manager and confine the manager to an office or desk until the union is satisfied the management will adequately address worker demands.[22] Routine forms of protest include slowdowns, in which workers do not leave work to go out on strike but slow down the production process by taking unusually long amounts of time to complete tasks, and gatherings in which workers hold placards and slogans. These four categories are not mutually exclusive, meaning

TABLE 4.4
Percentage of manufacturing companies experiencing various types of worker protest in four regional cases, 1991–2002

	Percent Experiencing			
Type of Protest	Sri Lanka	Maharashtra	Kerala	West Bengal
Stoppage of work	**51**	**27**	**24**	**25**
Strike	51	19	22	22
Lockout	13	10	6	14
Violent or extreme protest	**22**	**13**	**3**	**8**
Assault on manager	2	7	0	4
Assault on other workers	4	2	0	1
Damage to property	8	8	3	3
Threats to management	11	11	0	3
Obstruction/Occupation	**24**	**16**	**11**	**19**
Gherao	9	13	7	12
Climbing high structure	10	0	0	0
Fasting	2	1	1	0
Sit-in/Blocking gates	12	6	6	9
Routine protest	**52**	**36**	**34**	**42**
Slowdown	1	14	12	20
Gathering	48	20	26	27
Any form of protest	**55**	**37**	**36**	**48**

Source: Telephone survey of 385 managers and directors conducted between November 2002 and May 2004.

that workers can engage in more than one form of protest during a given protest event. When protesting for a wage increase, for instance, a union might strike, hold a gathering, and also damage company property.

The most interesting result of the survey data is that the use of violent forms of protest, including property damage, threats, and assaults are much less common in more democratic regions where political MPUs dominate the union movement than in the regions where NIUs constitute the primary form of worker representation. In Kerala only 3 percent of surveyed companies reported experiencing a violent or extreme form of union protest in one of their production units and in West Bengal the figure was 8 percent. In West Bengal, 4 percent of companies reported an assault on a manager and 1 percent an assault by a union on another group of workers. Three percent reported experiencing damage to company property and 3 percent reported experiencing threats to management. In Kerala, the only form of violent or extreme protest reported by manufacturing companies was damage to company property, which 3 percent had experienced. No companies reported any incidents of assault or threats to management.

By contrast, industrial relations are much more violent and chaotic in Sri Lanka and Maharashtra. Twenty-two percent of manufacturing companies in Sri Lanka and 13 percent of manufacturing companies in Maharashtra reported experiencing violent or extreme protest in one or more production units. In Maharashtra, 7 percent of companies reported an assault on management and 2 percent reported an assault by a union on other workers. Eight percent of manufacturing companies reported damage to company property. Eleven percent reported experiencing threats to management.

Sri Lanka, which has the lowest percentage of firms reporting the presence of MPUs, stands out for the high level of chaos experienced in its industrial relations. Whereas Maharashtra differs little from West Bengal and Kerala in terms of the frequency of other forms of protest, firms in Sri Lanka have experienced high levels of all forms of union protest. Fifty-one percent of companies reported a strike or lockout, 52 percent reported a routine form of protest such as a slowdown or a union gathering, and 24 percent reported obstruction of company property. Ten percent of companies in Sri Lanka reported experiencing an incident in which workers climbed to the top of a high structure such as a water tower, refusing to come down and, in many cases, threatening to jump if their demands were not met. Further, the level of violent and extreme protest in Sri Lanka was quite high. Two percent of manufacturing companies reported an assault against management and 4 percent reported an assault by a union on other workers. Eight percent of companies reported damage to company property and 11 percent reported experiencing a threat to a manager.

Dyadic Analysis of Industrial Conflict

To more firmly establish the relationship between union-party ties and worker protest, I draw on data from the in-depth survey to conduct an analysis of individual protest at the firm level, where the unit of analysis is the union-management dyad. As discussed earlier, 149 companies participated in the in-depth survey and 148 of these surveys yielded usable data.[23] Some companies had multiple union-management dyads, either because the same union operated in multiple production facilities or because more than one union had organized a production facility. If a group of workers was not unionized, they were counted as a separate dyad. The survey of 148 companies thus yielded information on a total of 368 dyads for the period 1991 to 2002. These data permit cross-section time-series (CSTS) models of the character of industrial protest at the level of the union-management dyad, yielding 4,416 potential observations. Missing observations are accounted for by the unavailability of data for some dyad-years and by the fact that some union-management dyads were not in existence for the entire period of the study.

Dependent Variables

For the analysis, each dyad-year is coded for whether the union in the dyad engaged in protest at all (1 if yes; 0 otherwise) and whether a union engaged in an extreme or violent form of union protest (1 if yes; 0 otherwise). "Extreme or violent" forms of protest include those listed under this category in table 4.4: assault on a manager, assault on other workers, damage to company property, or serious threats against the lives of managers. A third variable, the "level of protest" is coded 0 if no protest occurred, 1 if the union engaged in routine protest, and 2 if the union engaged in extreme or violent protest. This ordinal variable constitutes the main dependent variable of interest in most of the models in the analysis.

Independent Variables

The main independent variables in the analysis are a dichotomous variable for MPUs, coded 1 if the union is affiliated with a major political party and 0 otherwise, an ordinal variable for the degree of control an external federation exerts over shop-floor leaders and members, and a multiplicative interaction term (MPU*degree of external control). The degree of external control was measured by the aforementioned survey question, in which company managers were asked to assess, based on their interactions with the union during negotiations, whether the parent union "always," "sometimes," or "never" had control over the actions and behavior of the local union. Responses of "always" were coded as 2, responses of "sometimes" were coded as 1, and responses of "never" were coded as 0. The control variable is also coded 0 if workers have no affiliation with an external federation. Together, these three variables are used to test the hypothesis that NIUs will encourage more aggressive protest as they gain greater control over the union and the hypothesis that affiliation with an MPU reduces the tendency of individual union leaders to ratchet up protest. The analysis also includes an indicator variable for enterprise unions—coded 1 if workers in the dyad were organized by an enterprise union and 0 otherwise. This variable tests the hypothesis that enterprise unions are quiescent. This entails that the baseline union category is nonunionized dyads, that is, worker-management dyads in which workers do not belong to a union at all.

Control Variables

As discussed in chapter 3, scholars who study union behavior in developing countries have emphasized the competitiveness of the union movement as an important influence on union protest. Precisely how competition affects union behavior has been the topic of much discussion in the literature. One argument holds that the fragmentation of the union movement generates competition that, by providing workers with the option to defect to another union, forces political and union leaders to be more responsive to worker demands and thus results in more militancy (Burgess 2004; Tafel and Boniface 2003). Murillo (2001) distinguishes between organizational fragmentation of the union movement and partisan competition for union support. She argues that organizational fragmentation *undermines* the effectiveness of union protest by making it more difficult for workers to advocate a unified set of demands. However, partisan battles for control over the union movement augment the power of the union movement by undermining the state's control over workers. These theories have been tested with national and sectoral data but never with enterprise-level data. To test for the effect of union competition on union behavior at the enterprise level, I include a control for the number of active unions in the production unit at the time of the protest event. Since union competition at the enterprise level is typically between political unions of various stripes and independent unions, my data allow us to test whether these theories, which are often used to explain union protest in the political arena, also apply to industrial protest.

The analysis also includes controls for the number of workers in the production unit at the time of the dispute, which is intended to capture the effects of the more impersonal relationships between workers and management at a large factory. Since no comparable data are available on the product wage, real wages, or employment for Sri Lanka and India, I include regional measures of inflation and economic growth at the time of the protest event to control for overall economic conditions. Finally, I include fixed effects for regions and years to account for any unobserved heterogeneity and a time-trend to account for the effect time may have on respondents' memory of events. All of the regressions were run with robust standard errors, clustered by company.[24]

Results

Table 4.5 presents the results of the models. Models 1 and 2 are logit models of the effects of external federation control on nonviolent and violent protest. Model 3 is an ordered logit model of the effects of external federation control on the "level of protest" variable. Providing support for the argument that MPUs restrain protest while NIUs ratchet up militancy, the direct effects of the MPU variable and the degree of external control are positive and significant at the 0.001 level while the interaction effect is negative and significant at the 0.001 level. Providing support for the argument that enterprise unions are relatively quiescent, the coefficient for enterprise union is positive but not significant. In model 2 the enterprise union variable is dropped because enterprise unions never engage in violent protest. Of the control variables, inflation and growth are positively associated with protest in models 1 and 3, a finding that comports with the consensus in the strikes literature that strike protest is procyclical. The control for the number of unions positively predicts union violence but not routine protest. The time trend is positive and significant in all of the models, suggesting that respondents may have a greater propensity to report more recent events.

To facilitate the substantive interpretation of the results, I generated a series of predictions based on the results of model 3.[25] I generated predicted probabilities of routine and violent protest for MPUs and NIUs at high, moderate, and low levels of external control, as well as predictions for enterprise unions. These predictions and their associated 95 percent

TABLE 4.5
Logit and ordered logit models of worker protest

	(1) Routine Protest	(2) Violent or Extreme Protest	(3) Level of Protest
Major party union (MPU)	1.60***	1.831**	1.614***
	(0.423)	(0.624)	(0.425)
Degree of external control	1.178***	1.324***	1.194***
	(0.159)	(0.269)	(0.162)
Interaction term = MPU* degree of external control	−1.268***	−1.617***	−1.288***
	(0.284)	(0.379)	(0.282)
Enterprise union	0.804	—	0.798
	(0.500)	—	(0.505)
Number of workers	−0.0001	0.0003	−0.00009
	(0.0002)	(0.0002)	(0.0002)
Number of unions	0.099	0.485*	0.100
	(0.109)	(0.207)	(0.108)
Inflation	0.100*	0.023	0.099*
	(0.041)	(0.061)	(0.040)
Growth	0.068*	0.027	0.069*
	(0.031)	(0.043)	(0.031)
Time trend	0.244***	1.349***	0.244***
	(0.068)	(0.079)	(0.068)
Constant	−8.490***	−6.735	
	(1.067)	(7.172)	
Threshold α_1			8.494***
			(1.057)
Threshold α_2			10.098***
			(1.086)
Number of observations	3778	3778	3778
Number of clusters	148	148	148
Log likelihood	−665.74	−181.05	−761.00
χ^2	126.54	165.90	127.88

Notes: Regressions include fixed effects for states and years. Robust standard errors, clustered by company, in parentheses. * p < 0 .05, ** p < 0.01, *** p < 0 .001.

confidence intervals are presented in table 4.6. The predictions provide strong support for the central hypotheses regarding the behavior of union federations advanced in this article. Increasing external control by MPUs induces a modest decline in routine and violent protest, whereas increased control by NIUs results in a marked and statistically significant increase in routine and violent protest. Comparing the level of protest of MPUs and NIUs with high levels of control highlights the differences between these two types of unions. According to the results of the model, the predicted probability that a group of workers organized by an MPU will engage in routine protest is 0.04, and their predicted probability of engaging in violent protest is just 0.01. By contrast, the probability that

TABLE 4.6
Predicted probabilities of protest by major party, narrow interest, and enterprise unions

	Routine Protest	Violent Protest
Major party union		
High control	0.041	0.011
	(0.022, 0.061)	(0.005, 0.017)
Moderate control	0.045	0.012
	(0.031, 0.06)	(0.007, 0.017)
Low control	0.050	0.014
	(0.022, 0.078)	(0.005, 0.022)
Narrow interest union		
High control	0.130	0.041
	(0.084, 0.176)	(0.020, 0.063)
Moderate control	0.048	0.013
	(0.033, 0.062)	(0.007, 0.020)
Low control	0.015	0.004
	(0.008, 0.022)	(0.001, 0.007)
Enterprise union	0.033	0.009
	(0.007, 0.060)	(0.002, 0.016)
Wald tests		
MPU high = enterprise	$\chi^2 = 0.28$	$\chi^2 = 0.28$
	p = 0.598	p = 0.598
NIU high = enterprise	$\chi^2 = 13.84$	$\chi^2 = 8.27$
	p = 0.0002	P = 0.004
MPU high = NIU high	$\chi^2 = 13.26$	$\chi^2 = 8.24$
	p = 0.0003	p = 0.004

Notes: Predicted probabilities of worker protest based on models 3 in table 4.5. 95% confidence intervals in parentheses.

workers who are tightly controlled by an NIU will engage in routine protest is 0.13 and the probability of violent protest is 0.04. A Wald test presented at the bottom of the table demonstrates that the difference in the predictions for NIUs and MPUs with strong control over shop-floor leaders and members is statistically significant.

Comparisons between the two federation types and enterprise unions are also illuminating. According to the model, the predicted probability that enterprise unions will engage in routine protest is 0.03 and the predicted probability of violent protest is 0.009. Wald tests confirm that there is a statistically significant difference between the predictions for enterprise unions and those for NIUs. However, there is no statistically significant difference between the predicted probability of protest for MPUs with high control and enterprise unions. Thus the analysis of these data suggests that leaders of MPUs are just as conservative as enterprise unions in their protest behavior. This finding directly challenges the conventional wisdom in the policy literature, which argues that federated unions always bargain and protest more aggressively than enterprise unions, and that unions affiliated with political federations are the most aggressive unions of all.[26]

Tests of Alternative Explanations

The explanation of union behavior set forth in this article was tested against relative alternatives in an analysis that is discussed but, due to space constraints, is not displayed here.[27] The literature on the political economy of industrial protest identifies at least three alternative hypotheses that warrant serious consideration. The first hypothesis is that the incumbent status of the affiliated political party matters, and more specifically, that unions engage in restraint when their affiliated parties are in power, but ratchet up demands and protest when their affiliated parties are out of power.[28] To test this hypothesis, I created new indicator variables for major party unions that are in power and major party unions that are out of power in a given region and year. Each of these variables was then interacted with the degree of external control variable to determine whether the dampening effect on union protest is stronger for MPUs that are in power versus those that are out of power.

While the coefficient of the interaction term is more negative for in-power MPUs, the predictions based on the model suggest there is no difference in the behavior of MPUs when they are in power versus when they are out of power. The predicted probability of routine protest for an MPU exerting a high degree of control over shop-floor leaders and members when it is in power is 0.039, and the predicted probability of routine protest is 0.043 when it is out of power. Similarly, the probability of violent protest for an in-power MPU is 0.010 and for an out-of-power MPU it is 0.011. Wald tests confirm that there is no statistically significant difference in the protest behavior of in-power and out-of-power MPUs.

A second alternative hypothesis is that political ideology matters for union restraint. This argument can take one of two forms. One is that centrist and right parties are more likely to encourage restraint because of their conservative outlook on economic and social matters. The countervailing thesis is that left parties are more likely to succeed in mobilizing restraint because their deeper commitment to working-class issues engenders a unique bond of trust between workers and unions. To test these hypotheses, I created two indicator variables—one for MPUs affiliated with left political parties, and one for MPUs affiliated with nonleft political parties—and interacted these with the external control variable. The results suggest no difference in the protest behavior of left and nonleft MPUs. While the predicted probability of protest is less for left unions than for nonleft unions, Wald tests suggest that these differences are not statistically significant.

The third hypothesis is the standard Olsonian account of union behavior, which argues that worker restraint in the industrial relations arena is explained by the encompassing nature of the union, as opposed to the political party with which it is affiliated. As an approximate measure of union encompassment, data from the telephone survey are used to calculate the percentage of all manufacturing companies in which a given MPU has a reported presence.[29] To test the union encompassment hypothesis, I create an indicator variable for "high" and "low" levels of union encompassment and interact this variable with the measure of external control. For the purposes of this analysis, "high" encompassment is defined as a percentage above the mean level of encompassment for all MPUs. The results of this analysis suggest no statistically significant difference in the behavior of high versus low encompassing MPUs. This is not to suggest, however, that union encompassment never matters. The most encompassing union in the study is the CPM in West Bengal, which has representation in 66 percent of private sector manufacturing companies in the state, and the mean level of encompassment for all four regions is 17.3 percent—not a very high level of union encompassment relative to the LOs of Northern Europe, for example. Thus it may simply be that unions in South Asia are not encompassing enough to internalize the externalities of union militancy, so that the party is the more relevant encompassing organization.

Regional Robustness of the Results

The foregoing analysis rests on the assumption that the data from four regions of South Asia can safely be pooled and that no one regional case is driving the results. A critical reader may be skeptical about this assumption. Could it be, for example, that Sri Lanka, with its long history of civil conflict and strong presence of NIUs, is driving the relationship between NIU control and worker violence? Similarly, could it be that MPU dominance in West Bengal or Kerala is the entire reason behind the significance of the interaction term?

To test the regional robustness of the results, I first ran the ordered logit model dropping each regional case. Then, I ran the regression for Maharashtra by itself, which as table 4.3 suggests is unique in the diverse structure of its union movement, incorporating in almost equal measure, major party, narrow interest, and enterprise unions. The results (not shown here) suggest that the relationship between union type and patterns of strike protest are highly robust across regions.[30] The direction, magnitude, and significance of the coefficients do not change very much regardless of which regional case is dropped or whether the analysis is performed on Maharashtra by itself. Similarly, the predicted probability of routine and violent protest remains fairly constant across the models. Finally, the Wald tests confirm that, across regions, there are significant differences in the behavior of MPUs and NIUs, and between NIUs and enterprise unions; but as in the original analysis, MPUs do not differ from enterprise unions in their propensity to engage in protest.

The fact that the results hold for Maharashtra by itself also helps to dispel any concerns that worker self-selection might explain the results. Specifically, one concern might be that workers with higher skills, education, and thus more market power are more likely to engage in aggressive protest than uneducated workers. As it turns out, Maharashtra has a unique closed-shop law that requires the management to recognize and bargain with only one union.[31] This means that skilled workers must join the same unions as unskilled workers if they want to engage in collective bargaining with management. Thus the results for Maharashtra provide a high degree of confidence that it is the imperatives of the union leadership, rather than the bargaining power of particular groups of workers, that explain the relationship between party affiliation and worker restraint.[32]

The Validity of the NIU Category

Another untested assumption of the analysis is that two union subtypes, small-party unions and political independent unions, can legitimately be grouped into the broader category of narrow interest union. Again, the critical reader might be skeptical. Might small-party unions, which engage in policymaking, behave more like MPUs than independent unions? Or does their lack of organizational encompassment in fact cause them to behave more like NIUs?

To test the assumption that independent and small-party unions behave in a manner similar to one another, but different from that of MPUs, I coded a series of six dichotomous variables—a high control dummy and a low-to-moderate control dummy for each of the three union types. I then regressed the level of protest on these variables, generated predictions, and analyzed the difference between these predictions. The results of this exercise confirm the validity of the NIU category. While the predicted probability of routine and violent protest for independent unions is higher than it is for small-party unions, these differences are not statistically significant. In contrast, the lower predicted probability of protest for MPUs is significantly different from both small-party and independent unions.

Conclusion

Drawing on original data from four regions of South Asia, this chapter has demonstrated how union democracy and partisan ties condition union protest behavior. An analysis of strikes in fifteen Indian states demonstrated a relationship between measures of political competition and participation, on the one hand, and strike protest on the other. Analysis of survey data helped to establish the mechanism at work—union-party ties. Major political parties are encompassing organizations that internalize the externalities associated with the behavior of their members, including leaders of affiliated unions. Responding to new economic realities, political parties restrain the protest behavior of affiliated unions and restrict protest activities to include routine strikes and institutionalized forms of grievance resolution.

In contrast, without the constraints imposed by an encompassing political party, leaders of small-party and nonaffiliated union federations behave quite differently. These leaders are more likely to take advantage of economic challenges to ratchet up militancy and have a greater tendency to encourage the use of extreme and violent forms of protest. When routine forms of protest fail to extract concessions from management, these leaders often continue with their protest and condone or even encourage the use of extreme and violent forms of protest.

CHAPTER 5

Labor Institutions, FACB Rights, and Economic Performance in India

India needs to reform its absurdly restrictive labour laws, which hold back the expansion of manufacturing particularly.
—***Economist*** **magazine, "India Overheats"**

A national consensus has been emerging that India's archaic labour laws are hampering industry's ability to face international competition aggressively and successfully, particularly in the wake of rapid globalization and the liberalization of the Indian economy.
—**Confederation of Indian Industries, *Labour Reforms in Southern Region States***

It is apparent that much of the reasoning behind labor regulation was wrong-headed and led to outcomes that were antithetical to their original objectives.
—**Timothy Besley and Robin Burgess, "Can Labor Regulation Hinder Economic Performance? Evidence from India"**

In addition to the political impetus for restraining worker protest, chapter 3 discussed the benefits of associational rights for managing industrial unrest. Specifically, we saw that democracies typically enact more regulation to protect freedom of association and collective bargaining (FACB) rights and promote the institutionalized resolution of worker grievances. FACB rights are crucial to the effectiveness of institutions such as labor courts and tribunals, arbitration proceedings, conciliation proceedings, and legally binding collective bargaining agreements. And such institutions are effective in reducing exploitation and providing industrial relations stability where workers can assert their rights. Conversely where workers lack rights such institutions merely become a mechanism for state cooptation and control of organized labor. In such situations economic performance will suffer as employers engage sweated labor and resolve disputes in arbitrary and ad hoc ways.

Like most democracies, India has passed a lot of laws to protect worker rights and facilitate institutionalized grievance resolution. As the epigraphs at the opening of this chapter illustrate, India's labor laws have drawn the widespread ire of economists, the business community, and political elites in recent years for their perceived strictness. India's Industrial Disputes Act (IDA) has been at the center of this controversy. However the IDA is primarily designed to channel worker grievances through the state's industrial relations machinery—voluntary conciliation proceedings, voluntary and compulsory arbitration, labor courts and tribunals, and bipartite collective bargaining. If the theory developed in chapter 3 is correct, then the IDA should have a positive impact on economic performance rather than the deleterious effects that economic and political elites suggest it does. What explains this divergence between the growing consensus in the policy community and the arguments about the benefits of protective labor regulation made in this book?

This chapter serves as a corrective to previous studies by showing how core elements of the IDA do indeed promote economic growth. Previous studies have come to the wrong conclusion regarding the IDA because, quite simply, they mischaracterize the act, which results in the use of erroneous codings in their statistical models. Specifically, econometric studies have focused overwhelmingly on the impact of state-level employment protection provisions under chapter V-B of the act. Coding these provisions as "prolabor" and most other amendments to the act as "proemployer" has led to the conclusion that laws that protect worker rights impede investment and productivity.

The problem with this approach is twofold. First, one state—West Bengal—accounts for more than half of state-level employment protection amendments to the central act. While West Bengal's employment protection regulation has indeed been stringent, its economy has suffered for a variety of other reasons. Some of the reasons for slow growth, such as past worker militancy and an adverse relationship with the central government, have nothing at all to do with labor laws.

Second, and more important, it is incorrect to characterize amendments to other sections of the IDA (i.e., those outside of chapter V-B) as either "proworker" or "proemployer." Rather, other portions of the act are designed to facilitate state intervention in industrial relations. There is no way to predict a priori whether the state will intervene in a prolabor or proemployer fashion; and if the state is intervening appropriately it should do so as a neutral arbiter.

Instead of viewing labor law as inherently proworker or proemployer, social scientists should analyze specific provisions based on their intended purpose. The IDA defines three areas of law with implications for economic performance: employment protection law (EPL); the law relating to state intervention in industrial disputes (IDL); and the law pertaining to the ability of state and national governments to limit strikes by declaring industries "public utilities" (PUL). EPL, which has received the most attention in the literature, restricts flexibility in labor markets by making it difficult for employers to fire workers or close their factories. IDL, which has received less attention by social scientists, increases worker and employer access to industrial relations institutions, thereby enhancing the mediating role of the state. PUL, which has so far been completely ignored in the literature, restricts the ability of workers to strike in certain industries.

Each of these areas of law has very different implications for economic performance. The bulk of the provisions of the IDA, which facilitate third-party mediation and collective bargaining, positively affect investment, capital deepening, productivity, and industrial output. Conversely, PUL has negative effects on these outcomes in industries where it restricts FACB rights, because such restrictions encourage exploitation and undermine institutionalized grievance resolution. Finally, although there is evidence that state-level amendments in the area of EPL have adverse effects on economic outcomes, such amendments explain relatively little in terms of cross-regional variations in economic performance because so few states have enacted them.

The Standard Approach

Over the last five years, a number of studies have employed similar methodologies to examine the impact of labor regulation on economic performance in the Indian states. Specifically, these studies examine the effects of state-level amendments to the IDA, the primary piece of regulation governing the formal procedures to be followed by employers and unions in the event of an industrial dispute. Over time, state-level amendments to the central act have proliferated, and vary from those that make minor changes in the qualifications of industrial tribunal judges to those that place heavy restrictions on the ability of employers to hire and fire workers. Taken together, these amendments have resulted in a large amount of spatial and temporal variation in laws governing industrial relations, which economists have harnessed to address questions about the impact of labor laws on economic performance.

The seminal study is by Besley and Burgess (2004) who use panel regressions to analyze the economic impact of state-level amendments to the IDA during the period 1958–92. For their analysis Besley and Burgess (hereinafter "BB") developed an index of labor regulation by coding individual amendments to the IDA as "proworker" or "proemployer" and aggregating these codings to measure the direction of change in regulation for a given state/year. BB code a state-level amendment +1 if the direction of change in labor legislation in a given state-year is "proworker," 0 if it is "neutral," and −1 if it is "proemployer." These scores are then added to the previous year's score to measure the cumulative trend in the regulation of labor over the thirty-five-year period. BB purport to show that proworker regulation results in lower levels of investment, lower productivity, lower levels of employment, and reduced economies of scale.

The BB index has been employed in a number of subsequent studies to analyze the impact of labor laws on various aspects of economic performance in India. One set of papers uses the BB index to explore the extent to which restrictive labor law dampens the effects of beneficial economic policies, such as trade liberalization (Hasan et al. 2007; Topolova 2004) and industrial delicensing (Aghion et al. 2008). Similarly, Sanyal and Menon (2005) examine the effects of industrial disputes and labor laws on investment location decisions in the postreform era. Another group of studies explores the effects of labor law on economic performance in specific sectors. Amin (2009) combines the BB index with data from employer surveys to look at how labor laws impact unemployment in India's retail sector. Ahsan and Pagés (2009) analyze the effects of labor laws and dispute legislation on the performance of labor-intensive industries within manufacturing.[1]

Critiques of the Standard Approach

While studies employing the standard BB approach to analyzing the economic effects of state-level amendments to the IDA have been popular among Western economists and policymakers, the method has come under increasing scrutiny in the Indian academy. One set of critiques has emphasized the declining importance of employment protection provisions in recent years. The first point is that the enforcement of these provisions is not very robust—employers continue to hire and fire at will in spite of strict EPL (Deshpande et al. 2004; Sharma 2006; Sundar 2005). Additionally, in defiance of the standard neoliberal prediction that strict EPL results in artificially high wages, productivity has continued to outstrip wages in India from the late 1960s through the late 1990s (e.g., Kannan 1994; Papola 1994; Goldar and Banga 2005). The relationship between EPL and levels of employment is also not apparent. A number of scholars have pointed out that rates of employment growth in manufacturing have fluctuated despite the lack of any change in India's labor laws (e.g., Nagaraj 1994; Kannan and Raveendran 2009).

Another set of critiques, raised by Bhattacharjea (2006; 2009), relate to the BB method of coding labor regulation. Bhattacharjea asks whether the proemployer/proworker dichotomy adequately captures the substance of many state-level amendments to the IDA. Additionally, Bhattacharjea critiques the BB method of coding the "direction of legislative change" in a given year, as opposed to the actual number of amendments passed. These critiques are of substantial importance to the analysis presented in this chapter and are thus worth reprising here.

The "Proworker" versus "Proemployer" Dichotomy

A major difficulty the BB index is its false distinction between "proworker" and "proemployer" amendments to the IDA. Bhattacharjea (2006) notes the odd implications of coding amendments to the IDA along this dimension in terms of the index scores for individual states. For example, BB code Kerala, the state that was home to the first freely elected communist government in the world as proemployer, and Maharashtra and Gujarat, two of India's most popular investment destinations, as proworker. Closer scrutiny reveals that the BB yields such counterintuitive codings because a proemployer versus proworker dichotomy is not really evident in the law.

Admittedly some amendments to the IDA, especially those imposing restrictions on labor flexibility, constitute proworker legislation. For example, in 1980, Maharashtra passed an amendment to section 25C that requires employers to pay workers 100 percent of their wages for a period of forty-five days if they are laid off for any reason aside from a failure in the supply of electricity. Similarly, in 1984 Rajasthan passed an amendment to section 25Q stipulating that employers who lay off workers or reduce the size of their workforce without the permission of the government are subject to a penalty of up to three months imprisonment and/or a fine of up to two thousand rupees. In 1980, West Bengal passed an amendment to section 25C stipulating that laid-off workers are entitled to receive 50 percent of their salary indefinitely.

However, for the vast majority of provisions of the IDA, categorizing along a proworker versus proemployer dimension is much more problematic. For example, in 1982, Andhra Pradesh enacted an amendment to sections 11B-D of the IDA, expanding the ability of labor courts to enforce awards and settlements. Is this a proworker or proemployer amendment? The answer depends on whether we perceive labor courts as being biased in favor of employers or workers; but if we perceive courts as neutral arbiters, then the answer is "neither." The BB coding often exhibits confusion with respect to how the courts are biased. For example, the authors code amendments like the one described above as proemployer, but then code amendments that allow workers greater access to labor courts as proworker. Clearly it does not make sense to say that courts are biased in favor of workers when workers initiate proceedings but are otherwise biased in favor of employers.

In actuality, there is no systematic evidence to suggest that labor courts, labor tribunals, or ministries of labor harbor a systematic bias in favor of workers or employers. As was mentioned earlier, these institutions were created following Independence by the Indian National Congress as a tool for the political control of unions, and subsequent amendments were often enacted for a similar purpose. The general perception among employers, however, is that the labor courts, tribunals, and conciliation officers are the product of a socialist planned economy, where the state actively intervened in industrial relations to redress a power imbalance between workers and employers. For example, in a policy memo, the Confederation of Indian Industries (CII) once complained that historically, labor courts have been populated by activist judges who "interpreted the labour laws, invariably with a pro-labour tilt" (CII 2004, 2).

Another possibility is that the extent of any bias in favor of labor or employers depends on the politics of the state government in question. Left and center-left governments, for example, are probably more likely to appoint judges with a proworker orientation than governments of other political stripes. In the end, however, such arguments are highly speculative, and in the absence of systematic evidence that political ideology filters through the courts or ministries of labor, it is probably best to remain agnostic regarding whether India's labor institutions are biased one way or the other.

According to Bhattacharjea, the fact that the BB index lacks face-validity may not be devastating, since measurement error results in a downward bias of the estimates. But as I show below, the problem is greater than simple "noise" in the measurement of the independent variable. By coding Indian labor law along a more-or-less contrived dimension, the BB measure completely misses the actual impact of the IDL on economic performance.

Coding Direction of Change versus the Number of Amendments Passed

A second critique of the BB index relates to the fact that it measures the direction of legislative change in a given year, rather than the total volume of regulation adopted. In doing so, the index gives equal weight to the passage of a single amendment and the passage of a large volume of amendments. Additionally, states that pass the same regulation but in different years can end up with different scores on the index. Assuming the regulation passed in a given state/year is of similar importance, an additive index that counts the number of amendments passed would better reflect the degree of regulation in a given year.

The Ahsan and Pagés Coding Scheme

In their study of the impact of labor regulation on the performance of labor-intensive manufacturing industries, Ahsan and Pagés (2009) seek to improve on the BB coding by distinguishing between industrial disputes regulation and employment protection regulation. In making this distinction, Ahsan and Pagés (hereinafter "AP") are certainly on the right track, but they largely retain BB's original "proworker" versus "proemployer" coding within each of these categories. AP recharacterize amendments to the IDA in terms of their effect on efficiency and cost, but in the end this recharacterization amounts to little more than relabeling amendments that BB describe as "proemployer" as reducing the costs to industry, and those that BB label as "proworker" as increasing costs to industry. This simple recharacterization does little to address the critiques that have been raised regarding the index. In the same way that it is difficult to label labor courts or ministries of labor as "proemployer" or "proworker," it is problematic to make a priori assumptions about the implications of such institutions for efficiency and cost. Finally, the AP coding also retains the BB method of coding the direction of regulation change in a given state/year, as opposed to using the additive index described above.

Three Types of Labor Regulation

In this section, I present a new method of coding Indian labor law that helps to address the problems with previous indexes. To correct for the problems associated with making judgments about whom regulation may benefit, the method codes regulation based on its intended purpose. Additionally, the new index measures the total volume of regulation passed by a state legislature in a given/state year as opposed to the direction of change. Regulation under the IDA falls into three categories: (1) industrial disputes regulation; (2) regulation that designates specific industries (sectors) as "public utilities"; and (3) employment protection regulation.[2] Below, I discuss each type of regulation and describe how I will use them to analyze the effects of labor regulation on economic performance.

Industrial Disputes Law

Provisions pertaining to the government's power to intervene in industrial disputes constitute the bulk of the IDA. Sixteen out of the act's forty sections and over half of all state-level amendments to the IDA can be categorized as IDL. Within this body of law, there are two distinct subsets of amendments—amendments that increase the capacity of the judiciary (courts and industrial tribunals) to intervene in industrial disputes, and those that increase the capacity of state governments (ministries of labor) to intervene in industrial disputes. This regulation governs issues of jurisdiction—typically broadening it—as well as the capacity of courts, tribunals, and government officials to enforce judgments and to execute awards and settlements.

I coded state-level IDL provisions to create an index of the capacity for state intervention in industrial disputes according the following method. First, each state-level amendment in this area of law is coded for whether it facilitates greater judicial or government intervention in industrial disputes, either by expanding the jurisdiction of courts or ministries of labor, or by increasing the capacity of these institutions to enforce judgments or execute awards. Amendments are given a score of +1 if they increase the capacity for judicial or government intervention, −1 if they decrease the capacity for judicial or government intervention, and 0 if they do not affect the capacity for judicial or government intervention at all.

The IDL index is the sum of amendments facilitating state intervention minus the number of amendments that decrease the capacity for intervention over time. For example, in 1949, Andhra Pradesh and Tamil Nadu both adopted the following amendment to section 10 of the IDA:

> Where a Tribunal has been constituted under this Act for the adjudication of disputes in any specified industry or industries and a dispute exists or is apprehended in any such industry, the employer or a majority of the workmen concerned may refer the dispute to that Tribunal.[3]

This amendment gives industrial tribunals greater power to intervene in industrial disputes by giving workers and employers direct access to appeal for their intervention. Under the central act, only the government has the power to refer industrial disputes to a tribunal. Thus Andhra Pradesh and Tamil Nadu receive a score of +1 on the IDL index from 1949 onward until these states adopt further amendments to the IDA in the 1980s. In 1987, Andhra Pradesh adopted five new amendments, two of which expanded the capacity of the judiciary to intervene in industrial disputes, and three of which expanded the capacity of the ministry of labor to intervene in industrial disputes. Andhra Pradesh's score on the index thus increases from +1 to +6 on the state intervention index from 1987 onward. Tamil Nadu adopted two amendments that increase the capacity for state intervention in 1982 and two more in 1988. Thus Tamil Nadu jumps from +1 to +3 on the index in 1982, and increases to +5 in 1988.

Figure 5.1 presents graphs of the IDL index scores for each of the fifteen states from 1950 to 1997. As the figure shows, governments in half of India's largest states increased their capacity to intervene in industrial disputes. Most amendments that increased the government's intervention occurred during the turbulent early- to mid-1980s. States that increased capacity for intervention included many of the fast-growing states in the west and south, namely Andhra Pradesh, Gujarat, Maharashtra, and Tamil Nadu. India's two left-leaning states, Kerala and West Bengal, also adopted regulations to increase state intervention in industrial disputes, as did Madhya Pradesh. Rajasthan adopted interventionist regulations earlier than most states, when it passed an amendment to increase the capacity of the judiciary to enforce awards in the 1970s. No state governments enacted regulations that, on balance, diminished the state's capacity for intervention in industrial disputes.

The coding scheme developed in this section gives a very different picture of industrial disputes regulation than those used in previous studies. The closest approximation to my coding scheme is the aforementioned Ahsan and Pagés (AP) scheme, which disaggregate amendments into those that pertain to industrial disputes and those that pertain to employment protection. Despite the similarities in how we categorize regulation, the AP coding is frequently very different from my own. For example, Kerala (in 1979) and Tamil Nadu (in 1982) adopted very similar amendments to section 10B that permit the government to issue temporary binding resolutions, and to prohibit strikes and lockouts until an industrial court or tribunal issues a ruling on an industrial dispute. AP code this regulation −1 because it increases the amount of time needed to resolve a dispute, and thus the cost of resolving it. I code this piece of regulation as +1 because it increases government intervention in industrial disputes.

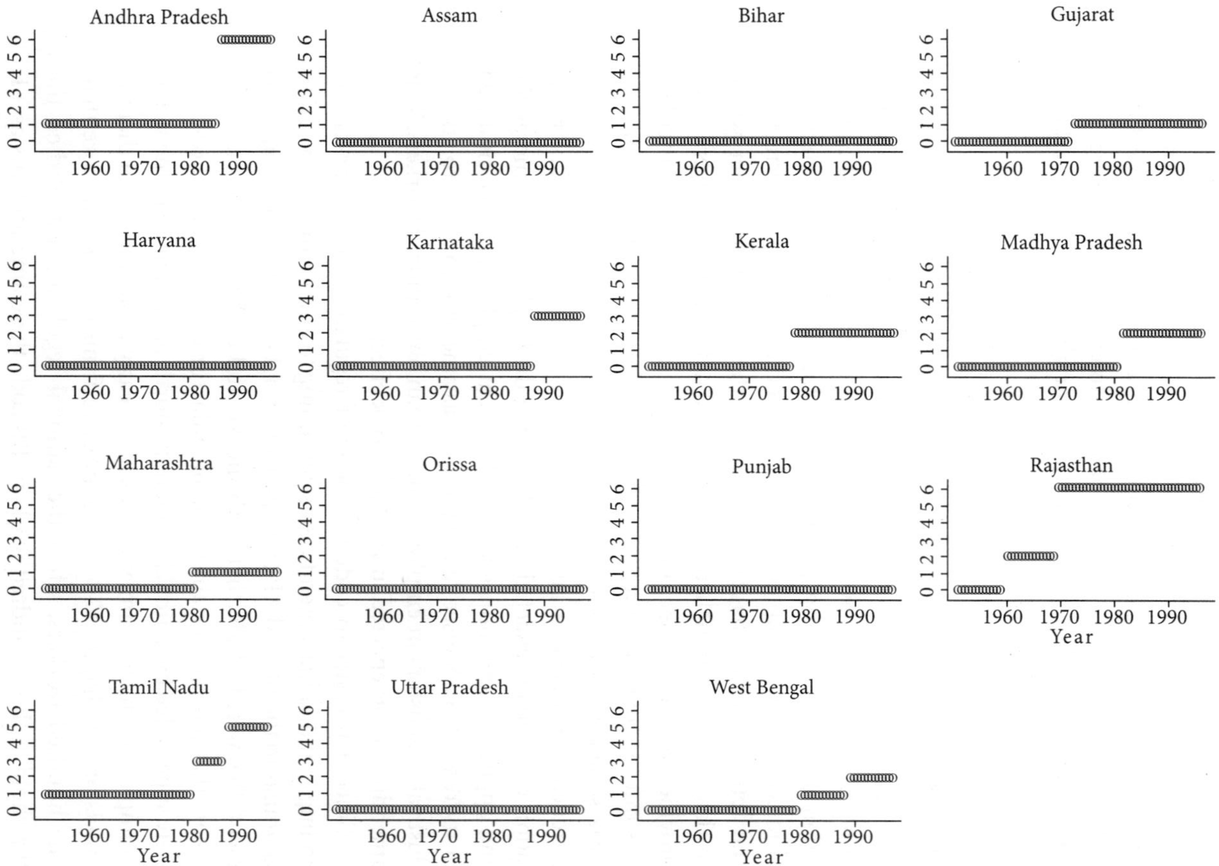

Figure 5.1: Industrial disputes law index

At the same time, my coding of industrial disputes is not simply the inverse of the AP coding, as there are many cases in which our codings of amendments are the same. For example, Rajasthan adopted an amendment to section 33c in 1970 that expanded the scope of awards for which workers could seek judicial assistance in obtaining money from employers. We both code this amendment as +1. Finally, there are a number of amendments that are relevant to my coding scheme but which AP do not include in their analysis. A full list of amendments, how they were coded for this index, and how they relate to the original BB as well as the AP coding is available in appendix B.

Employment Protection Law

In the academic literature as well as policy circles, the IDA's employment protection provisions have received more attention than any other regulation governing the employment relationship. The most contested provisions are those in chapters V-A and V-B of the act, which govern layoffs and retrenchment. Chapter V-A governs the conditions under which workers can be retrenched, the period of notice that employers must provide, and the compensation that workers are entitled to. Chapter V-B lays out the infamous provisions that require owners of medium- and large-scale factories to seek government permission before laying off or retrenching workers, or before shutting down their factories. The regulation was initially enacted in 1976 during the height of the Emergency and applied to any industrial establishment employing three hundred or more workers. Subsequently the law was amended to apply to any industrial establishment employing more than one hundred workers. This amendment was enacted in 1982 and took effect in 1984.

Since it is easier to code this body of regulation as proworker, my coding of individual amendments pertaining to employment protection is similar to the BB and AP codings. However, I do exclude some amendments that were included in the BB and AP studies. These include amendments that did not pertain to the manufacturing sector and those that were superseded by national regulation shortly after their enactment. For example, a number of amendments in the early 1980s stipulated that the provisions of chapter V-B would apply to firms employing more than one hundred workers, when the national regulation established the threshold at three hundred workers. BB code these amendments as +1, but I code them as 0 since the national regulation lowering the threshold from three hundred to one hundred workers took effect in 1984 rendering these state-level amendments redundant.

Each amendment that I include in the analysis is coded as +1 if the regulation increases restrictions on labor flexibility and −1 if it eases restrictions on flexibility. I then sum the individual amendments to create an additive index in the same manner that I do for industrial disputes regulation. Figure 5.2 presents graphs of the EPL index scores for each state from 1950 to 1997. As the figure illustrates, amendments designed to enhance the employment protection features of the IDA have not been an important area of regulation for most Indian states. The bulk of regulation featuring new limitations on labor flexibility has been enacted in West Bengal. It is also apparent from the figure that employment protection regulation does not correlate with economic performance in any obvious way since Andhra Pradesh and Maharashtra, both fast-growing states, have enacted more amendments in this sphere than many slow-growing states.

Public Utilities Law

An important area of labor regulation that has so far been overlooked by scholars is the special status of "public utility services" in the IDA. Section V of the act, governing the prohibition of strikes and lockouts, stipulates that workers and employers in public utilities must give at least two weeks notice before going on strike or declaring a lockout. Moreover, workers and employers in public utilities may not go on strike or declare lockouts while conciliation proceedings are underway, or within seven days after the conclusion of such proceedings.

In the original regulation (section 2 of the IDA), a "public utility service" is defined to include only a small number of services, including railways, ports, communications, sanitation, and services related to the supply of power, light, and water. Over time, however, chapter V of the IDA was used to restrict strike activity in a growing number of industries by adding them to the First Schedule—the official list of industries that the government may declare to be a public utility service. In the 1950s, the central government added a large number of manufacturing sectors to the First Schedule, including cement, textiles, foodstuffs, and iron and steel. To this, states have added their own lists of industries. The number of

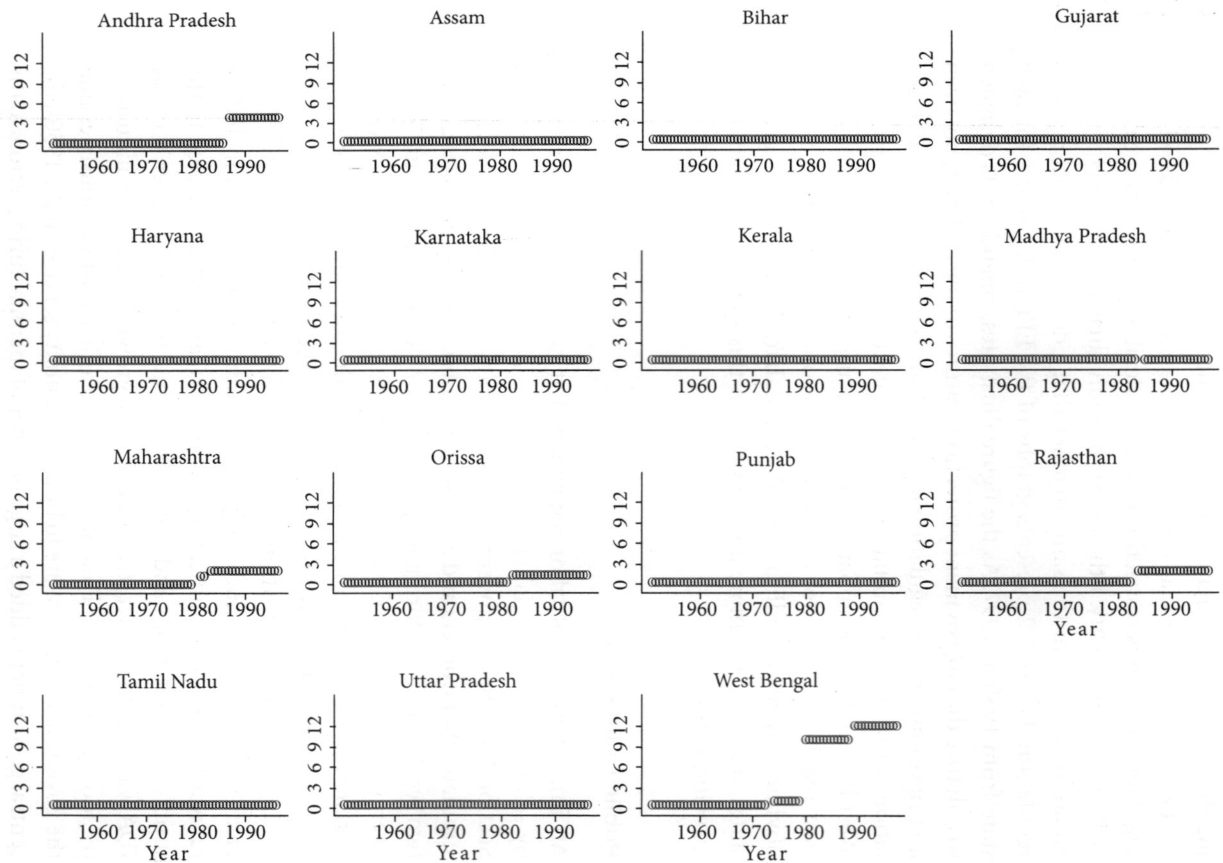

Figure 5.2: Employment protection law index

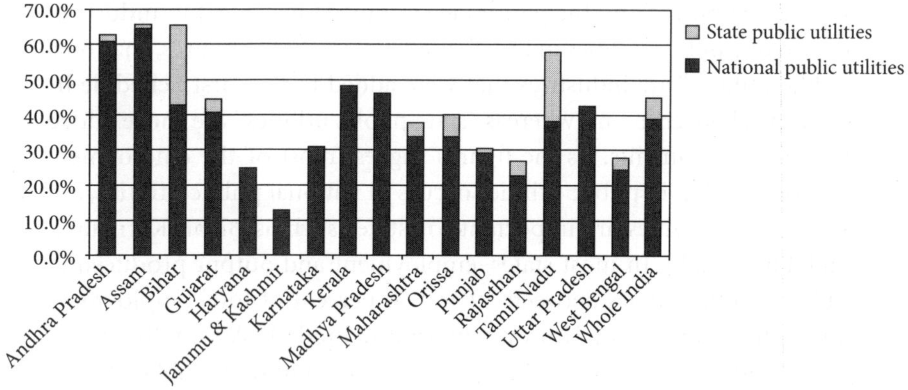

Figure 5.3: Percentage of workers employed in public utilities
Source: Original calculations based on data from the Ministry of Statistics and Programme Implementation, Government of India.

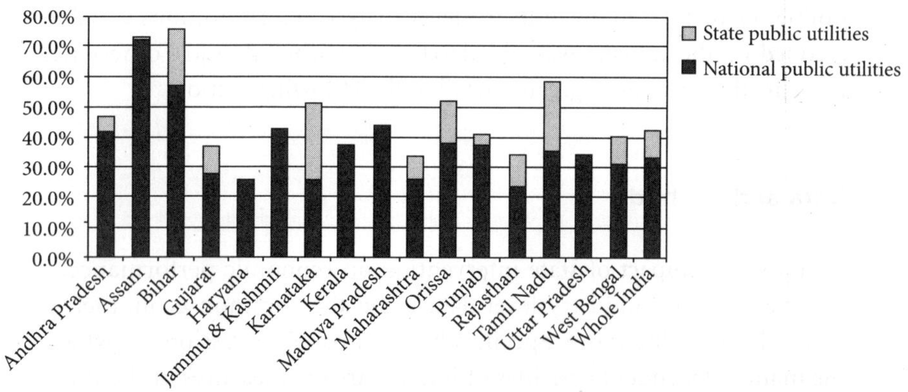

Figure 5.4: Percentage of output produced in public utilities
Source: Original calculations based on data from the Ministry of Statistics and Programme Implementation, Government of India.

industries added to the First Schedule ranges from zero (e.g., Kerala) to twenty-eight (Tamil Nadu).

There is a great deal of regional variation in the percentage of workers and industrial production affected by public utilities regulation. This is a result of the uneven effect of national-level regulation on Indian states and the variation in the number of industries declared as public utilities by state governments. Figures 5.3 and 5.4 present the percentage of workers employed and the percentage of output produced in industries declared as public utilities in India's major states. In the figures, "national public utilities" are industries that were added to the First Schedule by the central government, whereas "state public utilities" are those added by state governments. As the figures suggest most of the employment and production in public utilities occurs in national public utilities, but state public utilities are important for states such as Bihar, Karnataka, and Tamil Nadu. In most states, employment and output produced in public utilities ranges between 20 and 50 percent of total employment and output in industry. However, in Andhra Pradesh, Assam, Bihar, and Tamil Nadu the percentage of employment and output in public utilities is a good bit higher than in other states.

To explore the effects of public utilities regulation on economic performance, I analyze industry-level data. Thus I do not develop a state-level index or employ any other state-level measure of the prevalence of public utilities regulation. In my industry-level analysis, a dichotomous variable is coded 1 if the industry was added to the First Schedule and 0 otherwise. I discuss this analysis in greater detail in the following section.

Data and Methods

To assess the impact of state intervention on economic performance, I analyze state and industry-level data using the common econometric methods in the literature. Specifically, I run panel regressions in which the main independent variables of interest are the measures of the three types of labor regulation discussed above. I extend and make some improvements to the data; but in terms of model specification, I stay as close to the original BB analysis as possible in order to demonstrate that the differences in results are mainly due to the improvements I make in the coding of labor regulation. The analysis focuses on outcome variables most closely related to the arguments made here and in chapter 3, namely investment, productivity, and industrial output.

Some readers may wonder whether the analysis should also include measures of industrial conflict as in the previous chapter. Using the same specification as the model of strikes presented in chapter 4 (table 5.1), an analysis of the effects of labor regulation on protest (not shown here) provides some evidence of a positive relationship between IDL and strikes and a negative relationship between EPL and strikes. This suggests that state intervention in industrial disputes invites workers to air more grievances, and that increased EPL reduces protest, perhaps because the overwhelming leverage such regulation affords workers obviates the need for strikes.

While worth noting, these findings are not relevant to the argument developed in this book, which relates to the role of IDL in reducing exploitation and in institutionalizing protest. To the extent that IDL provides workers with increased associational rights and access to state mediation services, it would be reasonable to expect it to produce more routine protest. At the same time the earlier discussion suggests that state intervention will result in better industrial relations outcomes overall. Unfortunately the mechanisms through which IDL produces better industrial relations outcomes are difficult to measure. There are no state-level data for example on the character of industrial protest (whether routine, nonviolent, etc.). Nor is it possible to directly measure exploitation of workers or employer reliance on sweated labor, practices that by their very nature occur out of plain view. The mechanisms must therefore remain hypotheses since the best we can do is to measure the ultimate impact of labor regulation on economic performance.

Measures of Economic Performance

To test the argument that state intervention and FACB rights promote economic performance, I analyze the effects of labor regulation on four separate measures: (1) fixed capital investment per capita; (2) the capital-labor ratio; (3) total value added; and (4) value added per worker. Fixed capital investment measures the total level of investment in industry, while the capital-labor ratio measures the level of reliance on capital-intensive production. Total value added measures the total level of industrial output, and value added per worker measures the level of labor productivity.

To recap, our primary expectations are as follows. By improving the industrial relations climate, IDL will have positive effects on investment, output, and labor productivity. And by reducing employer reliance on sweated labor, IDL will force employers to invest in capital-saving technology. By contrast PUL, which undermines worker rights, will have adverse effects on economic performance. We should expect to see less investment and output as well as lower levels of productivity in sectors where PUL prevents workers from exercising their right to strike. Additionally, we would expect PUL to decrease investments in fixed capital because employers can more easily exploit workers when they cannot go on strike.

The data on the performance and structure of industry all come from the Annual Survey of Industries (ASI). In both the state-level and industry-level analysis, all variables pertaining to output and investment are expressed in log, real, and per capita terms.[4] Productivity is expressed in log real per worker terms.

Model Specification

The state-level analysis includes controls for political histories, state development expenditures, and population. Political histories are included to control for the possibility that some parties are more "progrowth" than others and are measured as a count of the number of years a given type of party is in power. The parties included in this analysis are the INC, left parties, and the BJP, although the results are robust to the inclusion of other party types. State development expenditures are included to control for infrastructural development.[5] I also included fixed state effects to control for any cultural, geographical, or historical factors unique to a given state, and fixed year effects to control for any temporal effects that are common across all states. Finally I include an indicator variable for the post-1979 period to control for the increased dynamism in the economy stemming from economic reforms.[6]

For the industry-level analysis, I include state-industry effects, year effects, and industry time trends. By state-industry effects, I mean the multiplicative interaction of an indicator variable for each state and an indicator variable for each industry. By year effects, I mean fixed effects for years. And by industry time trends, I mean the multiplicative interaction of a year counter and an indicator variable for each industry.

All regressions are OLS with robust standard errors. For the state-level analysis, the standard errors are clustered by states. For the industry-level analysis, the standard errors are clustered at the state-industry level.

Improvements to the Data

Although this analysis relies on the same data sources as previous studies, it benefits from four distinct improvements to these data. First, the period of analysis is a bit longer than previous studies, most of which stop in 1992. This not only provides more statistical leverage, it ensures that the analysis incorporates a substantial portion of the postreform period. For the state-level analysis, I analyze the period 1960–97.[7] The industry-level analysis is for the period 1973–97.[8] For the industry-level analysis, the extended time period permits the inclusion of between thirty-three thousand and thirty-four thousand observations for the industry-level regressions—about a third more observations than any previous study.

Second I cleaned the ASI for a number of unexplained jumps in the panels. An outlier was defined as an increase of 100 percent or more over the previous year, followed by a comparable decline the following year.[9] Third, previous studies have deflated industrial output and related data using the consumer price index for industrial workers (CPI-IW). This is potentially problematic since industrial output is more commonly deflated using the Wholesale Price Index (WPI). Thus I use CPI-IW to deflate wages but the WPI to deflate value added and investment figures.

Finally, the ASI data are comprised of two types of data—"census sector" data and "sample sector" data. Together the census and sample sectors comprise the "factory sector." The census sector includes large- and medium-scale factories, while the sample sector is comprised of smaller factories. Data on census sector factories is collected every year. Sample sector factories are surveyed periodically. An analysis of posted data suggests that previous studies have used only census sector data prior to the 1970s rather than data for the total factory sector. This is an understandable error that can be attributed to the fact that census and sample sector data were published separately prior to the 1970s; but only using census sector data for the early period produces an artificial jump in ASI figures in the 1970s once factory sector data are used. I therefore add the census and sample sectors to produce factory sector data for the 1960s. Where data for either the sample or census sector are unavailable, I treat the data as missing. This results in missing observations for three years during the 1960s.

Results of the State-Level Analysis

The results of the state-level analysis, which are presented in table 5.1, provide fairly strong evidence in support of the hypothesis that state intervention enhances the performance of industry. The state intervention index is positively and significantly correlated with overall measures

TABLE 5.1
State intervention, employment protection, and economic performance in the Indian states

	(1) Log Fixed Capital Per Capita	(2) Log Capital-Labor Ratio	(3) Log Value Added Per Capita	(4) Log Value Added Per Worker
IDL index$_{t-1}$	0.111***	0.074***	0.074**	0.038**
	(0.035)	(0.021)	(0.025)	(0.015)
EPL index$_{t-1}$	−0.008	−0.016	−0.026*	−0.033**
	(0.020)	(0.018)	(0.013)	(0.014)
Years of left government	−0.016	0.042**	−0.041***	0.017
	(0.186)	(0.016)	(0.013)	(0.010)
Years of BJP government	0.020	0.016	0.075*	0.072**
	(0.038)	(0.041)	(0.036)	(0.030)
Years of Congress government	0.018	0.029*	0.010	0.021***
	(0.017)	(0.015)	(0.012)	(0.005)
Log dev. expenditure per capita	0.206	0.158	0.107	0.059
	(0.175)	(0.145)	(0.109)	(0.061)
Log population	−0.288	−0.041	−0.791	−0.544
	(1.365)	(0.887)	(1.27)	(0.656)
Post-1979	1.447**	0.758	1.705**	1.02**
	(0.553)	(0.498)	(0.573)	(0.354)
Constant	2.633	9.864	7.092	7.923
	(13.40)	(8.91)	(12.93)	(12.93)
Observations	496	496	496	496
Number of states	15	15	15	15
Adj. R-squared	0.8760	0.8760	0.9335	0.8919

Notes: Regressions include fixed effects for states and years. Robust standard errors, clustered by state, in parentheses. * $p < 0.05$, ** $p < 0.01$, *** $p < 0.001$.

of performance including investment (fixed capital per capita), capital deepening (capital labor ratio), output (value added per capita), and labor productivity (value added per worker).

According the model, the substantive effect of IDL on these variables is quite large. Specifically, the model predicts that, on average, investment will be 11 percent higher after a state adopts an amendment promoting greater intervention in industrial disputes.[10] The effects of labor regulation on the capital-labor ratio suggest that state intervention also promotes capital deepening and output. Specifically, the model predicts that IDL amendments result in a 7 percent increase in these two variables. Finally, the model suggests that the IDL results in a 3.8 percent increase in productivity.

The state-level analysis also provides some evidence that employment protection regulation adversely effects output and productivity. The EPL index is negatively and significantly correlated with these two variables. The model suggests that EPL amendments result in a 2.6 percent decrease in output and a 3.3 percent decrease in productivity. EPL is not, however, a good predictor of investment or capital deepening. And further analysis reveals that the relationship between EPL and output drops out of significance when West Bengal is dropped from the analysis.

Additionally, the models show the effects of party ideology, although no systematic patterns emerge. States with entrenched left government have experienced more capital deepening and less output. During the period under analysis, an additional year of left government resulted in a 4 percent increase in the capital-labor ratio but a similar decline in output. BJP and INC rule positively correlate with productivity. An additional year of BJP government increased productivity by 7 percent and an additional year of INC rule increased productivity by about 2 percent.

Results of the Industry-Level Analysis

Table 5.2 presents the results of the industry-level analysis, which also provides very strong support for the hypotheses developed earlier. As in the state-level analysis, IDL positively correlates with output, investment, the capital-labor ratio, output, and productivity, suggesting that state intervention in industrial disputes boosts industrial performance. The magnitude of the effect of IDL is very similar to the state-level analysis, although the coefficients differ for some variables because they refer to economic performance in specific industries as opposed to entire states.

By contrast, the indicator variables for public utilities are negatively and significantly correlated with output, investment, productivity, and the capital-labor ratio. According to the models, the economic impact of designating an industry a public utility is quite substantial. Declaring an industry a public utility results in a 49 percent decline in investment, a 34 percent decline in the capital-labor ratio, a 33 percent decline in output, and a 23 percent decline in labor productivity. National public utilities perform even worse. The models in which the national government declares an industry a public utility show a 150 percent decline in investment, a 230 percent decline in the capital-labor

TABLE 5.2
The effects of three types of regulation on economic performance in India: An industry-level analysis

	Log fixed Capital Per Capita		Log Capital-Labor Ratio		Log Value Added Per Capita		Log value Added Per Worker	
	(1)	(2)	(3)	(4)	(5)	(6)	(7)	(8)
State public utility$_{t-1}$	−0.494***		−0.340***		−0.332***		−0.231***	
	(0.162)		(0.098)		(0.122)		(0.066)	
National public utility$_{t-1}$		−1.480**		−2.379***		−0.636		−1.602**
		(0.733)		(0.635)		(0.804)		(0.699)
IDL index$_{t-1}$	0.062***	0.059***	0.038***	0.036***	0.075***	0.073***	0.050***	0.048***
	(0.015)	(0.015)	(0.011)	(0.011)	(0.013)	(0.013)	(0.009)	(0.009)
EPL index$_{t-1}$	−0.063***	−0.062***	−0.026***	−0.025***	−0.073***	−0.072***	−0.034***	−0.0338***
	(0.008)	(0.008)	(0.006)	(0.006)	(0.007)	(0.007)	(0.005)	(0.005)
Observations	34438	34438	34368	34368	33176	33176	33153	33153
Adj. R-squared	0.8131	0.8131	0.6800	0.6804	0.8030	0.8030	0.5702	0.5705
F-test PU = SI	0.001	0.036	0.000	0.000	0.001	0.378	0.000	0.018
F-test PU = EP	0.008	0.053	0.001	0.000	0.034	0.483	0.003	0.025
F-test SI = EP	0.000	0.000	0.000	0.000	0.000	0.000	0.000	0.000

Notes: Regressions include state *industry effects, year effects, and industry time trends. Robust standard errors, clustered by state-industry, in parentheses. * $p < 0.05$, ** $p < 0.01$, *** $p < 0.001$.

ratio, a 60 percent decline in output, and a 160 percent decline in labor productivity.

The industry-level analysis also provides stronger evidence than the state-level models that EPL has adverse effects on economic performance. EPL is negatively and significantly correlated with the dependent variable in all of the models. For almost every outcome, the magnitude of the effect is the same as IDL but in the opposite direction. However, it is important to reiterate that this effect is being driven by a small volume of amendments passed in a handful of states.

In addition to coefficients and significance tests, the tables present F-tests that compare the effects of each of the three types of amendments (IDL, EPL, and PUL). These tests demonstrate that the three types of regulation have different effects on industrial performance. The joint F-tests are significant at the 0.001 level in all of the models, and virtually all of the paired tests confirm that these three types of regulation have very different effects on economic performance.

Endogeneity

An obvious concern is that the relationship between labor legislation and economic performance is endogenous. One possibility is that industrial law is a product of industrialization itself. Therefore governments may only adopt industrial disputes legislation when industrial unrest reaches a point that it becomes necessary to do so. A related scenario is that both labor legislation and economic performance are explained by unobserved factors relating to leadership. For example, states that perform well in the economic arena may also adopt smart industrial policy because they are more stable or more democratic.

I performed two checks with the state-level analysis to allay these concerns. First, I generated plots of lag and lead dummy variables to demonstrate the change in economic outcomes after the adoption of new amendments to the IDA.[11] Specifically, I ran the regressions keeping data from all states and years until the date at which a second amendment was adopted in a state, and dropping the year of the second change and all later years. But instead of regressing outcome variables on the IDL index variable, I instead regressed them on five-year lag and lead dummies to the first policy change in each state and plotted the coefficients for each dummy variable. These plots are displayed in figure 5.5.

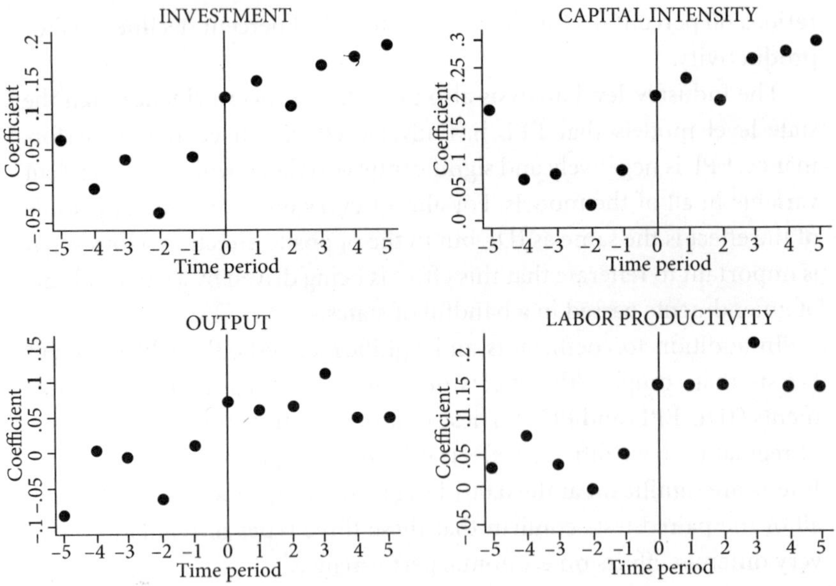

Figure 5.5: Plots of lag and lead dummies for state-level CSTS analysis of labor regulation and economic performance

As the plots suggest, the introduction of an IDL amendment (at time t_0) is associated with major jumps in all of the outcome variables.

The second check (not shown here) was a matching analysis in which states were paired based on initial levels of unionization. I then took the matched differences in outcomes between the pairs and regressed these on the IDL and EPL indexes. The results of the analysis were robust to this specification. The only notable difference in the results was for the EPL index, which positively correlated with investment and capital intensity in the matching analysis. However, since EPL is negatively associated with output and not related to productivity in the matching analysis, this result does not easily lend itself to interpretation.

Conclusion

This chapter has presented evidence that sheds substantial doubt on the standard neoliberal argument that labor regulation hampers economic performance. My analysis demonstrates that laws that facilitate third-party mediation and institutionalized grievance facilitate economic growth. Enhancing the voice function of unions not only boosts investment, it decreases employer reliance on sweated labor, thereby promoting capital-intensive production. Regulation that squelches the voice of workers has the opposite effect. In line with the theory developed in chapter 3, the analysis in this chapter suggests that prohibiting routine protest produces instability in industrial relations that, in turn, hampers productivity and induces capital flight. Such regulation also emboldens employers to engage in despotic labor relations, thereby reducing the incentive to invest in productivity-enhancing technology.

The analysis in this chapter shows why social scientists and the policy community need to adopt a more nuanced approach in their efforts to reform India's protective labor legislation. Although neoliberal dogma would suggest that India should scrap any laws that promote state intervention in the employment relationship, some of these laws have been quite helpful in promoting investment and productivity. The laws that economists, employers, and policymakers have been most focused on, namely the employment protection provisions of the IDA, negatively correlate with industrial output but have been of relatively little importance in most states. Public utilities law, by contrast, has had profoundly negative effects on economic performance across a number of industries in all states. The relative performance of national public utilities has been especially poor. Thus the analysis in this chapter makes it clear that rather than focusing solely on employment protection legislation, unions, employers, and policymakers should study the beneficial effects of industrial disputes legislation and add public utilities law to their reform agendas.

CHAPTER 6

The Deleterious Effects of Labor Repression in Sri Lanka

> The process of state formation is a long and contested one, and powerful transformative states can hardly be conjured up by the institution-building blueprints of the international development community. The developmental credentials of the East Asian states underscores the problem. Not only were they born of exceptional geopolitical circumstances and a unique historical lineage, but their transformative powers were largely a function of their authoritarian character. The so-called third wave of democratization has all but ruled out the authoritarian trajectory of rapid development.
> **—Patrick Heller, *The Labor of Development***

The last two chapters have demonstrated how democracies can draw on synergistic ties and labor institutions to manage worker protest in the context of rapid economic change. However, not all governments choose to respond to labor in this way. As we saw in chapter 5, even India's Industrial Disputes Act—famed for its highly protective provisions—includes public utilities provisions that violate workers' associational rights. In fact, the absence of robust political competition and union-party ties often entails that repression is the primary strategy for responding to organized labor in low- and middle-income countries, even those that have adopted the institutional trappings of democracy.

In Asia, a primary reason for the prevalence of repression as a state strategy for dealing with unions is the continued influence of the East Asian "model" of development. Social scientists have frequently attributed the rapid growth of East Asian economies to initial successes in low-end export production that depended on heavy doses of labor repression to keep labor costs low (Deyo 1987; Haggard 1990). Yet a central question arising from that experience is whether the labor-repressive tactics associated with East Asian development can produce positive growth outcomes in more socially mobilized settings (Evans 1995, chap. 10; Heller 1999, 30–36).

While a number of scholars have questioned the effectiveness of authoritarian responses to labor as a developmental strategy, there are few empirical studies detailing the effects of excluding organized labor from the policy arena and/or the repression of unions in the industrial relations arena. In this chapter, I provide concrete evidence of how labor repression can threaten political stability and economic development through an analysis of the recent history of state-labor relations in Sri Lanka.

From the late 1970s to the early 1990s, the Sri Lankan government adopted an export-oriented development strategy that closely resembled that of many East Asian countries. During this period, Sri Lanka focused intensively on shifting production into export processing zones (EPZs) that were designed to provide a large pool of docile, captive, and inexpensive female labor to produce low-end products for export. The EPZs proved especially attractive to the garment industry, which quickly eclipsed tea as Sri Lanka's number-one export earning industry.

However, in contrast to most East Asian countries, which faced little resistance from civil society at the time of embarking on a strategy of low-end, export-oriented development, Sri Lanka boasted one of the world's most vibrant democracies and a highly mobilized labor movement. An important feature of the Sri Lankan union movement was that unions in the private manufacturing sector were affiliated with Marxist parties that were key members of the governing United Front (UF) coalition. Sri Lankan Marxists had long abandoned aggressive class confrontation in the industrial arena to focus on the pursuit of a programmatic agenda in Parliament. Further, unions affiliated with Marxist parties were highly committed to institutionalized grievance resolution and negotiated a series of agreements with Employers' Federation of Ceylon (EFC) covering a majority of "manual grade" (blue collar) workers in the private manufacturing sector.

Despite these high levels of social mobilization, the United National Party (UNP) government launched a sustained campaign of repression against organized labor and civil society more generally. This dramatic change in the political landscape began with the election of the country's first executive president under the Gaullist constitution of 1978 and accelerated with the decision to suspend parliamentary elections in 1983. As Manor notes, "Many observers regarded [this decision], and the lawlessness and draconian treatment of the opposition which in their view attended it, as grave threats to democracy and to an open political order capable of arranging accommodation between antagonistic social groups, of which there is no shortage in Sri Lanka" (Manor 1983, 1). Repression was dealt to all groups that were perceived in any way as a threat to the government or its policies including, with tragic consequences, Marxist youth in the south and the Tamil minority in the north and east. The government only became more aggressive in its attempts to quell opposition as insurgencies broke out and the country descended into deep and protracted civil conflict.

The intense repression of organized labor during the UNP era eroded institutionalized channels of grievance resolution by undermining the credibility of traditional left parent union organizations and worker faith in the collective bargaining process. As a result, traditional left unions lost their ability to strategically restrain worker militancy for the purposes of collective bargaining, and workers began going on wildcat strikes and leaving traditional left unions to join unions with more aggressive leaders. This process culminated in the mid-1990s with an explosion of high-profile labor protest in which workers employed extreme and violent protest tactics, including assaults on managers, hostage takings, and threatened suicides. The extreme and violent forms of protest chased away hundreds of millions of dollars in much-needed new foreign direct investment (FDI) and led to the closure of dozens of existing factories.

The chaotic consequences of the Sri Lankan government's repression of organized labor give rise to two primary conclusions. The first conclusion is that prior democratic mobilization may make labor repression untenable over the long term, even if unions are successfully repressed in the short term. The second is that repression destroys the political and institutional foundations of class compromise. By eviscerating freedom of association and collective bargaining rights, state repression of left parties and left-affiliated unions erodes channels for institutionalized grievance resolution, producing bursts of highly visible and destabilizing protest, discouraging new investment and threatening existing ventures. And by undermining the confidence of workers in unions affiliated with mainstream parties, repression makes it difficult for major party unions (MPUs) to mobilize worker restraint. In short, the Sri Lankan case demonstrates that repressing unions in a democratic setting can backfire, undermining the rapid development of private industry, which was arguably the central goal of neoliberal reforms.

Neoliberal Reforms and Labor Repression in Sri Lanka

In the late 1970s, Sri Lanka began a dramatic transformation from a vibrant democracy to a brutally repressive authoritarian regime, and the widespread repression of labor was a prominent feature of this transition to authoritarianism. Sri Lanka's transition from a labor-friendly to a labor-repressive state was remarkable both in its extent and in its completeness. In the early-1970s, the dominant political force was the pro-poor, pro–working class United Front (UF) coalition built around the dominant Sinhalese nationalist Sri Lankan Freedom Party (SLFP). Marxist political leaders controlled the majority of labor unions, and Marxist parties were key members of the coalition, which aggressively pursued a socialist path to economic development that emphasized strict regulation of the economy, high levels of taxation, and the redistribution of wealth through social security and welfare expenditures. In the international community, Sri Lanka's welfarist approach to development was held up as a "model" for its ability to achieve exceptionally high levels of social and human development at very low levels of per capita income (Herring 1987, 325).

In the mid-1970s, an economic crisis led to a total reversal of the fortunes of the left and a frontal assault on Sri Lanka's closed economy. The root of the crisis lay in Sri Lanka's structural dependence on three export crops (tea, rubber, and coconuts) and its failure to maintain self-sufficiency in the production of rice. A dramatic fall in commodity prices combined with a rapid increase in international food prices and an unprecedented rise in the price of oil led to an extreme deterioration in the terms of trade, inflationary pressures, and a severe balance of payments crisis. In conjunction with these international economic pressures, the inability of traditional plantation agriculture to provide meaningful employment to an increasingly educated rural youth contributed to widespread social unrest and the substantial delegitimization of the left and its economic policies (Herring 1987, 327–28).

In 1977, voters responded to Sri Lanka's increasingly dire economic prospects by electing the UNP on its platform of economic reform. With the UNP winning 80 percent of the seats in Parliament, the victory was nothing short of a landslide and the mandate for the UNP's economic proposals was clear. Key among these proposals was the dismantling of the regulatory regime that supported Sri Lanka's import substitution industrialization (ISI) and the promotion of an export-oriented industrialization (EOI) strategy of development based on the production of low-end manufactured products. The UNP's radical shift from ISI to EOI put the party on a collision course with traditional left parties and their unions, whose ability to secure high wages and enforce rigid employment rules derived from soft budget constraints in the public sector and protectionist policies governing the private sector.

The struggle between the UNP and the left escalated in the late-1970s as the former UF parties and unions took their political struggle against the UNP to the streets by calling out a series of nationwide protests and strikes against the government. The struggle came to a head in the July 1980 General Strike, which began as a strike in support of a wage increase among railway workers, but quickly evolved into a full-scale standoff between UF unions and the UNP government.[1] D. W. Subasinghe, secretary-general of the Ceylon Federation of Trade Unions (CFTU), describes the strike in the following way:

> The CFTU leadership, after 1977, could not accept the victory of the United National Party.... There were a number of other like-minded trade unions at that time. All were of the opinion that we should try our best to bring the government down.... There was this intention of making it difficult for the government to rule. And we wanted to do our part to hasten the downfall of the government.... We didn't think that that strike would cause the government to fall.... But we wanted to discredit the government.[2]

Whether the UNP perceived the strike as a threat to its hold on power, or simply as an opportunity to crush the left, its response was to crack down hard. The UNP declared the strike illegal under emergency regulations and sent out police, soldiers, and members of the UNP-committed union, Jathika Seveka Sangamaya (JSS) to harass, intimidate, and physically assault the strikers.[3] In addition, the UNP used essential services orders under emergency regulations to declare strikes illegal and to expel strikers from their jobs. The UNP declared all the manufacturing and transport sectors as "essential services," issued a decree that all workers in the public sector participating in the strike had vacated their posts, and pressured private sector employers to follow suit.

It is difficult to overstate the setback these dismissals represented to left unions. By the end of the strike, upward of thirty thousand union members, including key committee members of local branches, had lost their jobs and were subsequently replaced by UNP loyalists. The strike also had substantial demonstration effects for the private sector where employers began to view a union-free environment as a legitimate goal and repressed organized labor knowing they could count on government support. Consequently, traditional left unions in the private sector lost members and became nonentities in the collective bargaining arena.[4]

Following the 1980 General Strike, the UNP continued its repression of worker protest for the entirety of its remaining fourteen years in power. This repression took two forms. The first was further repression and victimization of already unionized workers. Cyril Mathew, minister of industries under the UNP and leader of JSS, the UNP-committed union, led the continued charge against the left and center-left unions. Mathew's aim was to transfer total control of the union movement from the left and center-left unions to the JSS. To this end, Mathew transferred thousands of left and center-left union members in the public sector to remote locations and employed goons to harass and even physically assault union leaders. Under Mathew's guidance, the UNP froze union bank accounts and used essential services orders under emergency regulations to declare strikes illegal throughout their rule. At one point in the early-1990s, the UNP introduced legislation that would make all strikes illegal, with a ten-year prison term as penalty for violation of the law.[5]

The second strategy of reducing the strength of private sector unions involved discouraging the formation of unions in new firms. In large measure, this objective was accomplished by the establishment of what is now known as the Sri Lanka Board of Investment (BOI), a government organization that has the stated purpose of facilitating investment, but whose main function was arguably establishing a pool of docile labor for low-end export production.[6] The BOI shielded firms set up under its jurisdiction from Sri Lanka's many laws guaranteeing workers the right to form a labor union and engage in labor union activities by interfering with the functions of the Labor Department.[7] The BOI also encouraged firms under its jurisdiction to actively discourage workers from organizing unions and to dismiss workers who successfully organized unions, and pressured the commissioner of labor not to prosecute employers who refused to recognize or enter into collective bargaining negotiations with labor unions.[8]

Additionally, the BOI set up restricted and isolated economic zones, called export processing zones (EPZs), and guaranteed employers that unions would be effectively banned from the zones. In the year 2000, there were thirteen such zones and parks (BOI 2000). Workers in BOI companies located within EPZs face special logistical difficulties in terms of organizing and carrying out protest activities. Workers and visitors to factories inside the zone are not permitted to move freely in and out of the zones, which are surrounded by high barbed-wire fences and which require special forms of identification for entry.

For obvious reasons, such isolation makes it difficult for workers to engage in labor union activities. Outside union leaders cannot organize workers because they are prevented from meeting with them. Even if the union leaders can organize workers in the zone, the isolation of companies inside of the zone diminishes the utility of traditional protest methods such as pickets in front of company premises. Further, since the zones are in out-of-the-way rural or peri-urban locations, demonstrations attract less attention than pickets outside of a company in a heavily populated area.

Another tactic the BOI uses to discourage the formation of unions in new firms is to encourage companies to establish "workers' councils" for labor unions. As per BOI instructions, workers' councils are to be elected by their peers, meet every month, and make representations to the employer regarding issues of concern to workers; but widespread abuse by employers has rendered the councils ineffective. There are many reports of employers fixing elections, pressuring certain workers not to run for positions on the council, and pressuring workers to vote for representatives who are friendly to the interests of employers. Abuse of workers' councils has been widespread and visible enough to prompt a letter of complaint from the International Confederation of Free Trade Unions

(ICFTU), the European Trade Union Confederation (ETUC), and the World Confederation of Labor (WCL) to the Sri Lankan government in June 2002.

Yet even if the councils ran free from interference from employers, it is not clear that workers' councils would effectively represent worker interests, because they do not provide any proactive means of redressing grievances. Most notably, workers' councils do not have the ability to negotiate binding contracts and do not have the right to strike. The BOI instructs that the councils should "work together" with the management "in a spirit of mutual trust for the good of the enterprise and its employees" and recommends that councils should "refrain from doing anything likely to impair the efficiency and productivity of the enterprise" (BOI 2002, 7).

By the 1990s, the BOI controlled and confined the vast majority of workers in the manufacturing sector, producing what Laksiri Fernando refers to as Sri Lanka's "new industrial proletariat" (Fernando 1988). In 1995, Sri Lanka's manufacturing sector employed 263,900 workers (http://laborsta.ilo.org). Of these, 217,441, or 82 percent, were employed by BOI-controlled firms; 85,847 workers, 33 percent of workers in the manufacturing sector, were employed in EPZs (BOI 2000).

How Labor Repression Resulted in Industrial Relations Chaos

The imposition of authoritarian control over Sri Lanka's democratically mobilized workforce had dire consequences for industrial relations. Specifically, repression resulted in two destabilizing dynamics. The first was that repression eroded worker confidence in institutionalized grievance resolution. Rather than engaging in collective bargaining or resolving disputes through the state's industrial relations machinery, workers began taking matters into their own hands by engaging in wildcat strikes. Second, repression led to a destabilizing shift in union membership from traditional left unions to independent unions and unions with ties to smaller left parties, or narrow interest unions (NIUs), which behave more aggressively because they are not bound by the interests of a broader constituency.

Effects of Repression on Institutionalized Grievance Resolution

The most important effect of UNP repression was to draw conflict away from collective bargaining and institutionalized mechanisms of grievance resolution. Prior to the 1980 General Strike, the UF unions had formed the bedrock of institutionalized grievance resolution, signing collective bargaining agreements that covered the majority of manual employees in the private organized manufacturing sector. Specifically, industrial relations in the manufacturing sector were structured by a set of agreements signed in 1971 between the EFC and unions affiliated with parties in the UF coalition. These agreements provided for the payment of automatic cost of living adjustments, generous retirement benefits, forty-two days of paid casual and sick leave per year, paid leave for nine public holidays per year, check-off facilities for the payment of union dues, a monthly salary (as opposed to a daily wage) based on skill-level, and a comprehensive set of disputes resolution procedures.[9] The agreements initially benefited twenty-five thousand workers but were eventually extended to cover seventy-five thousand (mostly manufacturing sector) workers, or approximately 42 percent of the workforce in organized manufacturing in 1980.[10]

Following the UNP crackdown, this foundation of institutionalized bargaining was badly damaged. Traditional left unions were seldom given any opportunity to sign an agreement, and by the mid-1980s, most manufacturing companies no longer subscribed to the manual workers' collective agreements to which traditional left unions were the primary signatories (Amerasinghe 1994, 112). On the rare occasion that left unions engaged in collective bargaining, the agreement was signed "from a position of absolute weakness" in which whatever the EFC offered was "taken without resistance" (Amerasinghe 1997).[11]

By rendering traditional union leaders powerless in the collective bargaining arena or, in many cases, removing leaders from factories altogether, the UNP generated a massive legitimacy crisis for traditional left union leaders. As Franklin Amerasinghe, the former secretary-general of the EFC puts it, "The experience of the workers in July 1980 resulted in disenchantment with Trade Union leadership, which was a sad setback to the Trade Unions and which perhaps created a vacuum in leadership at the workplace level in several Companies" (Amerasinghe 1994, 76).

Ultimately, the disenchantment of the rank and file with traditional left leaders made it difficult for leaders of traditional left union federations to control the protest actions of local union leaders and members. Increasingly workers took matters into their own hands, ignoring the directives of party leaders and engaging in unauthorized strikes. This tendency was dramatically illustrated in the protest at Ansell Lanka (Pvt) that was related at the beginning of chapter 3; but examples of similarly chaotic wildcat strikes abound in the postliberalization period.

Effects of Repression on the Structure of the Union Movement

A second effect of the loss of faith in traditional union leaders was a massive shift in union membership away from unions affiliated with major left parties to NIUs with more aggressive leadership.[12] More specifically, membership shifted away from unions affiliated with parties in the former UF coalition that had participated in the 1980 General Strike—the CFTU, the Ceylon Federation of Labor (CFL), and the Sri Lanka Nidahas Sevaka Sangamaya, or "Sri Lanka Independent Workers Union" (SLNSS), hereafter referred to collectively as the "UF unions."[13] Two NIUs were especially effective at taking advantage of the loss of credibility suffered by traditional left unions during the 1980 General Strike. The first was the Ceylon Industrial Workers' Union (CIWU), which is affiliated with the Nava Sama Samaja Party (NSSP) or "New Social Equality Party." The second was the Inter-Company Employees' Union (ICEU), affiliated with the Janatha Vimukthi Peramuna (JVP) or "People's Liberation Front"—the radical Marxist party whose bloody insurgency resulted in as many as sixty-six thousand deaths between 1987 and 1989 (Shastri 1997). Primarily for convenience, I refer to these as "new left unions" in the subsequent discussion.

While the NSSP did not openly support violence, the ICEU appealed to workers through open advocacy of violent and extreme protest tactics. And while the JVP has evolved into a mainstream political party in recent years, its earlier radical posture had long-term implications for industrial relations in Sri Lanka (Venugopal 2009). Arguably, the JVP's radicalization of the union movement began even before the UNP left power, with the formation of JVP "action committees" in Sri Lankan factories during the mid-1980s. Repression of traditional left unions enabled the JVP to establish the control over the industrial sector that was crucial to the success of the uprising, and through its action committees, the JVP instituted a reign of terror in public and private sector industries, forcing companies into agreements through violence and intimidation. Thus although these committees were set up more for the purposes of armed insurrection as opposed to industrial relations, they arguably had a substantial effect on industrial relations in Sri Lanka as the industrial workforce began to absorb the violent tactics of the JVP.[14]

The shift in control from old guard left unions to new left unions continued through the 1990s. Table 6.1 reports the percentage of manufacturing firms reporting the presence of traditional and other left unions in manufacturing units in 2002. These figures are based on an original telephone survey of ninety-one manufacturing firms randomly selected from the Ceylon Chamber of Commerce members' directory, as discussed in chapter 4. The survey results show that the rise of new left unions has substantially eroded the control of UF unions over the Sri Lankan labor movement. Prior to UNP rule, one would have been hard pressed to find a manufacturing unit without workers represented by UF unions. In 2002, only 54 percent of companies reported the presence of UF unions, with 22 percent of firms reporting the presence of a CFTU-affiliated union, 24 percent of firms reporting the presence of an SLNSS-affiliated union, and a mere 11 percent of firms reporting the presence of a CFL-affiliated union. The survey results also demonstrate the increased dominance of the ICEU and the CIWU. These unions, which were nonexistent in the 1970s, now organize workers in nearly half of unionized companies in the manufacturing sector. Thirty-two percent of unionized companies reported the presence of an ICEU-affiliated union, while 22 percent reported the presence of a CIWU-affiliated union.

The dominance of new left unions had a dramatic effect on industrial relations. In many factories in the early- and mid-1990s, workers repeatedly pursued aggressive demands by employing extreme and violent protest tactics that, according to reports by managers and local union leaders, were supported rather than discouraged by leaders of new left unions. For example, in 1990, ICEU members at a metal packaging factory outside of Colombo went on strike in support of a wage demand and the strike quickly turned violent. A manager at this factory reported that, with the full support of ICEU leadership, ICEU members assaulted

TABLE 6.1
Structure of the union movement in Sri Lanka

Union	% Unionized Companies
United Front unions	54
CFTU	22
CFL	11
SLNSS	24
Narrow interest left unions	49
ICEU	32
CIWU	22
Other unions	57
CMU	35
JSS	14
Other	16

Notes: Figures represent the percentage of unionized companies reporting the presence of each type of union in one or more of their production units. The data are from a telephone survey of managers and directors of 91 randomly selected companies in the Sri Lankan manufacturing sector conducted during November and December of 2002.

nonstriking workers and management, ransacked one manager's home, and damaged company machinery.[15]

Similarly, in 1992, members of the Ceylon Industrial Workers' Union (CIWU) went on strike at a coir manufacturing facility in the city of Galle.[16] When the management did not grant the union's demand for a 42 percent wage increase, the workers threw rocks, sticks, and bottles at the management and went on a two-week slowdown. Failing to win their demand, the CIWU leadership continued its agitation and led the workers on strike a second time in 1994 when workers, in the presence of the union leadership, staged a fast atop the company's water tower and hurled missiles at management for a second time.

The Implosion of Institutionalized Grievance Resolution

These anecdotes are representative of a more general trend toward more chaotic and violent industrial relations in the postreform era. Figure 6.1 presents the trend in aggregated dispute volume in Sri Lanka's manufacturing sector from 1973 to 2001. Dispute volume is calculated as the number of workerdays lost to industrial disputes (strikes or lockouts) per one thousand workers and is the broadest measure of industrial

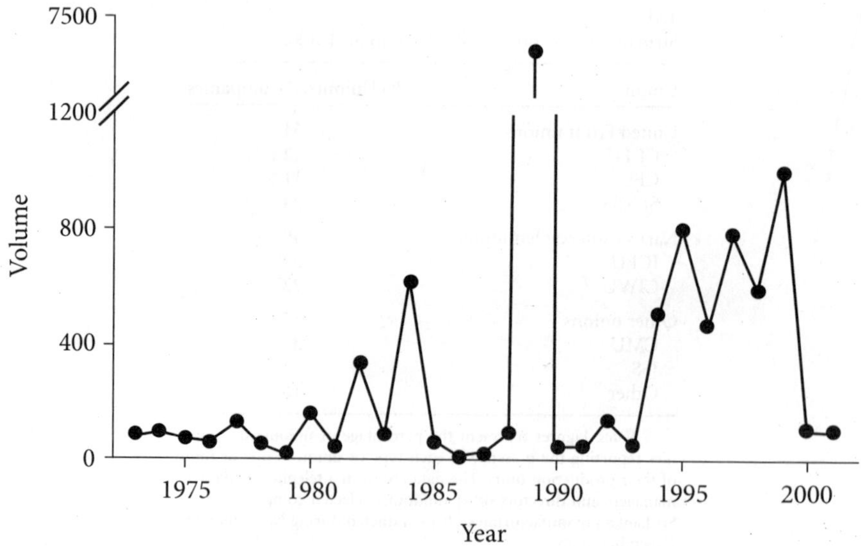

Figure 6.1: Dispute volume in Sri Lanka's manufacturing sector
Notes: Industrial dispute volume is the number of workerdays lost due to industrial disputes per 1,000 workers. The calculations displayed in this figure are specific to the manufacturing sector. The data are from the International Labor Organization's LABORSTA database, available online at http://laborsta.ilo.org.

protest.[17] Prior to the 1980 General Strike, industrial relations were extremely cordial, even by international standards. In most years during this period, dispute volume in the manufacturing sector was less than one hundred workerdays lost per thousand workers. This level of industrial peace rivals that of most countries, and is on par with the low levels of industrial conflict characteristic of postwar social democracies in Northern Europe (Hibbs 1987, 53–62).

During the course of UNP rule, dispute volume rose steadily, peaking at 7,458 disputes per 1000 workers during the height of the JVP uprising in 1989. Although the JVP period was exceptional, dispute volume continued to be high by Sri Lankan standards, even after the uprising ended. When the center-left People's Alliance (PA) government defeated the UNP in the 1994 elections, there was a sustained increase in industrial disputes. Relative to the UF era, dispute volume continued to be quite high during the mid- and late-1990s, ranging between 500 and 1,000 workerdays lost. The dispute volume witnessed in the post-UNP period is also moderately high by international standards, putting contemporary Sri Lanka on par with the famously contentious labor movements of France and Italy (Hibbs 1987, 61).

Yet as I have stated previously, dispute volume is only part of the story. There is also evidence of a widespread deinstitutionalization of industrial relations in the post-UNP era (see table 4.4). Industrial violence became exceedingly common. In the 1990s, 22 percent of companies experienced violent or extreme forms of protest in one or more of their production units. Eight percent of companies reported an industrial dispute in which workers damaged company property, while 11 percent reported threats against management by union members. Four percent of companies reported that union members physically assaulted other workers when they tried to cross the picket line, and 2 percent of companies reported a direct assault on managers.

Further, during the 1990s, many workers began engaging in nonviolent but highly nonroutine forms of protest. For example, 10 percent of companies reported that workers had climbed to the top of high structures such as water towers or office buildings during the course of a dispute, typically threatening suicide.[18] Other forms of obstruction and occupation of company premises were also common. Nine percent of companies experienced a *gherao,* a uniquely South Asian form of protest in which workers surround a manager, refusing to allow the manager to leave his/her desk (even to use the lavatory) until their demands have been addressed.[19] Twelve percent reported that workers had occupied or obstructed company gates so as to deny managers or owners access to the premises. Two percent of companies reported experiencing a fast. In all, 30 percent of companies reported experiencing some form of obstruction or occupation of company premises.

A Statistical Test of the Argument

To test the argument that repression eviscerated the foundations of institutionalized grievance resolution, I estimate a logistic model of industrial protest events of a form similar to the event-based models presented in chapter 4 (table 4.5) but focusing only on protest events in Sri Lanka. Specifically, I analyze whether workers that were controlled by UF unions were less likely to engage in routine or violent protest than

NIUs. The analysis also explores the protest dynamics associated with the loss of control by MPUs and the emergence of NIUs. If the argument developed in the preceding section is correct, then we should see more chaotic industrial relations as UF unions lose control and as NIU leaders gain control of local union leaders and members.

Data and Method

The data are derived from in-depth surveys of thirty-five companies in Sri Lanka selected via a random sample of the ninety-one participants in the telephone survey. These interviews yielded a sample of sixty-one industrial protest events reported to have occurred between 1991 and 2002 at the thirty-five companies participating in the in-depth interviews. The models are of the same form as in chapter 4—cross-section time-series dyadic models of strike protest.

As in the previous analysis, the dependent variables relate to the occurrence of routine and violent protest. Each dyad-year is coded for whether the union in the dyad engaged in protest at all (1 if yes; 0 otherwise) and whether a union engaged in an extreme or violent form of union protest (1 if yes; 0 otherwise). "Extreme or violent" protest include an assault on a manager, assault on other workers, damage to company property, or serious threats against the lives of managers. A third variable, the "level of protest" is coded 0 if no protest occurred, 1 if the union engaged in routine protest, and 2 if the union engaged in extreme or violent protest.

The main independent variables of interest are a measure of external federation control of union leaders and members, two categories of unions (UF versus NIU), and an interaction term (UF*degree of external control). The level of control exercised by a central union leadership over enterprise-level leaders and members is a qualitative assessment by the management of the firm experiencing the protest event. The management was asked whether the parent union "always," "sometimes," or "never" had control of the actions and behavior of the local union.[20] For the purposes of this analysis, the central union leadership was coded as having a "high" degree of control if the management responded that it "always" had control over firm-level leaders and members, a "moderate" degree of control if the management responded that the union "sometimes" controlled the behavior of the local union, and a "low" degree of control if the respondent said the management "never" exercised control over the branch union.

To recap, the category "UF union" pertains to unions affiliated with political parties that formed the UF coalition and that were on the receiving end of UNP repression in the aftermath of the 1980 General Strike. The UF union category is closely related to but is distinct from the "MPU" category that has been used throughout the book. First, the parties that formed the UF coalition were in power prior to 1991 and the MPU category was operationalized as a union affiliated to a party that had been in political power since the economic reforms began in India.[21] Second, and more important, the JSS is an MPU that is affiliated to the UNP and therefore is not included in the United Front category. This analysis thus goes beyond the broader analysis of MPU behavior in prior chapters to test the specific dynamics at work in the Sri Lankan context. Conceptually, the NIU category is the same as in the previous analysis. It is defined to include unions affiliated to small political parties and independent unions. During the period analyzed in this chapter, these included the CIWU, the ICEU, the Ceylon Mercantile Union (CMU), and a handful of smaller unions. There were no enterprise unions in the Sri Lanka sample.

The control variables are the same as in the previous analysis. I included the number of active unions in the production unit at the time of the protest event to control for the effects of union competition. The number of workers in the production unit at the time of the dispute captures the effects of a larger workforce and more impersonal management-worker interactions. To control for the impact of economic conditions on union violence, the analysis includes the rates of inflation and economic growth.[22] The analysis includes fixed year effects as well as a time trend to account for the possibility that respondents are more likely to report recent events than events that occurred in the past.

Results

The results of the basic analysis are presented in table 6.2. Providing support for the argument that UF unions discourage aggressive protest, the interaction term in all of the models is negative and significant.[23] Two other results of the analysis are worth noting. First, the number of unions is positive in the models of strike frequency and level of protest, suggesting that increased competition in the union movement that resulted

TABLE 6.2
Logit and ordered logit models of worker protest in Sri Lanka

	(1) Routine Protest	(2) Violent or Extreme Protest	(3) Level of Protest
United Front (UF) union	0.805***	1.778***	0.841***
	(0.224)	(0.498)	(0.236)
Degree of external control	1.316***	3.822***	1.442***
	(0.443)	(1.021)	(0.449)
Interaction term = UF union* degree of external control	−0.847**	−2.468***	−0.938***
	(0.349)	(0.618)	(0.352)
Number of workers	0.0002	0.001***	0.0003
	(0.0003)	(0.0002)	(0.0002)
Number of unions	0.423**	0.385	0.403**
	(0.182)	(0.344)	(0.173)
Inflation	−0.022	−0.042	−0.023
	(0.079)	(0.058)	(0.076)
Growth	−0.030	0.225**	−0.001
	(0.095)	(0.112)	(0.090)
Time trend	0.140	2.339**	0.160
	(0.110)	(1.127)	(0.107)
Constant	−5.077**	−34.137**	
	(1.997)	(13.469)	
Threshold α_1			5.311***
			(1.886)
Threshold α_2			6.532***
			(1.922)
Number of observations	969	749	969
Number of clusters	35	35	35
Log likelihood	−202.6	−75.04	−242.6
χ^2	83.75	75.85	85.47

Notes: Regressions include fixed effects for states and years. Robust standard errors, clustered by company, in parentheses. * p < 0 .05, ** p < 0 .01, *** p < 0 .001.

from UNP repression was related to an increased frequency of protest. Second, the time trend is significant in the violence model but not in the model of routine protest or the ordered logit model. If simple memory effects were driving this result, we would expect the time trend to be significant in all of the models, and not just in the violence model. The fact that it is only significant for violence depicts growing chaos in Sri Lankan industrial relations during the 1990s and early 2000s. This entails that the deleterious effects of repression were not limited to the period immediately following the 1980 General Strike but were progressively amplified over the twenty-five-year period covered by the analysis.

Predictions on the model of worker violence reveal some interesting patterns with respect to the dynamics of external federation control (see table 6.3). Specifically, the likelihood of violence decreases with increasing United Front control over branch-level leaders and members, but

TABLE 6.3
Predicted probabilities of protest by United Front and narrow interest unions

	Violent Protest
United Front union	
High control	0.032
	(0.002, 0.062)
Moderate control	0.060
	(0.030, 0.090)
Low control	0.107
	(−0.002, 0.008)
Narrow interest union	
High control	0.083
	(0.019, 0.148)
Moderate control	0.016
	(0.0002, 0.031)
Low control	0.003
	(−0.002, 0.008)
Wald tests	
UF high = NIU high	$\chi^2 = 2.36$
	p = 0.124
UF high = UF low	$\chi^2 = 2.77$
	p = 0.096
UF high = NIU low	$\chi^2 = 5.95$
	p = 0.015

Notes: Predicted probabilities of worker protest based on model 2 in table 6.2. 95% confidence intervals in parentheses.

increases with increasing NIU control. According to the model, workers controlled by a UF union have a 3 percent chance of engaging in violent or extreme protest actions. But workers that belong to a UF union that has lost control of its membership have more than a 10 percent chance of engaging in violence. Conversely, workers that belong to an NIU that has little control over its members behave like enterprise or nonunionized workers, that is, they have next to no chance of utilizing aggressive protest tactics. Finally, as NIU control increases so does the likelihood of violence. Workers controlled by an NIU have an 8 percent chance of engaging in violence according to the model. Wald tests shown at the bottom of the table reveal that these differences—between UF unions with high control and low control, and between NIUs with and high and low control—are statistically significant.

These results provide very strong evidence in favor of the argument that the UNP's efforts to undermine UF control of the union movement also gutted institutionalized bargaining in Sri Lanka. The loss of UF control is clearly associated with increased violence as is the strengthening of control by more aggressive NIUs. But one result remains unexplained. Why does the first Wald test show no difference between the likelihood of violence by UF unions and NIUs with tight control over their members? Arguably this result provides further support for the theory that UNP repression rendered the UF incapable of mobilizing restraint in the postreform era. While protest declines with UF control, it never drops below that of an NIU because workers do not fully trust in the effectiveness of UF leadership. But UF unions where the leadership has completely lost control of the membership are going to be even more violent than those guided by NIU leaders, who are more strategic in how they deploy aggressive protest tactics. Having overcome basic collective action problems, but not facing any constraints, such workers are likely to be the most violent of all. And this is precisely what the results of the model tell us.

The Economic Impact of Industrial Violence

In the short term, it is likely that repression boosted economic growth and investment. By dismembering the left labor union movement, the UNP deprived the traditional left of its last weapon against UNP-led economic reforms. Lacking the ability to call out general strikes, traditional left parties and unions were powerless to resist tough reform measures such as devaluations and reductions in rations. Further, for a period of time, the UNP's tough stance against unions made Sri Lanka more attractive to foreign investors. However, available evidence suggests that the initial success of a repressive strategy was counterbalanced by the resulting destabilization of industrial relations in the private sector. In particular, industrial violence had negative implications for FDI and led to a higher rate of factory closures in private manufacturing.

The events of the 1990s captured the attention of the international press, thereby hampering the efforts of the Sri Lankan government to attract new foreign investment. The headline of a *Financial Times* article reporting on the Ansell strike read "Investment Blow to Sri Lanka."[24] *Reuters* reported that South Textiles, a Canadian joint venture, threatened to pull out after strikers assaulted its managers and, in the same article, reported a hostage-taking at a Japanese porcelain factory.[25] In a report focusing

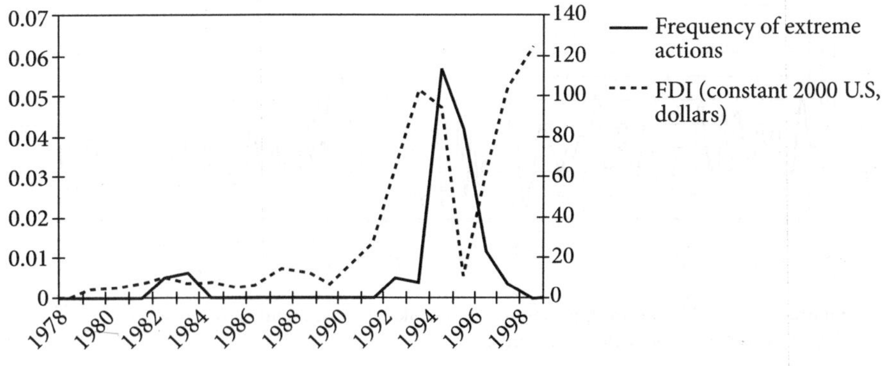

Figure 6.2: Trends in frequency of extreme protest and FDI in Sri Lanka
Notes: The frequency of extreme protest is measured as the number of extreme protest actions reported in the Sri Lankan press in a given year per 1,000 manufacturing sector workers. Data on extreme protest actions are original data collected from newspaper reports. The number of workers in manufacturing is from the ILO LABORSTA database, available online at http://laborsta.ilo.org. The FDI data are from *The BOI Sector: Statistical Abstract, 2001* published by the Sri Lanka Board of Investment.

on industrial violence in Sri Lanka's manufacturing sector, the *Journal of Commerce* focused on the desperate efforts of the Sri Lankan government "to calm fears of overseas investors" during a wave of strikes in 1994.[26]

Violent and extreme protest actions generate uncertainty for investors, and highly publicized violence tends to reduce the appeal of a country as a destination for FDI. It is therefore not surprising that the burst of industrial violence in the early-1990s resulted in a sharp decline in FDI in Sri Lanka. Figure 6.2 displays the trend in FDI and violent and extreme protest events appearing in the Sri Lankan press.[27] As the figure demonstrates, a dramatic reduction of new FDI followed directly on the heels of the extreme and violent protest in the mid-1990s. FDI fell from 103 million to 10 million constant 2000 U.S. dollars from 1993 to 1995, a decrease of about 90 percent in the span of two years. FDI eventually recovered, but the dramatic downturn put a substantial dent in the overall level of FDI. FDI inflows had gained quite a bit of momentum in the 1990s, and the rate of growth in new FDI was quite rapid—approximately 86 percent per year during the first five years of the 1990s. If the growth had continued at the same pace through the end of the 1990s, new FDI would have been \$2.1 billion in 2000 as opposed to the \$173 million that Sri Lanka actually received.

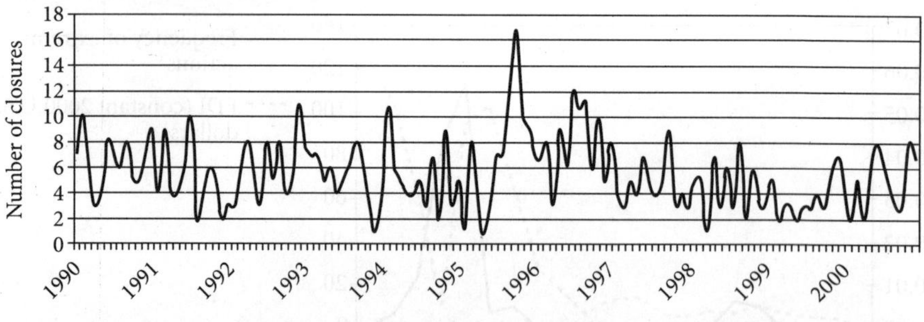

Figure 6.3: Monthly closure applications in Sri Lanka's private manufacturing sector
Source: Ministry of Labor closure records.

In addition to chasing away new investment, the industrial chaos of the 1990s resulted in the closure of already existing production units. Microdevices, the largest joint venture electronics plant in Sri Lanka, closed up shop after a number of women working at the plant assaulted senior managers and did extensive damage to company property.[28] Two diamond-cutting factories pulled out of Sri Lanka following violent strikes. Blue Diamonds left after workers occupied the factory,[29] and Keells Diamonds closed after workers violently clashed with strikebreakers.[30] The wave of violent strikes also struck at the heart of the BOI-controlled EPZs. Regency Garments, Youngi and Ones, and Korea Ceylon are just three examples of BOI-controlled garment manufacturers that closed down due to factory occupation, hostage takings, damage to property, or other violence.[31]

These anecdotes are representative of a wave of closures brought about by the surge in extreme and violent protest in the mid-1990s. The effect of industrial violence on closures was more lasting than its impact on FDI. Figure 6.3 displays the monthly number of applications for closure to the Ministry of Labor in the private manufacturing sector. The records show a spike in the monthly number of applications during the period of severe labor unrest in the mid-1990s, rising as high as seventeen closure applications in one month in 1995, and hovering around ten a month through 1996.

Conclusion

In this chapter, I have argued that the recent history of state-labor relations in Sri Lanka provides evidence of the adverse effects of pursuing a labor-repressive, export-oriented strategy of development in a democratically mobilized setting. In the short term, the UNP's narrow focus on developing a docile pool of low-wage labor attracted investment in low-end, export-oriented industries, especially to the garment sector. Over the long term, the strategy had substantially negative implications for Sri Lankan industrial relations and, ultimately, investment in Sri Lankan industry. The repression and harassment of traditional left leaders rendered institutionalized forms of grievance resolution ineffective and eroded the confidence of the working class in collective bargaining and routine strike activities. Some workers began taking matters into their own hands, employing extreme and violent protest tactics to win their demands. Other workers joined unions with more aggressive leaders who encouraged the use of violence. The result was a surge in high-profile standoffs between management and workers in the 1990s that chased away new investment and forced the closure of hundreds of production units.

The Sri Lankan experience casts doubt on the notion that East Asian style labor-repressive strategies might produce positive developmental outcomes in other regions. Instead, as Heller (1999) notes, the developmental strategies of East Asian states were more likely "the product of a very specific state-society balance" that cannot be successfully replicated in more socially and politically mobilized settings (34). Moreover, by demonstrating that the denial of institutionalized grievance resolution destabilizes industrial conflict, the Sri Lankan case can help to explain the surge in labor protest and the instability of industrial relations noted to have occurred during and shortly after democratic transitions in East Asia itself (Freeman 1993; Evans 1995).

CHAPTER 7

Conclusion

Theoretical and Policy Implications

Like most developing democracies, national and regional governments throughout South Asia have struggled to manage the social tension and conflicts inherent in periods of rapid economic transition. There has been great variation in the nature and effectiveness of these attempts. Some, like the southwestern state of Kerala, provide examples of how democratic governments can forge class compromise without substantially undermining worker interests. Others, like Sri Lanka, have only fomented greater instability through their efforts to eliminate working-class opposition to economic reforms. This book has demonstrated that the effectiveness of government strategies in managing industrial conflict is directly related to the depth of political democracy. Competitive elections promote the development of mutually beneficial union-party ties that enable parties to mobilize worker restraint. Robust freedom of association and collective bargaining (FACB) rights, also a feature of mature democracies, serve as the foundation for the institutionalized resolution of worker grievances.

The analysis upends conventional wisdom regarding state-labor relations and economic development. While few would advocate the outright repression of organized labor, employers, social scientists, and policymakers have frequently argued that the political mobilization of the working class hinders economic growth. Employers express concern that union partisan ties result in undue political interference in industrial relations. Economists and international development organizations denounce union advocacy of protective labor legislation and opposition to neoliberal reforms. Although these concerns do not equate to union smashing, they frequently serve as a justification for the political repression and exclusion of organized labor.

The results of this study suggest reasons to be more optimistic about the ability of democratic countries to balance the interests of organized labor against those of a broader constituency. After all, balancing competing interests and priorities is precisely what democracy is designed to do. Ties between unions and major political parties do not promote the undue influence of a distributional coalition so much as they contribute to the stability of the industrial relations environment. This is because major parties internalize the externalities of affiliated organizations, including unions. Moreover, this moderating tendency is only enhanced by competitive party systems and elections.

Also contrary to the conventional wisdom, this study demonstrates how protective labor legislation benefits economic performance. Specifically, legislation facilitating state intervention in industrial disputes boosts investment, capital deepening, productivity, and industrial output. This is because such legislation helps to institutionalize industrial conflict and reduces the tendency of employers to rely on sweated labor. In contrast, repressive "public-utilities" legislation, designed to prevent strikes in certain industries, has exactly the opposite effect of legislation that facilitates state intervention in industrial disputes. Such legislation undermines FACB rights, thus enabling employers to exploit workers and undermining institutionalized grievance resolution.

South Asia is in many ways the perfect laboratory for studying the effects of party-union ties in developing democracies. As the world's most populous democracy and the developing world's most stable democratic country, India is arguably the most important case for understanding the dynamics of state-labor relations in a developing democracy. South Asia is also home to less stable democracies and to countries that have been governed for long spells by authoritarian regimes. The less democratic experiences of these countries permit a comparison of the effects of India's voluntary union-party ties with the strategy of political domination, repression, and exclusion of organized labor typically practiced by authoritarian and hybrid regimes. In this book, India's democratic experience was contrasted with that of Sri Lanka, where state-labor relations were characterized by a high degree of repression and exclusion during the 1980s and early 1990s.

The history of Sri Lankan state-labor relations shows how the forcible exclusion of the working class from politics can give rise to a union movement dominated by narrow interest unions (NIUs), which tend to be guided by the interests of one or a handful of union leaders. Such unions behave more aggressively than unions with ties to major political parties because the leadership benefits from a show of force but is not constrained by the broader interests of a political party. NIUs are therefore more likely to present larger demands and to utilize violent and extreme forms of protest in order to enhance their reputation for toughness and extract larger rents from the management.

The remainder of this chapter explores some additional implications of these findings and addresses some remaining issues. I first discuss the theoretical implications for the study of democracy and the developmental state. I then turn to a discussion of the implications of the analysis for states' reversing of capital flight by comparing the experiences of Kerala and West Bengal—both so-called "red states" that have endeavored to overcome their reputations for worker militancy. This leads to a discussion of whether investment promotion entails the co-optation of workers and the subjugation of their interests to the party. Finally, I end by noting the implications of my findings for future reforms in India and abroad.

Democracy and Development: Beyond Autonomy and Embeddedness

The findings of this study speak to academic and policy debates about the relationship between democracy and economic development. Previous studies have not found a straightforward relationship between democracy and economic growth; but it is also clear that quality of governance matters for economic outcomes. The development studies literature has long been concerned with "state autonomy," defined as the ability of state actors to craft economic policies absent interference from powerful distributional coalitions, as a key factor contributing to the emergence and effective implementation of economic reforms. Understanding the best method of achieving state autonomy has gained urgency as more developing countries have simultaneously adopted democratic institutions and market reforms.

A dominant perspective in political economy holds that the authoritarian exclusion of distributional coalitions is the key to state autonomy and effective policymaking. A countervailing perspective holds that a developmental strategy that relies entirely on repression and exclusion may be less likely to succeed than one which relies on social "embeddedness" or the development of "synergistic" ties between the state and powerful groups (Evans 1995 and 1996; Heller 1999). This book pushes this debate forward in two distinct ways.

The book's first contribution to this debate is to show that repression and exclusion of organized labor are a suboptimal strategy for achieving policy autonomy. Repression destroys the faith of workers in political parties, thereby eroding the mutually beneficial ties that enable governments to engineer a strategic withdrawal of militancy among affiliated unions. Further, repression makes it impossible for the state to institutionalize industrial conflict. It quite simply becomes difficult to resolve grievances equitably so long as workers are prevented from expressing them or employers are provided with artificial external leverage in negotiations. The resulting denial of justice generates a dangerous backlash among workers that can easily derail efforts to compete over private sector investment. Additionally, labor repression results in rampant exploitation of workers that reduces productivity and industrial output.

The book's second major theoretical contribution is to point to specific mechanisms that enable democracies to manage pressures from highly mobilized interests. Ties to distributional coalitions are indeed of critical importance, but it is competitiveness of the political system combined with the organizational encompassment of political parties that make such ties effective in influencing their behavior. First, competitive elections provide an incentive for political parties to mobilize the working class as an electoral constituency. Whereas dictators may be able to alienate organized labor with little cost, it is difficult for parties to do so in democracies, where the working-class constitutes an important block of votes and unions a key resource for mobilizing those votes. Elections force political parties to find more sophisticated ways of managing organized labor because they are likely to lose votes when they rely on repression as their primary strategy for controlling labor. This explains why, generally speaking, synergistic union-party ties, labor institutions, and robust protections of FACB rights are more prevalent in democracies than authoritarian countries. Second, in the context of free and fair elections, political parties have more reason to be concerned with the externalities associated with militant unionism. In short, democracy helps to neutralize the influence of distributional coalitions by making political actors responsive to the demands of the voters that benefit from increased investment and employment opportunities in the private sector.

This logic has obvious applications in the realm of development policy, including how low- and middle-income countries can improve industrial relations as part of an investment promotion strategy that respects rather than violates worker rights. The importance of policies that foster a stable industrial relations environment cannot be overstated. A successful strategy of economic growth depends on rapid industrialization, which in turn depends on investment in manufacturing. From the perspective of Indian development policy, one might argue that the key problem has been a lack of focus on the growth of the organized manufacturing sector. Instead of making the infrastructural investments and policy adjustments conducive to the development of organized manufacturing, the Indian government has alternatively focused on fostering growth in the informal and small-scale sectors, or on growth in the service sector and particularly the high-wage, high-skill information technology (IT) sector. Francine Frankel aptly refers to this latter aspect of the Indian development strategy as an attempt to "leapfrog the industrial revolution" (Frankel 2005).

Ultimately, developmental strategies that ignore the health of the organized manufacturing sector are bound to fail. Jobs that provide low-skill workers with good pay and benefits cannot be found in the informal economy and the spillover benefits of IT are unlikely to be enough to benefit the vast majority of South Asians. In India, the output of the IT sector represents just 3 percent of GDP and the vast majority of IT employees are relatively well-off university graduates. Comparing the Indian economy with China's, Jean Drèze and Amartya Sen aptly state the argument this way:

> Even if India were to take over the bulk of the world's computer software industry, this would still leave its poor, illiterate masses largely untouched. It may be much less glamorous to make simple pocket knives and reliable alarm clocks than to design state-of-the-art computer programmes, but the former gives the Chinese poor

> a source of income that the latter does not provide—at least not directly—to the Indian poor. (1995, 39)

Thus one the most important tasks for the Indian government is to develop an easily trainable workforce that can produce manufactured products for export.

There are many ways to promote the development of human capital, including investments in education and training. However, it is obvious that basic education is only one aspect of training a productive workforce. As the findings of this study suggest, worker productivity depends in large measure on the industrial relations climate at individual companies. Politically affiliated unions play a key role in assisting management in fostering an industrial relations climate and in negotiating productivity-linked wage agreements, while labor laws are crucial for decreasing employer reliance on sweated labor and encouraging investments in new technology. It is crucial for policymakers to recognize the role these factors play in providing the productivity-enhancing industrial relations environment so critical to the success of industry.

If You Build It They Will Come Back: Industrial Relations and Private Sector Investment

This book has provided systematic evidence of how synergistic union-party ties and labor legislation can promote investment and growth. A tougher question is whether improvements in the way states manage industrial relations can attract capital back to a given region once it has fled. Is the reputational damage of militant unionism permanent, or can states recover their image by mobilizing restraint and intervening more effectively in industrial disputes? If policymakers transform a region's industrial relations environment, is a new influx of capital likely to follow?

The importance of this question is illustrated by the plights of Kerala and West Bengal, which are generally thought to have suffered a loss of investment due to labor militancy in the 1970s and early 1980s. Prior to the onset of India's economic reforms, Kerala and West Bengal were home to two of the most militant union movements in the world.

Following the reforms, both governments embarked on a campaign to radically transform their industrial relations culture and to attract private manufacturing investment to their states. Although the strategies of the two state governments were identical, they have had very different postreform experiences in terms of attracting new investment, with Kerala faring better than West Bengal.

In the postreform period, the rate of growth in fixed capital investment increased in Kerala from an average annual rate of 7.7 percent to 8.5 percent.[1] By this measure, Kerala went from being the eighth most popular investment destination in the prereform period to the fifth most popular destination in the postreform period. In West Bengal, by contrast, the average annual growth rate in fixed capital investment declined from 8.4 to 4.1, and West Bengal went from having the sixth highest growth rate in fixed investment in the prereform period to the second lowest in the postreform period.

Why did Kerala experience such a quick and dramatic turnaround with respect to investment flows in the postreform period whereas West Bengal did not? One potential argument is that West Bengal has enacted more stringent employment protection legislation (EPL) than other states. West Bengal has implemented twelve EPL amendments to the Industrial Disputes Act, which are more EPL provisions than were passed in all other states combined. Some of these provisions are strict to the point of being absurd. For example, an amendment to section 2A of the act stipulates that "refusal of employment" is grounds for an industrial dispute. An amendment to section 25Q increases the maximum jail term for laying off workers without government permission from one month to three months. Kerala, by contrast, has passed no EPL provisions since Independence.

But as was noted in chapter 5, state governments have not rigorously enforced EPL provisions in recent years. Thus some other explanation for why Kerala has fared better must be sought. A plausible explanation is that Kerala has done a better job of managing industrial conflict. While Kerala and West Bengal had similar levels of industrial conflict in the prereform period, the total volume of industrial conflict has gone down in Kerala while it has risen in West Bengal (figure 7.1).

Additionally, industrial relations have been somewhat more institutionalized in Kerala than in West Bengal (see table 4.4). In Kerala, only

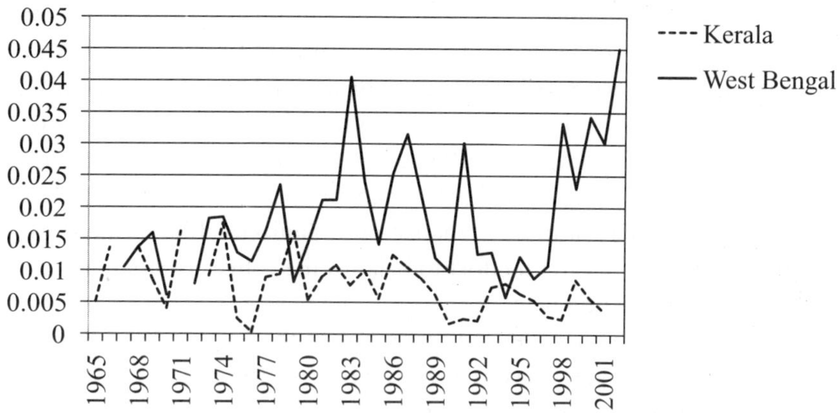

Figure 7.1: Dispute volume in Kerala and West Bengal
Notes: Dispute "volume" is the number of workdays lost to industrial disputes per 1,000 workers. Data on industrial disputes are from the Indian Labor Yearbook. Data on the number of workers in industry are taken from the Annual Survey of Industries.

3 percent of companies experienced any form of violent or extreme protest and no companies reported an assault on management. In West Bengal, by contrast, 8 percent of companies had experienced violent or extreme protest. Other forms of nonroutine protest, such as *gheraos* and sit-ins, were also more common in West Bengal than in Kerala.

Finally, in West Bengal, general strikes, or *bandhs,* are more typical than in Kerala or any other state for that matter. The consensus of employers with whom I spoke was that production is affected by *bandhs* approximately six times per year. While general strikes are short (typically half a day or less) they cause highly visible interruptions of production that do not occur elsewhere. In spite of the best efforts of the CPM to attract investment to the state, frequent general strikes send a very negative signal to potential investors, and particularly those who export a substantial percentage of their output.

The fact that West Bengal has not done as well as Kerala in mobilizing worker restraint is at least partially explained by the theory developed throughout this book. As measured by vote shares, the CPM is a more encompassing party in West Bengal than in Kerala, but this encompassment is not complimented by a highly competitive political system. While it is true that winning margins in elections are narrow, the CPM has held power continuously since 1977, and the lack of turnover has decreased the responsiveness of the party. In other words, political parties in West Bengal are more encompassing but less constrained by voter preferences than in Kerala. In Kerala the party system has historically been more of a multiparty democracy, with CPM-led, left-front coalitions competing for power against Congress-led centrist coalitions. This competition has not only entailed a continued reliance on organized labor for political support, but a more careful effort to balance the concerns of labor with those of other constituencies.

In addition, the unchallenged hegemony of the CPM in West Bengal has meant that the party has frequently run roughshod over workers in a way the government in Kerala has not. A good example of the party's indifference to the concerns of affiliated unions is the party's unbridled support for the development of export processing zones (EPZs) to attract new investment to the state. As was discussed in chapter 6, EPZs are typically designed to be union-free zones in which employers can skirt protective labor laws. CPM support of EPZs has naturally resulted in dissent among local CITU leaders and members, thus presenting challenges to the CPMs effort to mobilize restraint in existing factories. Arguably, the resulting industrial unrest has undermined the CPM's efforts to attract investment to West Bengal.

Do Union Partisan Ties Entail the Co-optation of Organized Labor?

The previous discussion raises the question of the implications of union partisan ties for the representation of worker interests. Do workers benefit from their ties with parties, or are their interests more frequently overridden by those of the party? Throughout this book I have tried to emphasize that the strength and degree of reciprocity in union-party ties is a direct function of the depth of democracy. The less democratic a government becomes the more likely it is to simply veto the interests of important groups in favor of its development objectives. However, as a general matter many have viewed the relationship between parties and unions in India in a negative light, and it is those objections that I intend to address here.

Frequently social scientists have treated organized labor in India as a relatively unimportant social and political actor. This treatment is largely the result of some faulty historical analysis that portrays organized labor as highly fragmented and therefore weak. Chronic failures of collective action, it is said, prevent workers from successfully pursuing their collective interests in both the industrial relations and political arenas. Moreover, this weakness is thought to be progressive, meaning that the working class has become increasingly factionalized and ineffective over time.

The supposed source of this lack of organizational strength is the political incorporation of labor. It is argued that strong ties to political parties generate political infighting in what would be an otherwise united labor movement, and that the progressive fragmentation of the party system in turn results in greater fragmentation of the labor movement (e.g., Rudolph and Rudolph 1987). Additionally, strong ties between parties and unions result in the political domination and exclusion of working-class interests (e.g. Crouch 1966; Raman 1967). According to this view, the relationship between parties and unions is a zero-sum game in which *either* party interests *or* working-class interests find representation in the collective bargaining and political arenas. It is assumed that parties dominate unions and that as a result working-class interests get marginalized at the collective bargaining table through the introduction of extraneous political issues or, still worse, the complete programming of branch-level leaders and members. For this reason, some observers have viewed the union-party tie as being more pernicious than synergistic. In one of the more colorful statements of this view, Raman writes that

> In the struggle for the control of labor, the outside leaders fitted with political boots have trampled the very bed of grass that they purportedly set out to develop into a Garden of Eden, filled with many a luscious fruit traditionally forbidden for labor to eat. (Raman 1967, 166)

A related concern is that the political domination of the union movement increases the salience of the state's industrial relations machinery at the expense of bipartite collective bargaining (Ramaswamy 1983, 25). This is arguably a negative outcome because workers can more freely present their demands and utilize the strike weapon in direct negotiations with management.

Although consistent and logical, these arguments have largely been debunked in previous analysis (Teitelbaum 2008). The argument regarding union multiplicity derives from poor union statistics. The observed increase in the number of registered unions since Independence is due, quite simply, to poor record keeping. Unions frequently remain listed in the government registry even after they fail to submit returns while the number of unions actually submitting returns has been fairly constant. The notion that India's labor movement faces severe collective action difficulties due to enervating political divisions thus turns out to be a fiction perpetuated by a misinterpretation of government data. The phenomenon of union fragmentation that has been witnessed by scholars is not due to increasing union competition but rather the accumulation of nonfunctioning unions in the government registry. As the original survey data presented in table 4.2 suggest, the vast majority of workers belong to a relatively limited number of federations.

The fear of undue political interference in industrial relations is also largely unfounded. In my survey, I asked a series of questions designed to get at the extent to which political intervention in the union movement may have led to the co-optation of worker interests. First, a comparison of workers organized by MPUs and NIUs in the sample for this study reveals no statistically significant difference in the level of wages paid to each group. My survey data also suggest a continued vibrancy of collective bargaining, as opposed to the heavy reliance on compulsory adjudication and arbitration that many observers have assumed prevails in Indian industrial relations.

The Industrial Disputes Act of 1947 provides the state with a broad range of powers to settle industrial disputes. These include (a) voluntary mechanisms, such as voluntary nonbinding conciliation proceedings or voluntary binding arbitration proceedings and (b) compulsory arbitration and adjudication. Voluntary conciliation proceedings are typically presided over by a labor commissioner, but are sometimes conducted by a specially appointed board. Labor courts and industrial tribunals conduct arbitration and adjudication proceedings. While they have overlapping jurisdiction on some issues, labor courts are primarily responsible for adjudicating disputes pertaining to individual workers whereas industrial tribunals adjudicate collective disputes between the management and a union.

I asked managers whether they were covered by a collective agreement and whether they had any disputes referred for compulsory adjudication or arbitration (collective or individual) in the last year. Sixty-four percent of companies reported that they were currently bound by a collective bargaining agreement but only 15 percent reported having a dispute referred for compulsory adjudication or arbitration in the previous year.

I also asked managers whether they had any collective disputes referred to an industrial tribunal (which have jurisdiction over collective disputes) for compulsory adjudication since 1991. Only 16 percent reported that one or more collective disputes had been referred to an industrial tribunal for compulsory adjudication *since 1991*, suggesting that the bulk of disputes being referred for compulsory adjudication in the previous year were disputes between companies and individual workers and not collective disputes.

In addition to questions about compulsory adjudication and arbitration, I asked managers questions about how frequently they rely on voluntary state-sponsored mechanisms to resolve industrial disputes. Only 8 percent of companies reported a dispute that had been referred for voluntary arbitration proceedings since 1991. And while 31 percent of companies reported bringing one or more industrial disputes before the labor commissioner for conciliation proceedings since 1991, only 38 percent of these disputes had been successfully resolved in conciliation. The remaining disputes were shunted back into the collective bargaining arena for further bipartite negotiation. These results suggest that like compulsory adjudication and arbitration, voluntary state-sponsored tripartite mechanisms of dispute resolution constitute dispute resolution mechanisms that are used to compliment rather than replace collective bargaining.

The notion that political ties result in the co-optation of organized labor is also refuted by the continued ability of workers to press their demands in collective bargaining and in politics. As was noted in chapter 2, the capacity of organized labor to call out strikes was undermined by increased competition in product and labor markets following a long rise in worker militancy that lasted through the mid-1980s. If forcible co-optation of unions was causing increasing quiescence, then the total volume of industrial disputes would have remained constant after Independence when the right wing of the INC endeavored to subdue organized labor.

Moreover, if either party gained "undue influence" in the other's affairs, we would have to conclude that organized labor got the upper hand. Labor's political strength is clearly evidenced by its large body of protective labor legislation. It is hard to imagine that such a large body of labor legislation could have been passed through national and state legislatures, or have been consistently enforced, if labor were fragmented and politically weak. It is also notable that twenty years following its watershed economic reforms, India has not substantially "reformed" its labor law, despite consistent calls for reform by employers and international development organizations to do so. Additionally, union resistance has slowed the pace of broader economic reforms. Most notably, the privatization of central government enterprises has been very slow. Within the first nine years of the privatization process, Candland notes that India had "not completed the privatization of any of its 248 enterprises," whereas in Pakistan, where unions have less political influence, privatization "has been anything but cautious" (Candland 2001, 78). For all of these reasons, it is difficult to characterize labor in India as "co-opted" or "politically weak."

Implications for Future Reforms

In chapter 5 of this book, I examined the impact of labor laws on economic performance in the Indian states. I began with a discussion of previous studies, which focus primarily on the effects of the Industrial Disputes Act (IDA) on the performance of the industrial sector. These studies have yielded a consensus among economists and policymakers that India's protective labor legislation adversely affects economic performance; but they are based on a flawed conceptualization of the legislation. I suggested a new method of conceptualizing the IDA and demonstrate how legislation facilitating specific types of state intervention in industrial relations is correlated with better economic performance. Namely, legislation that facilitates third-party mediation in industrial disputes through the expansion of worker access to the state's industrial relations machinery has positive effects on economic outcomes.

However, not all types of intervention benefit the economy. I analyzed the effects of a previously overlooked body of labor law pertaining to the government's ability to inhibit strikes in an industry by declaring it a "public utility." I show that the policy of discouraging strike protest in these industries actually undermines economic performance by eroding worker rights.

These findings have significant implications for India's economic reforms. There has been increasing discussion of reforming Indian labor laws, and the IDA has been at the center of this discussion. Mostly, the business community and policy elites have focused on the deleterious effects of employment protection provisions that make it difficult for employers to fire workers or close their factories. But as I have pointed out, the enforcement of such legislation has been increasingly lax, and this area of law has been of relatively little importance at the state level. Reform of employment protection provisions, therefore, will likely have little impact on economic performance.

My findings suggest that policymakers would do better to focus their efforts on industrial disputes and public utilities provisions of the IDA. Policymakers could learn from the examples of states in the South, like Andhra Pradesh, Karnataka, and Tamil Nadu that have promoted industrial growth by expanding the jurisdiction of and access to conciliation proceedings, labor courts, labor tribunals, and arbitration. It would be beneficial if some of these provisions were adopted at the national level, and if the government placed more emphasis on third-party mediation as a strategy for resolving industrial disputes. It is also clear from my analysis that restrictive public utilities provisions, and particularly those enacted by the national government, have had extremely adverse effects on economic performance. These should be lifted and workers should be able to form unions and exercise their right strike in all but the most essential public services.

Conclusion

This book began with some thoughts about how governments have struggled with the question of how to achieve labor peace since the birth of industry. It is an issue that will not disappear so long as factory production relies on human labor. The history of state-labor relations in

South Asia provides rich insights into which state strategies for managing industrial unrest work and which do not. While there are still improvements to be made, India has effectively balanced the imperatives of economic reform with the needs of industrial workers in the postreform period. It has done so because electoral pressures make it imperative to mobilize the support of the working class but also make it imperative to restrain worker protest in favor of broader developmental objectives. Political parties have cultivated ties to organized labor without their political agendas being hijacked by unions, and without undermining the effectiveness of unions. This strategy, combined with the development of sophisticated industrial relations machinery and robust protections for worker rights, has been quite successful in reducing and institutionalizing industrial conflict. It has also reduced exploitation of workers in industry while achieving the policymaker's goal of attracting investment and promoting economic growth. There are obvious lessons to be taken from this experience by academics, employers, trade unions, and governments within South Asia and abroad.

APPENDIX A

Survey Methods and Response Rates

Telephone Survey

Kerala

The sample for the Kerala telephone survey was drawn from two sources—the Confederation of Indian Industries (CII) member directory and the Kerala State Industrial Development Corporation (KSIDC) Manufacturer's Directory.

There were 515 companies listed in the KSIDC directory and 83 companies listed in the CII directory. I drew a random sample of 50 percent of the 515 firms without replacement from the KSIDC directory and took all 83 companies from the CII directory for a total sample of 292 companies.

These 292 companies yielded 102 completed surveys.

The breakdown of the 292 selected firms for the purposes of calculating the minimum response rate is as follows:

(A) Completed	102
(B) Noninterviews (explicit "no's")	6
(C) Unknown Eligibility	137
No Answer/Wrong Number	102
No Contact/Avoidance	29
Language/Communication Problems	8
(D) Ineligible	44

Not in Private Sector	9
No Manufacturing/Manufacturing in Another Region	24
Not in Organized Sector	7
Closed	1
Listed Twice Under Different Names	3

Based on the standards of the American Association for Public Opinion Research (AAPOR), the minimum response rate should be calculated as (A)/((A)+(B) +(C)), or the number of completed interviews divided by the number of completed interviews plus the number of noninterviews plus the number of cases of unknown eligibility.

Using the AAPOR standard, the response rate of the survey is 41.63 percent.

Maharashtra

The sample for the Maharashtra telephone survey was drawn from the Bombay Chamber of Commerce (BCC) member directory.

There were 777 companies listed as manufacturers in the BCC directory. I randomly selected a sample of 20 percent without replacement from this list of 777 manufacturers for an initial list of 156 firms. When this list was exhausted, I selected 25 percent of the remaining 621 companies without replacement for an additional sample of 156 firms. This yielded a total sample of 312 companies from the initial list of 777.

These 312 companies yielded 102 completed surveys.

The breakdown of the 312 selected firms for the purposes of calculating the minimum response rate is as follows:

(A) Completed	102
(B) Noninterviews (explicit "no's")	7
(C) Unknown Eligibility	113
No Answer/Wrong Number	52
No Contact/Avoidance	58
Language/Communication Problems	3
(D) Ineligible	90
Not in Private Sector	0

No Manufacturing/Manufacturing in Another Region	78
Not in Organized Sector	2
Closed	3
Listed Twice Under Different Names	7

Based on the standards of the American Association for Public Opinion Research (AAPOR), the minimum response rate should be calculated as (A)/((A)+(B)+(C)), or the number of completed interviews divided by the number of completed interviews plus the number of noninterviews plus the number of cases of unknown eligibility.

Using the AAPOR standard, the response rate of the survey is 45.95 percent.

Sri Lanka

The sample for the telephone survey of manufacturing firms for Sri Lanka was drawn from the Ceylon Chamber of Commerce (CCC) member directory CD ROM.

First, I selected all manufacturing firms from the directory using the CD ROM's automatic sorting function. This yielded 243 manufacturing firms.

From the 243 manufacturing firms, I selected an initial sample of 124 firms randomly without replacement. When this list was exhausted, I selected an additional 74 firms from the remaining unselected 170 manufacturing firms in the CCC directory, randomly and without replacement. Thus a total of 198 firms were selected for participation from 243 manufacturing firms listed in the directory.

Of these 198, 120 interviews were completed and 29 were lost due to a computer failure, yielding a total of 91 completed surveys.

The breakdown of the 198 selected firms for the purposes of calculating the minimum response rate is as follows:

(A) Completed	120
(B) Noninterviews (explicit "no's")	6
(C) Unknown Eligibility	31
No Answer/Wrong Number	17

No Contact/Avoidance	12
Language/Communication Problems	2
(D) Ineligible	41
Not in Private Sector	4
No Manufacturing/Manufacturing in Another Region	23
Not in Organized Sector	0
Closed	2
Listed Twice Under Different Names	12

Based on the standards of the American Association for Public Opinion Research (AAPOR), the minimum response rate should be calculated as (A)/((A)+(B) + (C)), or the number of completed interviews divided by the number of completed interviews plus the number of noninterviews plus the number of cases of unknown eligibility.

Using the AAPOR standard, the response rate of the survey is 76.43 percent.

West Bengal

The sample for the West Bengal telephone survey was drawn from two sources—The Bengal Chamber of Commerce and Industry (BCCI) member directory and the Chamber of Commerce and Industry (CII) member directory.

The BCCI member directory listed 49 manufacturers and the CII member directory listed 201 manufacturers. The two directories listed twenty-four manufacturers in common, leaving 226 manufacturing firms listed by the two directories. These 226 companies were sampled at 100 percent, meaning I contacted all 226 companies to request participation in the survey.

These 226 firms yielded 92 completed surveys.

The breakdown of the 226 selected firms for the purposes of calculating the minimum response rate is as follows:

(A) Completed	92
(B) Noninterviews (explicit "no's")	15
(C) Unknown Eligibility	67
No Answer/Wrong Number	41

No Contact/Avoidance	20
Language/Communication Problems	6
(D) Ineligible	52
Not in Private Sector	7
No Manufacturing/Manufacturing in Another Region	35
Not in Organized Sector	4
Closed	2
Listed Twice Under Different Names	4

Based on the standards of the American Association for Public Opinion Research (AAPOR), the minimum response rate should be calculated as (A)/((A)+(B) + (C)), or the number of completed interviews divided by the number of completed interviews plus the number of noninterviews plus the number of cases of unknown eligibility.

Using the AAPOR standard, the response rate of the survey is 52.87 percent.

In-Depth Employer Survey

Kerala

I selected 55 of the 102 companies participating in the telephone survey to contact for in-depth interviews. The firms were selected with a stratified random sample, the strata being whether the workers had engaged in any form of protest. I selected 100 percent of the 35 firms experiencing protest and randomly selected 30 percent of the 67 firms not experiencing protest.

These 55 companies yielded 37 completed interviews. One additional company was chosen for an interview, but was not randomly selected, for a total of 38 completed interviews.

The breakdown of these interviews for the purposes of calculating response rates is as follows:

(A) Completed	37
(B) Noninterviews (explicit "no's")	4
(C) No Contact/Avoidance	14

Based on the standards of the American Association for Public Opinion Research (AAPOR), the minimum response rate should be calculated as (A)/((A)+(B) +(C)), or the number of completed interviews divided by the number of completed interviews plus the number of noninterviews plus the number of cases of unknown eligibility.

Using the AAPOR standard, the minimum response rate to the surveys selected from respondents to the telephone survey was 67.27 percent.

Maharashtra

I selected 89 of the 102 companies participating in the telephone survey to contact for in-depth interviews. Because of the lower response rate in Maharashtra relative to other regional cases, these companies were selected in four stages of sampling as each list of companies became exhausted.

The first set of companies were selected in four stages with a stratified random sample, the strata being whether the workers had engaged in any form of protest. I selected 100 percent of the 38 firms experiencing some form of protest and randomly selected 15 percent of the 65 firms that did not experience protest for a total of 48 firms to contact.

When the first list of companies was exhausted, I selected an additional 30 percent of the 55 remaining firms not experiencing protest for an additional 17 firms to contact.

In the third stage of sampling, I selected 25 percent of the remaining 38 companies for an additional 10 firms to contact.

In a fourth stage of sampling, I selected 50 percent of the remaining 28 companies for an additional 14 firms to contact.

These 89 companies yielded 37 completed interviews.

The breakdown of these interviews for the purposes of calculating response rates is as follows:

(A) Completed	37
(B) Noninterviews (explicit "no's")	6
(C) No Contact/Avoidance	46

Using the AAPOR standard, the minimum response rate to the surveys selected from respondents to the telephone survey was 41.57 percent.

Sri Lanka

I selected 54 of the 91 companies participating in the telephone survey to contact for in-depth interviews. The firms were selected with a stratified random sample, the strata being whether the workers had engaged in any form of protest. I randomly selected 90 percent of the 50 firms experiencing protest (for a total of 46 firms that experienced protest) and 20 percent of the 42 firms that did not experience protest (for a total of 8 firms that did not experience protest) to contact for in-depth interviews.

These 54 companies yielded 39 completed interviews. The breakdown of these interviews for the purposes of calculating response rates is as follows:

(A) Completed	39
(B) Noninterviews (explicit "no's")	1
(C) No Contact/Avoidance	14

Using the AAPOR standard, the minimum response rate to the surveys selected from respondents to the telephone survey was 72.22 percent.

A number of events were of special interest from the perspective of this study, and so I decided to include a small number of companies experiencing extreme or violent protest reported on in the press. Thus an additional twenty-four companies were selected randomly from a list of firms reported to have experienced strike protest in the Sri Lankan press that were not selected for the telephone survey. Unfortunately, most of these companies had closed since the time of the event reported in the press and this process only resulted in five completed interviews. The breakdown of the interviews selected from the list of firms selected from the newspaper is as follows:

(A) Completed	5
(B) Noninterviews (explicit "no's")	0
(C) No Contact/Avoidance	1
(D) Wrong numbers/Closed	17

The minimum response rate for the surveys selected from firms listed in the newspapers was 21.74 percent.

West Bengal

I selected 58 of the 92 companies participating in the telephone survey to contact for in-depth interviews. The firms were selected with a stratified random sample, the strata being whether the workers had engaged in any form of protest. I selected 100 percent of the 44 firms experiencing protest and 30 percent of the 48 firms that did not experience protest (for a total of 14 firms that did not experience protest) to contact for in-depth interviews.

These 58 companies resulted in 40 completed interviews. The breakdown of these interviews for the purposes of calculating response rates is as follows:

(A) Completed	40
(B) Noninterviews (explicit "no's")	7
(C) No Contact/Avoidance	11

Using the AAPOR standard, the minimum response rate to the surveys selected from respondents to the telephone survey was 68.97 percent.

APPENDIX B

Labor Law Coding

I. State intervention index

State/No.	Year	Section	Description & Discussion of Amendment	BB Code	AP Code	IDL	IDLΔ
Andhra Pradesh	1949						+1
1		2	Gives government the right to declare any sector a public utility. Public utilities legislation constitutes a distinct form of government intervention, and is analyzed in a separate framework. See text.	−1	−1	0	
2		10	Provides direct access to tribunals for workers and employers.	−1	−1	+1	
Andhra Pradesh	1968						0
3		2	Declares hospitals and dispensaries public utilities. Does not apply to manufacturing.	−1	0	0	
Andhra Pradesh	1987						+5
4		2A	Individual workers are given the right to petition labor courts for adjudication. This expands access to the courts.	+1	+1	+1	
5		10B	Allows government to issue temporary binding resolutions, including work orders, prohibition of strikes, and prohibitions of lockouts until such time as an industrial tribunal or labor court makes a ruling.	−1	0	+1	
6		29A	Backs up section 10B with penalties; violations punishable by a prison term of no less than six months and a fine of an unspecified amount. Expands the power of the government to enforce its orders.	−1	−1	+1	
7		11B	A labor court or tribunal is granted the power of a civil court to execute its award or any settlement as a decree of a civil court.	−1	0	+1	
8		33c	In place of the collector, the chief judicial magistrate or the chief metropolitan magistrate (as appropriate) is authorized to recover money for an award as if it were a fine imposed by a magistrate.	+1	+1	+1	

Gujarat	1973						+1
9		2 & 30	Amendments enforce the creation of joint management councils as stipulated under Gujarat Act 21 of 1972. Mandates penalty of Rs 50 if management fails to designate representatives for council and Rs 50 per day for a continuing violation. Expands power of government to intervene in firm-level industrial relations.	+1	+1	+1	
Karnataka	1953						0
10		10A	Gives government the ability to transfer an industrial dispute under consideration in one tribunal to any tribunal constituted by the government for adjudication, and the ability to mandate that a case proceed *de novo*. Increases power of government at expense of courts, so net gain to power of state is zero.	−1	−1	0	
Karnataka	1988						+3
11		10	Individual workers are given the right to petition labor courts for adjudication within 6 months of the dispute. Expands worker access to courts.	+1	+1	+1	
12		10B	See Andhra Pradesh 1987 (5).	−1	−1	+1	
13		11	Expands the conciliation officer's power to enforce attendance at hearings and compel production of documents by delineating penalties for failure to comply of up to 3 months imprisonment, fines of up to Rs 500, or both.	−1	−1	+1	
Kerala	1979						+2
14		10B	See Andhra Pradesh 1987 (5).	−1	−1	+1	
15		29A	See Andhra Pradesh 1987 (6).	−1	−1	+1	

I. State intervention index—Cont.

State/No.	Year	Section	Description & Discussion of Amendment	BB Code	AP Code	IDL	IDL∆
Madhya Pradesh	1982						+2
16		7	Expands the jurisdiction of labor courts beyond the IDA to a new, specially constituted 'Part B' of the Second Schedule of the IDA, which includes 16 areas of central government labor legislation.	−1	−1	+1	
17		11A-D	Gives labor courts the ability to hear criminal cases by giving them the powers under the Code of Criminal Procedure of a judicial magistrate of the first class. Gives industrial tribunals the powers of the High Court to hear appeals in criminal cases. These powers are required for courts to hear cases related to the central government legislation listed in the 1982 amendment to Section 7 (above); thus not a distinct piece of legislation. Coded 0 to avoid double counting.	−1	0	0	
18		34	Stipulates that violations of the central act and of acts covered in Madhya Pradesh's specially constituted Part B of the Second schedule must be tried locally. Enhances authority of local courts by reducing "venue shopping," i.e., the ability of parties in a dispute to seek out the most favorable venue to hear a case.	−1	−1	+1	
Madhya Pradesh	2003						−2
19		7 & 11	Amendments remove provisions that expanded the jurisdiction of labor courts enacted in 1982.			−1	
20		34	Eliminates stipulation that all violations to the IDA and acts under Madhya Pradesh's specially constituted Part B of the Second Schedule of the IDA be tried locally, thus increasing venue shopping.			−1	
Maharashtra	1982						+1

21		10A, 18 & 19	Amendments create "closed-shop" policy, in which only settlements by the one recognized union in each company are binding under the law and only the recognized union can terminate a contract or file complaints under the IDA. Amounts to major intervention in structure of firm-level industrial relations and collective bargaining.			+1	
Rajasthan	1960						+2
22		2	Legislation makes four amendments to Section 2 relating the scope of the act: The first defines union as a trade union of employees registered under the *Indian Trade Unions Act of 1926*. The second appoints a registrar of unions. The third expands the definition of "employer" to include employers of contract workers. The fourth expands the definition of "workers" to include contract workers. The first two provide minor clarifications regarding the role of unions while the second two amendments greatly expand the scope of court jurisdiction, assuming the prevalence of contract labor.	−1	−1	+1	
23		3	Requires that the state government appoint a Registrar of Unions, perhaps to clarify who can represent workers on "works committees." This is ultimately a very minor expansion of judicial or government authority, partly because it is difficult to assume the prevalence of works committees.	−1	−1	0	
24		10B-J	Introduces sections 10B-J (after section 10A), which gives the state the right to refer disputes to an industrial tribunal, even if arbitration is in progress. Unions prohibited from striking and employers prohibited from locking out workers once dispute is referred to tribunal.	−1	−1	+1	
Rajasthan	1970						+4
25		9C	Expands the responsibilities of the registrar of unions to include enforcing closed-shop provisions.	−1	−1	+1	
26		10K	Grants state government authority to enforce work orders and bar strikes and lockouts, which can then be challenged within three months in an industrial tribunal.	−1	−1	+1	

I. State intervention index—Cont.

State/No.	Year	Section	Description & Discussion of Amendment	BB Code	AP Code	IDL	IDLΔ
27		30-30A	Introduces penalties of up to one-year imprisonment or 2,000 rupees in fines for failure to comply with a state government order in reference to an industrial dispute.	−1	−1	+1	
28		33C	Widens the scope of awards for which the worker can obtain judicial help securing money from employers to include awards made by the state government in orders resolving industrial disputes.	+1	+1	+1	
Tamil Nadu	1949						+1
29		2	See Andhra Pradesh 1987 (1).	−1	−1	0	
30		10	Provides direct access to tribunals for workers and employers. Gives greater power to the courts to intervene in industrial disputes.	−1	−1	+1	
Tamil Nadu	1982						+2
31		10A-K	See Andhra Pradesh 1987 (5).	−1	−1	+1	
32		29A	See Andhra Pradesh 1987 (6).	−1	−1	+1	
Tamil Nadu	1988						+2
33		2A	See Andhra Pradesh 1987 (2A).	+1	+1	+1	
34		11	Expands the conciliation officer's power to enforce attendance at hearings and compel production of documents.	−1	−1	+1	
West Bengal	1980						+1
35		2	Expands definition of workers to include sales promotion workers and supervisors making < Rs 1,000 (under the central act, threshold was Rs 500). Not significant because it does not pertain the industrial workforce.	+1	+1	0	

36		12	The report of the conciliation officer is due within 60 days, an increase from 14 days after commencement of conciliation proceedings. Gives conciliation officer more time to decide whether to intervene in a dispute, thereby reducing the likelihood of state intervention.	+1	+1	−1	
37		20	Effectively gives conciliation officer more time to conciliate before proceedings are referred to the labor court or tribunal. Decreases the likelihood of judicial intervention in a dispute, but increases the discretion of the ministry of labor. Net effect for state power is zero.	+1	+1	0	
38		11B	See Andhra Pradesh 1987.	−1	−1	+1	
39		17A	Appropriate government has the right, on grounds of national economy or social justice, to modify or void any award made by an arbitrator, labor court, or tribunal. The amendment increases the power of the government at the expense of the judiciary. Overall effect on state intervention is zero.	+1	+1	0	
40		33C	See Andhra Pradesh 1987 (row 8)	+1	+1	+1	
West Bengal	1986						0
41		15	Requires courts to issue interim relief order within 60 days of hearing from the parties to a dispute. Also requires courts to follow tighter procedural guidelines in keeping with amendment to section 17AA. Increases the power of the government at the expense of the courts. See amendment to Section 17A, 1980 for details.	+1	+1	0	
West Bengal	1989						+1
42		10	Gives individual parties to a dispute the right to petition the conciliation officer to certify pendency of resolution of the dispute. If the conciliation officer does not respond within 7 days, or if following the conciliation officer's certification, another 60 days passes without resolution of the dispute, the dispute shall be referred to the labor court or tribunal. This is an expansion of judicial authority.	+1	+1	+1	

Note: Numbers in parentheses refer to row numbers in left-hand column.

II. Employment protection index

State	Year	Section	Description & Discussion of Amendment	BB Code	AP Code	EPL	EPLΔ
Andhra Pradesh	1987						+4
43		9A	Increases notice period for changes to workers.	+1	+1	+1	
44		25FFF	Prior payment of compensation to workers is a condition for closure of an undertaking.	+1	+1	+1	
45		25H	When a closed firm is reopened, workers who were on the rolls given preference in employment.	+1	+1	+1	
46		25HH	When a worker is reinstated by award of a labor court or tribunal, his wages will be paid from the date specified in that award, regardless of whether s/he has been reinstated by an employer.	+1	+1	+1	
Karnataka	1988						0
47		25K	At the discretion of the appropriate government, rules for retrenchment, layoffs, and closure may be applied to firms with seasonal employment of not less than 100 workers. Under the central act, this clause did not apply to firms of a seasonal character. This provision has very little relevance for manufacturing, because most manufacturing enterprises are not seasonal in character.	+1	+1	0	
Madhya Pradesh	1983						0
48		25O	Undertakings dealing with construction of buildings, bridges, roads, canals, dams, or other construction are no longer exempted from procedures for closing down undertakings. Does not apply to manufacturing.	+1	0	0	

Maharashtra	1981					+1
49		2	Expands conditions when a worker may be laid off to include discontinuation or reduction of the supply of electricity. Under the central act, the valid reasons for layoff include "shortage of coal, power, or raw materials or the accumulation of stocks or breakdown of machinery," so this amendment clarifies that electricity is to be considered a "shortage of power" and therefore a valid reason for layoff. This amendment is integral to a simultaneous amendment to Section 25C (below), so I code it 0.	+1	+1	0
50		25C	If a worker is laid off because of loss of electricity, s/he shall receive 100% of wages s/he would otherwise receive. For any other valid reason for layoff employers are required to pay 50% of wages.	+1	+1	+1
51		25K	At the discretion of the appropriate government, rules for retrenchment, layoffs, and closure may be applied to firms with more than 100 workers. In 1983 the threshold under the central act was 300 workers; but in 1982, the central act was nationally amended to lower the threshold to 100 workers. Since the state-level provision only differed from the national provision for one year, it is unlikely to explain differences in economic performance.	+1	+1	0
Maharashtra	1983					+1
52		25O	Any employer or worker affected by the decision to close down an enterprise is permitted, for 30 days from the date on which permission for closure is granted, to appeal the decision to an Industrial tribunal.	+1	+1	+1

II. Employment protection index—Cont.

State	Year	Section	Description & Discussion of Amendment	BB Code	AP Code	EPL	EPLΔ
Orissa	1983						+1
53		25K	See Maharashtra 1981 (51).	+1	0	0	
54		25O	See Maharashtra 1983 (52).	+1	+1	+1	
Rajasthan	1984						+2
55		25K	See Maharashtra 1981 (51)	+1	0	0	
56		25M	Removes condition that employer must apply to continue layoffs of mine workers beyond 30 days in event of fire, flood, or gas explosion. Under the central act, no government approval was necessary only for first 30 day. Does not apply to manufacturing.	−1	−1	0	
57		25N	Requires that the employer give the government three month's notice before retrenching workers. Stipulates reasons that state governments may reject applications to retrench workers, etc.	+1	+1	+1	
58		25O	See Madhya Pradesh 1983 (48).	+1	+1	0	
59		25P	Under the central act, appropriate government had the authority to order the restarting of an undertaking if it closed before 1976 and failed to meet certain conditions. This amendment allows those orders to be appealed to an industrial tribunal. Likely irrelevant due to eight-year time lag in implementation.			0	
60		25PP	The state government may order the rehiring of workers retrenched in the six months prior to the enactment of the Industrial Disputes Rajasthan Amendment Act of 1984 if it deems that the retrenchment was without adequate reasons. Likely irrelevant due to eight-year lag between enactment and implementation.			0	
61		25Q	Increases penalty for layoff and retrenchment of workers without permission.	+1	+1	+1	

62		25S	The procedures for layoff and retrenchment specified in Chapter V-A of the central act are deemed to be applicable to industrial establishments of a seasonal character. Under the central act, the provisions of Chapter V-A do not apply to establishments of a seasonal character. This provision has very little relevance for manufacturing, because most manufacturing enterprises are not seasonal in character, so we code this "0."	+1	+1	0	
West Bengal	1974						+1
63		2	Amends central act so that if workers are provided work in first half of the shift, they cannot be laid off for the day.	+1	+1	+1	
West Bengal	1980						+9
64		2	Expands definition of retrenchment to include termination of workers on grounds of poor health.	+1	+1	+1	
65		9A	See Andhra Pradesh 1987.	+1	+1	+1	
66		25C	Removes proviso wherein workers and employers and workers may sign an agreement limiting layoff compensation to 45 days.	+1	+1	+1	
67		25E	When a layoff extends for more than seven days, the worker only has to present himself once a week at the plant in order to be entitled to compensation for that week. Under the central act, the worker is required to present himself daily.	+1	+1	+1	
68		25FFF	See Andhra Pradesh 1987 (44).	+1	+1	+1	
69		25H	See Andhra Pradesh 1987 (45).	+1	+1	+1	
70		25HH	See Andhra Pradesh 1987 (46).	+1	+1	+1	
71		25K	The rules of Section 25 on layoffs, retrenchments, and closure are applied to industrial establishments employing more than 50 workers, reduced from 300 workers in the central act. Note that in 1982, the central act was nationally amended to lower the threshold to 100 workers. The 1982 national amendment to the central act took effect in 1984.	+1	+1	+1	
72		25M	The period after which, if the appropriate government has not responded, the employer can commence layoffs (i.e. treat his application as granted) is extended from 2 to 3 months.	+1	+1	+1	

II. Employment protection index—Cont.

State	Year	Section	Description & Discussion of Amendment	BB Code	AP Code	EPL	EPLΔ
West Bengal	1989						+2
73		2A	Refusal of employment is added as grounds for an individual worker to enter into an industrial dispute with an employer.	+1	0	+1	
74		25O	Requires an employer's application to close down an undertaking to contain specifications of how payment of compensation to workers shall be made, as required under the 1980 amendment to Section FFF. Also expands definition of compensation owed to workers to include benefits.	+1	+1	+1	
75		25P	See Rajasthan 1984 (59).			0	

Notes: Since most of my coding of EPL legislation is largely in agreement with BB and EP, I only provided extended discussion when my coding differs. Numbers in parentheses refer to row numbers in left-hand column.

Notes

Chapter 1

1. Cingranelli and Richards code 195 countries for the degree to which core worker rights are protected on a three point ordinal scale—"fully protected," "somewhat protected," and '"severely restricted"; Cingranelli-Richards Human Rights Dataset, downloaded 2006, URL: http://www.humanrightsdata.org.

2. Examples from other regions include the Chinese government's concern regarding the threat industrial unrest may pose to investment and export-oriented growth, and the concern among leaders of bureaucratic authoritarian regimes that labor unrest could upend import substitution industrialization schemes in Latin America. For a discussion of China, see Gallagher (2005). For a discussion of Latin America, see O'Donnell (1978).

3. Bardhan (1998) notes that reforms faced little opposition from public sector workers due to the slow pace of privatization and little opposition from large-scale industry because new avenues of investment counterbalanced the loss of protected markets.

4. For a discussion of the timing and scope of India's reforms, see Jenkins (1999) and Kohli (2006).

5. Herring (2001) attributes the absence of widespread resistance to reforms to their departure from neoliberal orthodoxy. Reductions in subsidies were offset by large increases in public spending in other areas, much of which was supported by generous international development assistance.

6. By the end of the 1990s, the number of jobs in public sector manufacturing had dropped by about 30 percent, from 1.9 million in 1992 to 1.4 million in 2000 (Statistical abstracts of India, various issues).

7. All measures of electoral competition reported in this and subsequent paragraphs are based on data from state election reports published by the Election Commission of India (ECI). Averages are calculated across 15 major Indian states that account for approximately 95% of the population.

8. In the literature on party systems, the primary measure of party fragmentation is the standard Laakso and Taagepera (1979) "effective number of parties" measure, or $1/\sum x_i^2$ where x_i refers to the percentage of votes (or seats) captured by the ith party.

9. For Maharashtra, the average turnout in post-Emergency elections is 62%.

Chapter 2

1. Indian Labour Yearbook, various issues.

2. Interview with union activist, June 2002.

3. "A Raw Deal and Desperate," *Frontline* (*The Hindu*), April 14–27, 2001.

4. Details of the assault can be read in the Order of the Mumbai High Court, *Dr. Dattatraya Narayan Samant and Others vs. State of Maharashtra,* 1982 (1) BomCR 1. Datta Samant was found not guilty of conspiring to assault N. P. Godrej and his family. One union member was found guilty of committing the assault and three others were found guilty of abetting the crime.

5. All available evidence indicates that in the Taloja incident, employers were just as culpable as the union in fomenting industrial violence (Pendse 1980).

6. One prominent example is Arun Gawli (a.k.a. "Daddy"), leader of the Akhil Bharatiya Kamgar Sena. A thorough discussion of independent union leaders and their backgrounds is provided in chapter 3.

7. "Deadly Labor Wars Hinder India's Rise," *Wall Street Journal,* November 24, 2009.

8. "136 Charged With Murder of CEO in Noida," *Indian Express,* September 23, 2008.

9. "India Food Strike, Fatal Riots Hobble Push to Export Auto Parts," *Bloomberg,* November 13, 2009.

10. "Strikes Roil India Auto Sector," *Wall Street Journal,* October 21, 2009.

11. Herring (2001) provides a thorough characterization of the proposed reforms and how strictly Sri Lanka adhered to neoliberal orthodoxy. While privatization moved ahead and organized labor was subdued, the central government continued to spend heavily on social welfare and public infrastructure projects.

12. The general consensus among political scientists has been that economic reform was initially an elite-led process that only later gained popularity among the broader public. Jenkins (1999) has famously argued that the reforms were undertaken by "stealth" without the explicit consent of voters. Varshney (1998) states that the adoption of reforms in the early 1990s was primarily an elite-led process that was little understood by the broader public. Similarly, Byres (1998, 2–6) suggests that in policy circles, the primary advocates for neoliberal reforms were economists and politicians with strong connections to the World Bank and International Monetary Fund.

13. Figures for growth in registered manufacturing in this paragraph are based on figures for GDP (value added) in registered manufacturing reported in the National Accounts Statistics, Ministry of Statistics and Programme Implementation (MOSPI), Government of India.

14. For a detailed discussion of Nehruvian tenure reform policy, see Herring (1983).

15. The discussion of the political mobilization of rural voters around agrarian development policy presented here is largely based on the account provided by Varshney (1998b).

16. The gross terms of trade index (GTT) is superior to indices based on surveys or baskets of goods (barter terms of trade (BTT) indices) because it measures the returns to investment and corrects for productivity increases in both sectors. Additionally, the GTT index is a broader and more consistently accurate indicator of terms of trade than BTT indices. This is because (a) the baskets of goods, commodity weights, and groups surveyed for BTT indices change or become less representative of the economy over time and (b) the quality of goods produced in a basket of goods is not uniform across firms. Nonetheless, in the Indian context, the movements and turning points of the gross and barter terms of trade indices closely mirror one another (Hazell, Misra, and Hojatti 1995).

17. The belief that incentives to small-scale industry would occur solely or even primarily in rural areas was an article of faith based on the Gandhian ideal of rural development. In fact, a slight majority of small-scale sector production occurs in urban areas. According to the Ministry of Small Scale Industry's 2000 sample survey, 53 percent of small-scale sector units operated in areas designated as "urban" and 47 percent in areas designated as "rural." Yet, as I have demonstrated elsewhere (Teitelbaum 2007), the expansion of the productive capacity in the small-scale sector has the effect of driving up competition in product markets regardless of the actual location of the small-scale units.

18. Author's own calculations, based on Annual Survey of Industries data.

19. These figures were downloaded from the ILO Laborsta Database in July 2009.

20. For good discussions of this literature, see Kennan (1986) and Franzosi (1995), chap. 2.

21. The Indian Labour Yearbook lists as separate categories statistics for strikes related to wages, bonus, personnel, and retrenchment. For ease of analysis, these four categories were grouped into two.

Chapter 3

1. Interview with senior manager at a tire factory in Kerala, October 7, 2003.
2. Reported in an interview with management, February 3, 2003.
3. Reported in an interview with management, March 13, 2003.
4. Interview, April 19, 2004.
5. Interview with management, April 8, 2004.
6. Interview with management, October 1, 2003.
7. Interview, July 24, 2003.
8. Interview, June 10, 2003.
9. Interview, August 6, 2003.
10. Amerasinghe remarked that the quality of the EFC-CMU relationship is so good that their last agreement was negotiated "purely by very informal discussions, some of which took place on the telephone" (Amerasinghe 1994, chap. 5).
11. Interview, March 13, 2003.
12. Interview, April 8, 2004.

13. I provide a detailed discussion of these provisions in chapter 6.

14. The measure is = $1/\sum x_i^2$ where x_i refers to the percentage of votes (or seats) captured by the ith party.

15. See, for example, Pencavel (1997). Pencavel argues that developing countries should discourage unions from federating and encourage enterprise unionism, because federations are more aggressive in the industrial relations arena and adversely influence economic policy.

16. See, for example, Cameron (1984), Lange and Garrett (1985), and Calmfors and Driffill (1988).

17. Olson (1982), 52.

18. The figures for union density in industry are taken from Teitelbaum (2008). Figures for unionization rates in the organized sector and among nonagricultural workers are based on figures from 2005 downloaded from Indiastat.com, accessed May 26, 2010.

19. See chapter 7 for a discussion of state-labor dynamics in Sri Lanka.

20. Interview, September 16, 2003.

21. Interview, July 23, 2003.

22. Interview, August 12, 2003.

23. Interview, August 4, 2003.

24. Interview, June 24, 2003.

25. Interview, August 5, 2003.

26. Interview, August 6, 2003.

27. Ibid.

28. Interview, March 30, 2004.

29. Interview, March 31, 2004.

30. Interview, October 10, 2003.

31. Interview, October 20, 2003.

32. Interview, April 15, 2004.

33. Interview, February 29, 2004.

34. Interview, March 23, 2004.

35. Since 2004, more than thirty papers have appeared in peer-reviewed journals (Djankov and Ramahlo 2009).

36. The 1982 amendment took effect in 1984.

37. Several studies followed the Fallon and Lucas approach of estimating the effects of labor legislation at the national level through the 1980s, and arrived at similar conclusions. See, for example, Aggarwala (2002) and Dutta Roy (2002).

38. See section 10 (1) of the act.

Chapter 4

1. Andhra Pradesh, Assam, Bihar, Gujarat, Haryana, Karnataka, Kerala, Madhya Pradesh, Maharashtra, Orissa, Punjab, Rajasthan, Tamil Nadu, Uttar Pradesh, and West Bengal. Together these states are home to approximately 95 percent of India's population and produce a similar percentage of its economic output.

2. In a standard normal distribution, observations exceeding three standard deviations will account for approximately 0.3% of all observations. The extreme observations were in Assam and Kerala, and the results are robust to their inclusion.

3. In the sample, the standard deviation for ENPV is 1.34.

4. In the sample, the standard deviation for ENPS is 1.14.

5. In the sample, the standard deviations for winning margins and voter turnout are 12.88 and 10.72 respectively.

6. In the sample, the standard deviation for the product wage is .29.

7. In the sample the standard deviations of real wages and workers are .37 and .28 respectively.

8. Some surveys were discarded because the firm was not in the organized sector or did not in fact manufacture anything. For more details regarding the selection process and response rates, see appendix A.

9. Companies experiencing protest comprised approximately three-quarters of the sample for the in-depth survey, and companies experiencing no protest comprised approximately one-quarter of the sample. For more details, see appendix B.

10. Of the remaining 119 calls, 52 were ineligible, typically because the firm was not in the private manufacturing sector, and 67 were of unknown eligibility. Of these, 41 were not contactable due to a nonworking number and 6 could not be surveyed due to language barriers or other communications problems. Only 20 potential respondents could not be contacted at all. For more details on response rates, see appendix A.

11. This is not to say, however, that in a future study, surveys and intensive interviews of shop floor union leaders and members would not constitute a valuable tool for obtaining information on industrial protest.

12. Elections Commission of India, *Statistical Report on General Election, 1965 to the Legislative Assembly of Kerala.*

13. Elections Commission of India, *Statistical Report on General Election, 1996 to the Legislative Assembly of Kerala.*

14. The Trinamool Congress is officially known as the All India Trinamool Congress (AITC). It was formed by Mamata Banerjee in 1998 and recently merged with a faction of the Nationalist Congress Party (NCP) to form the Trinamool Congress Party (TCP) in 2004.

15. Yet it is important to note that the Congress Party led the fifteen-member coalition with a little less than 27 percent of the 543 seats in the Lok Sabha, reflecting the oft-noted trend away from a centralized political system and the increasing dominance of regional "cleavage-based" parties. In 2004 the UPA was primarily comprised of regionally based political parties, including the Rahstriya Janata Dal (RJD), Dravida Munnetra Kazhagam (DMK), the Nationalist Congress Party (NCP), the Marumalarchi Dravida Munnetra Kazhagam (MDK), and the Kerala Congress (KC). The alliance depended on "external" support from four left parties: the Communist Party of India, Marxist (CPM), the Communist Party of India (CPI), the Revolutionary Socialist Party (RSP), and the All India Forward Bloc (AIFB).

16. Datta Samant was gunned down on January 17, 1997, by a group of contract killers. It is unclear who was responsible for his murder.

17. Reported in an interview with Ashok Paradkar, secretary of the Indian National Trade Union Congress (INTUC), Maharashtra Branch in July 2003.

18. While the JVP's support has grown in recent years, it did not win a large enough percentage of the seats in parliament for it to qualify as a "major political party" during the period of this study.

19. The heavy presence of the BJP-affiliated BMS is surprising considering Kerala's reputation as a bastion of secularism and the CPM's dominance of Kerala's labor movement.

20. Many companies reported having "workers' councils," which are designed to replace unions. Since management sets up and heavily controls workers councils, these were not counted as unions in the survey.

21. In Maharashtra, the AITUC was counted as a small-party union since representatives from its affiliated party (the CPI) have not been elected to national office or to any State Assembly seat in Maharashtra.

22. I found in my interviews that a modern gherao typically lasts less than one working day, which is why the gherao is categorized as a form of obstruction or occupation, and not a form of violent protest. In the past, *gheraos* could last longer than this.

23. Companies experiencing protest constituted approximately three-quarters of the sample for the in-depth survey, and companies experiencing no protest constituted approximately one-quarter of the sample.

24. I cluster the standard errors by company to deal with unobserved company-level effects on the error term. Clustering standard errors by region is problematic, because as Donald and Lange note, standard asymptotics do not apply when the number of groups is small. Here the number of regions is four. Wooldridge argues that the solution is to use a fixed effects estimator. See Donald and Lange (2007); and Wooldridge (2003).

25. I generated the predictions using the "margins" command in Stata 11. For logit and ordered logit models, the "margins" command returns the average predicted probability (the mean of the marginal effects) based on the results of the regression and uses the delta method to obtain standard errors for these predictions. For a general discussion of this approach, see Bartus (2005).

26. See, for example, Pencavel (1997).

27. For the tables associated with this analysis, see Teitelbaum (2010).

28. See, for example, Alvarez, Garrett, and Lange (1991).

29. Ideally the measure would be based on the actual percentage of workers organized by each union in a given region, but unfortunately union data are self-reported and therefore are a poor tool for assessing the membership strength of any one union. For a discussion, see Teitelbaum (2008).

30. The regional robustness checks, along with predictions and Wald tests, are presented in an online appendix, http://home.gwu.edu/~ejt.

31. See sections 12(2) and 14 of the Maharashtra Recognition of Trade Unions and Prevention of Unfair Labour Practices Act 1971.

32. Another possibility is workers in some sectors are more skilled than others, with the result that more aggressive unions are more likely to appear in sectors dominated by skilled workers. However, the intersectoral structure of unions in South Asia makes this an unlikely scenario. The MGKU, for example, is an independent union that has organized substantial numbers of textile (low-skill) workers, as well as the engineering sector (moderate- to high-skill) workers. Similarly, the CITU and INTUC organize workers in traditional agro-industries like coir and tea, as well as workers in the modern engineering sector and chemical sectors.

Chapter 5

1. As in my analysis, Ahsan and Pagés disaggregate regulation according to type. However, the authors largely retain the original "proworker" versus "proemployer" schema within each category of regulation and consequently their findings therefore do not differ significantly from the original BB study. Ahsan and Pagés also do not address public utilities legislation. I discuss the Ahsan and Pagés coding scheme in greater detail below.

2. A group of amendments to section 7 of the IDA, dealing with minor changes in the terms and qualifications of judges, is excluded from the analysis.

3. See Malik (2004), 1811.

4. More precisely, output and investment figures are presented in lakh (100,000) rupees per 1,000 capita terms.

5. BB also include installed electrical capacity as an infrastructural control. I do not do this for two reasons. The first is that spending on electrical grids is subsumed by the development spending measure, which makes the installed electrical capacity measure redundant. Second, there is a lot of missing data in the installed electrical capacity series. This results in a lot of dropped state-years from the regressions, a trade-off that does not seem worth it, considering the high quality of the development spending measure.

6. For a more in-depth discussion of economic reforms and their effects on industrial relations, see chapter 2.

7. It would be nice to go beyond 1997 but the methods ASI uses to collect data change in 1998 and unfortunately the new data are not comparable to the earlier period. Also, I dropped 1958 and 1959 because the data were spotty and of poor quality. The state-level analysis also excludes the state of Jammu and Kashmir because it is missing data and because the conflict in the state entailed that the economy has not been functioning normally for many years.

8. Like BB I exclude sectors with fewer than 10 observations.

9. There are several jumps in the state-level ASI data from the 1960s of greater than 50 percent without a corresponding decline that were not removed from the dataset. These jumps are likely the result of the implementation of a new methodology, as opposed to an error in data entry.

10. Since the dependent variable is log transformed and the independent variable is not, we can interpret the coefficient in percentage terms by multiplying the coefficient by 100.

11. I thank Leila Agha for suggesting this approach.

Chapter 6

1. This account of the 1980 strike is based on newspaper articles appearing in the *Daily News,* the *Island,* and the *Sun* in July 1980 as well as multiple interviews I had with union leaders, employers, and government officials in Sri Lanka during the 1997–98 academic year and in 2003.

2. Interview, March 2003.

3. There were also a number of incidents of union harassment that preceded the 1980 General Strike. For example, in two protests leading up the 1980 strike,

workers were attacked with bats, knives, and bicycle chains. An SLFP politician named Alawi Maulana and a CFTU member named Somapala suffered serious stab wounds. Somapala died from his wounds.

4. In interviews conducted in 2003, the leaders of the CFTU, affiliated with the Communist Party, and the Ceylon Federation of Labor (CFL), affiliated with the Lanka Sama Samaja Party, each said that they lost more than 1,000 workers in the private sector because of dismissals following the 1980 strike. Mr. Siriwardena, the leader of the CFL, said that virtually all of those lost were branch-level committee members.

5. This legislation was withdrawn following threats of mass protest from trade union leaders and opposition leaders.

6. The BOI began as the Greater Colombo Economic Commission (GCEC) and was established by law No. 4 of 1978 (later known as the "BOI law"). Section 16a of the BOI law provides it with sweeping powers to "do all such acts or take such steps as may be necessary or conducive to the attainment of the objects [sic] of the Commission" (i.e., the GCEC). Section 16f somewhat redundantly establishes the power of the GCEC in astoundingly broad terms: "The Commission shall have the power…generally to do all such acts or things as are incidental to or consequential upon the exercise, performance and discharge of its powers, duties and functions under this law." A great deal of this "incidental" power was used to quell trade union activities.

7. The right to form a trade union is guaranteed as a basic right in chapter 3, section 18(2) of the 1978 Sri Lankan Constitution, and further guarantees regarding trade union activities are provided by the Trade Unions Ordinances No. 14 of 1935 and No. 3 of 1946, the Trade Union Acts No. 15 of 1948, No. 18 of 1958, and No. 24 of 1970, and the Industrial Disputes Act of 1950.

8. Reported in a letter to the Sri Lanka Government from the International Confederation of Trade Unions, the European Trade Union Confederation, and the World Confederation of Labor, dated June 18, 2002. The letter was in response to Sri Lanka's application for special trade privileges under the EU's Generalised System of Preferences.

9. It should be noted that the unions were not always in perfect compliance with these agreements. For example, during the 1974–75 fiscal year there were 55 strikes in violation of the agreements, and from 1971 to 1977 the total number of violations recorded by the EFC totalled 199 (Amerasinghe 1994, 111). At the same time, most of these strikes were "short in duration and arising out of trivial issues" (Amerasinghe 1994, 111).

10. According to ILO data, there were 180,000 paid employees in Sri Lanka's manufacturing sector in 1980 (http://laborsta.ilo.org).

11. The argument that UNP repression led to a breakdown in collective bargaining is further supported by the exceptionalism of the Ceylon Mercantile Union (CMU), which did not participate in the 1980 strike and as a result, was never a target of state repression during the 1980s and early 1990s.

12. Even prior to the 1980 General Strike, union switching had long been a feature of industrial relations in Sri Lanka. Kearney (1971, 88), noted that "the members' weak discipline and the uncertain commitment to the union, combined with

intense rivalry among unions, lead to frequent desertions and shifts to rival unions." Yet the nature of union switching following the 1980 General Strike was distinct from union switching prior to the strike. First, a good deal of the union switching that occurred in the 1960s and 1970s occurred in the public sector, where workers have direct incentives to switch unions based on which party is in power. In contrast, most of the union switching that occurred in the post–General Strike period was in the private sector, where union switching has traditionally been less common. Second, the direction of the shift was different. In the 1960s and 1970s, workers were shifting from one traditional left union to another, all of which were equally committed to collective bargaining and institutionalized forms of grievance resolution. In the 1980s and 1990s, workers were switching to more radical unions that actively encouraged the deinstitutionalization of industrial relations through the use of violent and extreme protest tactics. Finally, as I demonstrate below, there was a difference in the degree of the shift. Traditional left unions sustained a loss of members that was unprecedented in earlier periods.

13. The CFTU is affiliated with the Communist Party, the CFL to the Lanka Sama Samaja Party (LSSP), and the SLNSS to the Sri Lanka Freedom Party (SLFP).

14. However, it is notable that in manufacturing companies where traditional left unions were strong, the "action committees did not gain a foothold" (Amerasinghe 1994, 82).

15. Details pertaining to disputes at this company are taken from an interview with management, March 10, 2003.

16. Details regarding disputes at this company were provided during an interview with management and trade union leaders at the factory, February 28, 2003.

17. Dispute volume is the product of three dimensions of industrial disputes: size (number of workers per dispute); duration (number of workerdays lost per worker involved in a dispute); and frequency (number of disputes per 1,000 workers). See Hibbs (1987, 19–22) for a more detailed discussion of the measurement of industrial conflict.

18. It is, therefore, no wonder Amerasinghe described the new industrial relations climate as imbued with a "water-tower culture" (1994, 82).

19. *Gherao* means "encirclement" in Hindi.

20. For a more detailed discussion of this measure and the data used to construct it, see chapter 4.

21. See chapter 4. The term MPU was operationalized to include unions affiliated with parties that had been leading members of a coalition after 1991.

22. Data on annual inflation and growth rates are from *Economic and Social Statistics of Sri Lanka, 2002,* published by the Central Bank of Sri Lanka.

23. The violence model includes 220 fewer observations than the other two models. This is because the fixed year effects predict failure perfectly for two years in which the UNP was in power (1991 and 1993) and one year in the mid-1990s (1996).

24. *Financial Times,* January 3, 1995.

25. "Investors Want Action on Lankan Labor Unrest," *Reuters,* February 14, 1995.

26. "Sri Lanka Acts to Prevent Strikes in Export Zones," *Journal of Commerce,* September 19, 1994.

27. These original data are from the Lake House Press archives in Colombo, Sri Lanka. The archives maintain files of newspaper clippings by subject area, including industrial disputes.

28. Reported in the *Daily News* on January 13, 1996; June 12, 1996; and June 18, 1996, and the *Sunday Times,* January 21, 1996.

29. Reported in the *Island* on November 23, 1995.

30. Reported in the *Island* on June 4, 1995.

31. The Regency Garments closure was reported in the *Island* on February 27, 1995; the Youngi and Ones closure in the *Observer* on February 3, 1995; and the Korea Ceylon closure in the *Daily News* on June 20, 1995.

Chapter 7

1. Figures on fixed capital investment are taken from the Annual Survey of Industries, Central Statistical Office (Industrial Statistics Wing), Department of Statistics, Ministry of Programme Implementation, Government of India.

Works Cited

Books, Journals, and Published Working Papers

Agarwala, R. 2008. "From Work to Welfare: A New Class Movement in India." In Rina Agarwala and Ronald Herring, eds., *Whatever Happened to Class? Reflections from South Asia.* New York: Routledge.

Aggarwala, S. C. 2002. "Labour Demand Function for the Indian Organized Industry: An Instrument Variable Approach." *Indian Journal of Labour Economics* 37(2): 209–220.

Aghion, P., Y. Algan, P. Cahuc, and A. Shleifer. 2008. "Regulation and Distrust." Cambridge: Department of Economics, Harvard University, working paper.

Ahluwalia, I. J. 1998. "Contribution of Planning to Indian Industrialization." In T. J. Byres, ed., *The State, Development Planning, and Liberalization in India.* New Delhi: Oxford University Press.

Ahsan, A., and C. Pagés. 2009. "Are All Labour Regulations Equal? Evidence from Indian Manufacturing." *Journal of Comparative Economics* 37: 62–75.

Aidt, T., and Z. Tzannatos. 2002. *Unions and Collective Bargaining: Economic Effects in a Global Environment.* Washington, DC: World Bank.

Alvarez, M., G. Garrett, and P. Lange. 1991. "Government Partisanship, Labor Organization, and Macroeconomic Performance." *American Political Science Review* 85(2): 539–556.

Amerasinghe, F. 1994. *Employer's Federation of Ceylon: 1929–1994.* Colombo, Sri Lanka: Aitken Spence.

——. 1997. *The Changing Face of Trade Union Unionism in Sri Lanka.* Colombo, Sri Lanka: Institute of Policy Studies.

Amin, M. 2009. "Labour Regulation and Employment in India's Retail Stores." *Journal of Comparative Economics* 37: 47–61.

Anant, T. C. A., and K. Sundaram. 1998. "Wage Policy in India: A Review." *Indian Journal of Labour Economics* 41(4): 815–834.

Ashenfelter, O., and G. E. Johnson. 1969. "Bargaining Theory, Trade Unions, and Industrial Strike Activity." *American Economic Review* 59(1): 35–49.

Banerji, A., and H. Ghanem. 1995. "Political Regimes, Trade, and Labor Policies in Developing Countries." Working Paper No. 1521. Washington, DC: World Bank.

Bardhan, P. 1998. *The Political Economy of Development in India.* Delhi: Oxford University Press.

Bartus, T. 2005. "Estimation of Marginal Effects Using Margeff." *Stata Journal* 5 (May): 309–329.

Basu, S. 2004. *Does Class Matter? Colonial Capital and Workers' Resistance in Bengal, 1890–1937.* Oxford: Oxford University Press.

Battacharjee, D. 1987. "Union-type Effects on Bargaining Outcomes in Indian Manufacturing." *British Journal of Industrial Relations* 25(2): 247–263.

Besley, T., and R. Burgess. 2004. "Can Labor Regulation Hinder Economic Performance? Evidence from India." *Quarterly Journal of Economics* 119(1): 91–134.

Bhalotra, S. 1998. "The Puzzle of Jobless Growth in Indian Manufacturing." *Oxford Bulletin of Economics and Statistics* 60(1): 5–32.

Bhattacharjea, A. 2006. "Labour Market Regulation and Industrial Performance in India: A Critical Review of the Empirical Evidence." *Indian Journal of Labour Economics* 49(2): 211–232.

——. 2009. "The Effects of Employment Protection Legislation on Indian Manufacturing." *Economic and Political Weekly* 44(22): 55–62.

Bhowmik, S. K. 1998. "The Labour Movement in India: Present Problems and Future Perspectives." *Indian Journal of Social Work* 59(1): 147–165.

Burgess, K. 2004. *Parties and Unions in the New Global Economy.* Pittsburgh: Pittsburgh University Press.

Byers, T. J. 1998. "State, Class, and Development Planning in India." In Terence J. Byers, ed., *The State, Development Planning, and Liberalisation in India.* New Delhi: Oxford India.

Calmfors, L., and J. Driffil. 1988. "Bargaining Structure, Corporatism, and Macroeconomic Performance." *Economic Policy* 3(6): 13–61.

Cameron, D. R. 1984. "Social Democracy, Corporatism, Labour Quiescence, and the Representation of Economic Interest in Advanced Capitalist Society." In J. H. Goldthorpe, ed., *Order and Conflict in Contemporary Capitalism.* Clarendon: Oxford University Press.

Candland, C. 2001. "The Cost of Incorporation: Labor Institutions, Industrial Restructuring, and New Trade Union Strategies in India and Pakistan." In C. Candland and R. Sil, eds., *The Politics of Labor in a Global Age: Continuity and Change in Late-Industrializing and Post-socialist Economies.* Oxford: Oxford University Press.

——. 2007. *Labor, Democratization, and Development in India and Pakistan.* New York: Routledge.

Chandra, K. 2004. *Why Do Ethnic Parties Succeed? Patronage and Ethnic Headcounts in India.* Cambridge: Cambridge University Press.

Chhibber, P. K. 1999. *Democracy without Associations: Transformations of the Party System and Social Cleavages in India.* Ann Arbor: University of Michigan Press.

Chhibber, Pradeep, and Irfan Nooruddin. 2004. "Do Party Systems Count? The Number of Parties and Government Performance in the Indian States." *Comparative Political Studies* 37(March): 152–187.

Chibber, V. 2003. *Locked in Place: State-Building and Late Industrialization in India.* Princeton: Princeton University Press.

Collier, R. 1992. *Contradictory Alliance: State-Labor Relations and Regime Change in Mexico.* Berkeley: University of California Press.

Collier, R. B., and D. Collier. 1979. "Inducements versus Constraints: Disaggregating 'Corporatism.'" *American Political Science Review* 73(4): 967–987.

——. 1991. *Shaping the Political Arena: Critical Junctures, the Labor Movement, and Regime Dynamics in Latin America.* Princeton: Princeton University Press.

Crouch, H. 1966. *Trade Unions and Politics in India.* Bombay: Manaktala and Sons Private Ltd.

De Long, B. 2003. "India since Independence: An Analytic Growth Narrative." In D. Rodrik, ed., *In Search of Prosperity: Analytic Narratives on Economic Growth.* Princeton: Princeton University Press.

De Schweinitz, K. 1959. "Industrialization, Labor Controls, and Democracy." *Economic Development and Cultural Change* 7(4): 385–404.

de Silva, K. M. 1980. *A History of Sri Lanka.* Delhi: Oxford University Press.

Desphande, L., A. Sharma, A. Karan, and S. Sarkar. 2004. *Liberalization and Labour: Labour Flexibility in Indian Manufacturing.* New Delhi: Institute for Human Development.

Deyo, F. 1984. "Export Manufacturing and Labor: The Asian Case." In C. Bergquist, ed., *Labor in the Capitalist Economy.* Beverly Hills, CA: Sage.

——. 1987. "State and Labor: Modes of Political Exclusion in East Asian Development." In F. Deyo, ed., *The Political Economy of the New Asian Industrialism.* Ithaca: Cornell University Press.

——. 1989. *Beneath the Miracle: Labor Subordination in the New Asian Industrialism.* Berkeley: University of California Press.

Djankov, S., and R. Ramalho. 2009. "Employment Laws in Developing Countries." *Journal of Comparative Economics* 37(1): 3–13.

Donald, S., and K. Lange. 2007. "Inference with Difference-in-Difference and Other Panel Data." *Review of Economics and Statistics* 89(2): 221–233.

Drake, P. 1996. *Labor Movements and Dictatorships: The Southern Cone in Comparative Perspective.* Baltimore: Johns Hopkins University Press.

Drèze, J., and A. Sen. 1995. *India: Economic Development and Social Opportunity.* Oxford: Oxford University Press.

——. 1996. *Indian Development: Selected Regional Perspectives.* Oxford: Oxford University Press.

Dutt, R. 2003. *Lockouts in India.* New Delhi: Institute for Human Development.

Dutta Roy, S. 2002. "Job Security Regulations and Worker Turnover: A Study of the Indian Manufacturing Sector." *Indian Economic Review* 37(2): 141–162.

Etchemendy, S. 2004. "Repression, Exclusion, and Inclusion: Government-Union Relations and Patterns of Labor Reform in Liberalizing Economies." *Comparative Politics* 36(3) (April): 273–290.

Evans, P. 1995. *Embedded Autonomy: States and Industrial Transformation.* Princeton: Princeton University Press.

——, ed. 1996. *State-Society Synergy: Government and Social Capital in Development.* Berkeley: University of California.

Fallon, P., and R. Lucas. 1991. "The Impact of Changes in Job Security Regulations in India and Zimbabwe." *World Bank Economic Review* 5(3): 385–419.

——. 1993. "Job Security Regulation and the Dynamic Demand for Labor in India and Zimbabwe." *Journal of Development Economics* 40: 241–275.

Farber, H. S. 1986. *The Analysis of Union Behavior.* New York: Elsevier Science.

Fernando, L. 1988. "The Challenge of the Open Economy: Trade Unionism in Sri Lanka." In R. Southall, ed., *Trade Unions and the New Industrialization of the Third World.* Pittsburgh: Pittsburgh University Press.

Fields, G. 1994. "Changing Labor Market Conditions and Economic Development in Hong Kong, the Republic of Korea, Singapore, and Taiwan, China." *The World Bank Economic Review* 8(3): 395–414.

Fisher, P. 1961. "The Economic Role of Unions in Less Developed Areas." *Monthly Labor Review* 84(9): 951–956.

Frankel, F. 2005. *India's Political Economy, 1947–2004: The Gradual Revolution.* New Delhi: Oxford University Press.

Franzosi, R. 1995. *The Puzzle of Strikes: Class and State Strategies in Postwar Italy.* Cambridge: Cambridge University Press.

Freedman, R. 1960. "Industrialization, Labor Controls, and Democracy: A Comment." *Economic Development and Cultural Change* 8(2): 192–196.

Freeman, R. 1980. "The Exit-Voice Tradeoff in the Labor Market: Unionism, Job Tenure, Quites, and Separations." *Quarterly Journal of Economics* 94(4): 643–674.

——. 1993. "Does Suppression of Labor Contribute to Economic Success? Labor Relations and Markets in East Asia." World Bank Policy Research Department Working Paper Series on the East Asian Miracle. Washington, DC: The World Bank.

Freeman, R., and J. Medoff. 1979. "The Two Faces of Unionism." *Public Interest* 57: 69–93.

——. 1984. *What Do Unions Do?* New York: Basic Books.

Frenkel, S. 1993. *Organized Labor in the Asia-Pacific Region: A Comparative Study of Trade Unions in Nine Countries.* Ithaca: ILR Press.

Frenkel, S., and S. Kuruvilla. 2002. "Logics of Action, Globalization, and Changing Employment Relations in China, India, Malaysia, and the Philippines." *Industrial and Labor Relations Review* 55(3): 387–411.

Galenson, W., ed. 1959. *Labor and Economic Development.* New York: John Wiley and Sons.

Gallagher, M. E. 2005. *Contagious Capitalism: Globalization and the Politics of Labor in China.* Princeton: Princeton University Press.

Garrett, G. 1998. *Partisan Politics in the Global Economy.* Cambridge: Cambridge University Press.

Garrett, G., and P. Lange. 1986. "Performance in a Hostile World." *World Politics* 38 (July): 517–545.

Geddes, B. 1991. "How the Cases You Choose Affect the Answers You Get: Selection Bias in Comparative Politics." *Political Analysis* 2: 131–150.

Goldar, B., and R. Banga. 2005. "Wage-Productivity Relationship in Organized Manufacturing in India: A State-Wise Analysis." *Indian Journal of Labour Economics* 48(2): 259–272.

Golden, M. A. 1997. *Heroic Defeats: the Politics of Job Loss.* Cambridge: Cambridge University Press.

Griffin, J. I. 1939. *Strikes: a Study in Quantitative Economics.* New York: Columbia University Press.

Haggard, S. 1990. *Pathways from the Periphery.* Ithaca: Cornell University Press.

Hasan, R., D. Mitra, and K. V. Ramaswamy. 2007. "Trade Reforms, Labor Regulations, and Labor-Demand Elasticities: Empirical Evidence from India." *Review of Economics and Statistics* 89(3): 466–481.

Hausman, J., B. Hall, and Z. Griliches. 1984. "Econometric Models for Count Data with an Application to the Patents-R&D Relationship." *Econometrica* 52(4) (July): 909–938.

Hazell, P., V. N. Misra, and B. Hojatti. 1995. "Role of Terms of Trade in Indian Agricultural Growth: A National and State Level Analysis." Environment and Production Technology Division Paper No. 15. Washington, DC: International Food Policy Research Institute.

Heller, P. 1999. *The Labor of Development: Workers and the Transformation of Capitalism in Kerala, India.* Ithaca: Cornell University Press.

——. 2000. "Degrees of Democracy: Some Comparative Lessons from India." *World Politics* 52(4): 484–519.

Herring, R. 1983. *Land to the Tiller: The Political Economy of Agrarian Reform in South Asia.* New Haven: Yale University Press.

——. 1987. Economic Liberalisation Policies in Sri Lanka: International Pressures, Constraints, and Supports. *Economic and Political Weekly* 22(8): 325–333.

——. 1999. "Embedded Particularism: India's Failed Developmental State." In Meredith Woo Cummings, ed., *The Developmental State.* Ithaca: Cornell University Press.

——. 2001. "Making Ethnic Conflict: The Civil War in Sri Lanka." In Milton J. Esman and Ronald J. Herring, eds., *Carrots, Sticks, and Ethnic Conflict: Rethinking Development Assistance.* Ann Arbor: University of Michigan Press.

Hibbs, D. 1976. "Industrial Conflict in Advanced Industrial Societies." *American Political Science Review* 70(4): 1033–1058.

——. 1978. "On the Political Economy of Long-Run Trends in Strike Activity." *British Journal of Political Science* 8(2): 153–175.

——. 1987. *The Political Economy of Industrial Democracies.* Cambridge: Harvard University Press.

Hicks, J. R. 1948. *The Theory of Wages.* New York: Peter Smith.

Jenkins, R. 1999. *Democratic Politics and Economic Reform in India.* Cambridge: Cambridge University Press.

Johnson, C. 1982. *MITI and the Japanese Miracle: The Growth of Industrial Policy, 1925–1975.* Stanford: Stanford University Press.

Joshi, V., and I.M.D. Little. 1996. *India's Economic Reforms: 1991–2001.* New Delhi: Oxford University Press.

Jurkat, E. H., and D. B. Jurkat. 1949. "Economic Functions of Strikes." *Industrial and Labor Relations Review* 2(4): 527–545.

Kaldor, N. 1956. "Alternative Theories of Distribution." *Review of Economic Studies* 23: 83–100.

Kammen, D. 1997. *A Time to Strike: Industrial Strikes and Changing Class Relations in New Order Indonesia.* Ph.D. Diss., Cornell University.

Kannan, K. P. 1994. "Leveling Up or Leveling Down? Labour Institutions and Economic Development in India." *Economic and Political Weekly* 29(30): 1938–1946.

Kannan, K. P., and G. Raveendran. 2009. "Growth sans Employment: A Quarter Century of Jobless Growth in India's Organised Manufacturing." *Economic and Political Weekly* 44(10): 80–91.

Kapur, D., and R. Ramamurti. 2002. "Privatization in India: The Imperatives and Consequences of Gradualism." Working Paper No. 142. Stanford: Stanford University.

Kearney, R. 1971. *Trade Unions and Politics in Ceylon.* Berkeley: University of California Press.

Keidel, Albert. 2005. "The Economic Basis for Social Unrest in China." Manuscript presented at the Third European-American Dialogue on China, The George Washington University, Washington, DC (May 26–27).

Kennan, J. 1985. "The Duration of Strikes in U.S. Manufacturing." *Journal of Econometrics* 28(1): 5–28.

——. 1986. *The Economics of Strikes.* New York: Elsevier Science.

Kennedy, V. D. 1966. *Unions, Employers, and Government.* Bombay: P.C. Manaktala and Sons.

Kim, W., and J. Gandhi. 2010. "Co-opting Workers under Dictatorship." *Journal of Politics* 72(3): 646–658.

Knowles, K. G. J. C. 1952. *Strikes: A Study in Industrial Conflict.* Oxford: Basil Blackwell.

Kohli, A. 1990. *Democracy and Discontent: India's Growing Crisis of Governability.* Cambridge: Cambridge University Press.

——. 2004. *State Directed Development: Political Power and Industrialization in the Global Periphery.* Princeton: Princeton University Press.

——. 2006. "The Politics of Economic Growth in India, 1980–2005." *Economic and Political Weekly* 41(14): 1361–1370.

Korpi, W., and M. Shalev. 1980. "Strikes, Power, and Politics in the Western Nations, 1900–1976." *Political Power and Social Theory* 1: 301–334.

Kothari, R. 1964. "The Congress System in India." *Asian Survey* 4(12): 1161–1173.

Kucera, D. 2001. "The Effects of Core Workers Rights on Labor Costs and Foreign Direct Investment: Evaluating the 'Conventional Wisdom.'" Decent Work Research Programme Working Paper No. 130/2001. Geneva: International Labour Organization.

——. 2007. "Measuring Trade Union Rights by Violations of These Rights." In D. Kucera, ed., *Qualitative Indicators of Labour Standards: Comparative Methods and Applications.* Netherlands: Springer.

Kucera, D., and R. Sarna. 2006. "Trade Union Rights, Democracy, and Exports: A Gravity Model Approach." *Review of International Economics* 14(5): 859–882.

Kurtz, M. 2004. "The Dilemmas of Democracy in the Open Economy: Lessons from Latin America." *World Politics* 56(2) (January): 262–302.

Kuruvilla, S. 1993. *Industrialization Strategy and Industrial Relations Policy in Malaysia.* Ithaca: Cornell University Press.
——. 1996. "Linkages between Industrialization Strategy and Industrial Relations / Human Resource Policies: Singapore, Malaysia, Philippines, and India." *Industrial and Labor Relations Review* 49(4): 635–657.
Laakso, M., and R. Taagepera. 1979. "Effective Number of Parties: A Measure with Application to Western Europe." *Comparative Political Studies* 12: 3–27.
Lakha, S. 2002. "Organized Labor and Militant Unionism: The Bombay Textile Workers' Strike of 1982." In G. Shah, ed., *Social Movements and the State.* New Delhi: Thousand Oaks.
Lange, P., and G. Garrett. 1985. "The Politics of Growth: Strategic Interaction and Economic Performance in the Advanced Industrial Democracies, 1974–1980." *Journal of Politics* 47(3): 792–827.
Levitsky, S., and L. Way. 1998. "Between a Shock and a Hard Place: The Dynamics of Labor-Backed Adjustment in Poland and Argentina." *Comparative Politics* 30(2): 171–192.
Malhotra, O. P. 2004. *O. P. Malhotra's the Law of Industrial Disputes.* New Delhi: LexisNexis.
Malik, P. L. 2005. *Industrial Law.* Lucknow: Eastern Book Company.
Mehta, A. 1957. "The Mediating Role of the Trade Union in Underdeveloped Countries." *Economic Development and Cultural Change* 6(1): 16–23.
Mooij, J. 1999. *Food Policy and the Indian State: the Public Distribution System in South India.* New Delhi: Oxford University Press.
Murillo, V. 2001. *Labor Unions, Partisan Coalitions, and Market Reforms in Latin America.* Cambridge: Cambridge University Press.
Myers, C. 1958. *Industrial Relations in India.* Bombay: Harvard University Press.
Nagaraj, R. 1994. "Employment and Wages in Manufacturing Industries: Trends, Hypothesis and Evidence." *Economic and Political Weekly* 29(4): 177–186.
——. 2000. "Organised Manufacturing Employment." *Economic and Political Weekly* 38(38): 3445–3448.
Nikolenyi, Csaba. 2009. *Minority Governments in India: The Puzzle of Elusive Majorities.* New York: Routledge.
Nurkse, R. 1953. *Problems of Capital Formation in Underdeveloped Countries.* Oxford: Basil Blackwell.
O'Donnell, G. 1973. *Modernization and Bureaucratic Authoritarianism: Studies in South American Politics.* Berkley: University of California Institute of International Studies.
——. 1978. "Reflections on the Patterns of Change in the Bureaucratic Authoritarian State." *Latin American Research Review* 13(1): 3–38.
Olson, M. 1971. *The Logic of Collective Action: Public Goods and the Theory of Groups.* Cambridge: Harvard University Press.
——. 1982. *The Rise and Decline of Nations: Economic Growth, Stagflation, and Social Rigidities.* New Haven: Yale University Press.
Papola, T. S. 1994. "Structural Adjustment, Labour Market Flexibility, and Employment." *Indian Journal of Labour Economics* 37(1): 3–16.
Pencavel, J. 1997. "The Legal Framework for Collective Bargaining in Developing Economies." In S. Edwards and N. C. Lustig, eds., *Labor Markets in Latin*

America: Combining Social Protection with Market Flexibility. Washington, DC: Brookings Institution Press.

Pendse, S. 1980. "Industrial Violence: A Case Study." *Economic and Political Weekly* 15(11): 546–548.

Przeworski, A. 1986. *Capitalism and Social Democracy.* Cambridge: Cambridge University Press.

Przeworski, A., M. Alvarez, J. Cheibub, and F. Limongi. 2000. *Democracy and Development: Political Institutions and Well-Being in the World, 1950–1990.* Cambridge: Cambridge University Press.

Przeworski, A., and F. Limongi. 1993. "Political Regimes and Economic Growth." *Journal of Economic Perspectives* 7(3): 51–69.

——. 1997. "Democracy and Development." In A. Hadanious, ed., *Democracy's Victory and Crisis.* Cambridge: Cambridge University Press.

Przeworski, A., and J. Sprague. 1986. *Paper Stones: A History of Electoral Socialism.* Chicago: University of Chicago Press.

Rajagopal, A. 2001. *Politics after Television: Religious Nationalism and the Reshaping of the Indian Public.* Cambridge: Cambridge University Press.

Rakshit, M. 2004. "Some Macroeconomics of India's Reform Experience." In Kaushik Basu, ed., *India's Emerging Economy: Performance and Prospects in the 1990s and Beyond.* Cambridge, MA: The MIT Press.

Raman, N. P. 1967. *Political Involvement of India's Trade Unions.* Bombay: Asia Publishing House.

Ramaswamy, E. A. 1983. "The Indian Management Dilemma: Economic vs. Political Unions." *Asian Survey* 23(8): 976–990.

Rees, A. 1952. "Industrial Conflict and Business Fluctuations." *Journal of Political Economy* 60(5): 371–382.

——. 1963. "The Effects of Unions on Resource Allocations." *Journal of Law and Economics* 6(1): 69–78.

Robertson, G. 2004. "Leading Labor: Unions, Politics, and Protest in New Democracies." *Comparative Politics* 36(3): 253–272.

——. 2007. "Strikes and Labor Organization in Hybrid Regimes." *American Political Science Review* 101(4) (November): 781–798.

——. 2011. *The Politics of Protest in Hybrid Regimes: Managing Dissent in Post-Communist Countries.* Cambridge: Cambridge University Press.

Rodrik, D., and A. Subramanian. 2004. "From Hindu Growth to Productivity Surge: the Mystery of the Indian Growth Transition." National Bureau of Economic Research Working Paper No. 10376. Cambridge, MA: NBER.

Rudolph, L., and S. H. Rudolph. 1987. *In Pursuit of Lakshmi: The Political Economy of the Indian State.* Chicago: University of Chicago Press.

Sachs, J., N. Bajpai et al. 2002. "Understanding Regional Economic Growth in India." Working Paper No. 88. Cambridge: Harvard University Center for International Development.

Sachs, J., A. Varshney et al., eds. 1999. *India in the Era of Economic Reforms.* New Delhi: Oxford University Press.

Saez, L., and A. Sinha. 2009. "Political Cycles, Political Institutions, and Public Expenditure in India, 1980–2000." *British Journal of Political Science* 40: 91–113.

Samaraweera, V. 1981. "Sri Lankan Marxists in Electoral Politics: 1947–1978." In K. M. de Silva, ed., *Universal Franchise: 1931–1981, the Sri Lankan Experience.* Colombo: Department of Governmental Printing.

Sanyal, P., and N. Menon. 2005. "Labor Disputes and the Economics of Firm Geography: A Study of Domestic Investment in India." *Economic Development and Cultural Change* 53(4): 825–854.

Schneider, F. 2002. "Size and Measurement of the Informal Economy in 110 Countries around the World." Paper presented at a workshop of the Australian National Tax Centre, ANU, Canberra, Australia, July 17.

Schrank, A. 2007. "Labor Standards and Human Resources: A Natural Experiment in an Unlikely Laboratory." Presented at the Department of Sociology, Harvard University, May 8.

Seidman, G. 1994. *Manufacturing Militance: Workers' Movements in Brazil and South Africa, 1970–1985.* Berkeley: University of California Press.

Sharma, A. 2006. "Flexibility, Employment, and Labour Market Reforms in India." *Economic and Political Weekly* 41(21): 2078–2085.

Sharma, B. 1985. *Aspects of Industrial Relations in ASEAN.* Singapore: Institute for Asian Studies.

Shastri, A. 1997. "Transitions to a Free Market: Economic Liberalization in Sri Lanka." *Round Table* 344(1): 485–511.

Shorter, E., and C. Tilly. 1971. "The Shape of Strikes in France, 1830–1960." *Comparative Studies in Society and History* 13(1): 60–86.

——. 1974. *Strikes in France: 1830–1968.* Cambridge: Cambridge University Press.

Sinha, A. 2005. *The Regional Roots of Developmental Politics in India: a Divided Leviathan.* Bloomington: Indiana University Press.

Stern, N. 2001. *A Strategy for Development.* Washington, DC: World Bank.

Sturmthal, A. 1960. "Unions and Economic Development." *Economic Development and Cultural Change* 8(2) (January): 199–205.

Sundar, S. 2004. "Lockouts in India, 1961–2001." *Economic and Political Weekly* 39(39): 4377–4385.

——. 2005. "Labour Flexibility Debate in India: A Comprehensive Review and Some Suggestions." *Economic and Political Weekly* 40(22): 2274–2285.

Sundaram, K. 2007. "Employment and Poverty in India, 2000–2005." *Economic and Political Weekly* 42(30): 3121–3131.

Tafel, H., and D. Boniface. 2003. "Old Carrots, New Sticks: Explaining Labor Strategies toward Economic Reform in Eastern Europe and Latin America." *Comparative Politics* 35 (3): 313–333.

Tarrow, S. 1998. *Power in Movement: Social Movements and Contentious Politics.* Cambridge: Cambridge University Press.

Teitelbaum, E. 2007. "In the Grip of a Green Giant: How the Rural Sector Tamed Organized Labor in India." *Comparative Political Studies* 40(6): 638–664.

——. 2008. "Was the Indian Labor Movement Ever Co-opted? Evaluating Standard Accounts." In Rina Agarwala and Ronald Herring, eds., *Whatever Happened to Class? Reflections from South Asia.* New York: Routledge.

——. 2010. "Mobilizing Restraint: Economic Reform and the Politics of Industrial Protest in South Asia," *World Politics* 62(4): 676–713.

Tilly, C. 1995. *Popular Contention in Great Britain: 1758–1834.* Cambridge: Harvard University Press.

Topolova, P. 2004. "Trade Liberalization and Firm Productivity: The Case of India." IMF Working Paper No. WP/04/28. Washington, DC: International Monetary Fund.

Ulph, A., and D. Ulph. 1989. "Union Bargaining: a Survey of Recent Work." In D. Sapsford and Z. Tzannatos, eds., *Current Issues in Labour Economics.* London: MacMillan Press.

Unel, B. 2003. *Productivity Trends in India's Manufacturing Sectors in the Last Two Decades.* IMF Working Paper No. 03/22. Washington, DC: International Monetary Fund.

Urdal, H. 2008. "Population, Resources, and Political Violence: A Sub-National Study of India, 1956–2002." *Journal of Conflict Resolution* 52(4) (August): 590–617.

Varshney, A. 1998a. "Mass Politics or Elite Politics? India's Economic Reforms in Comparative Perspective." *Journal of Economic Policy Reform* 2(4): 301–335.

——. 1998b. *Democracy, Development, and the Countryside: Urban-Rural Struggles in India.* Cambridge: Cambridge University Press.

Venkata Ratnam, C. S. 2001. *Globalization and Labour-Management Relations: Dynamics of Change.* New Delhi: Response Books.

Venugopal, Rajesh. 2009. "Sectarian Socialism: The Politics of Sri Lanka's Janatha Vimukthi Peramuna (JVP)." *Modern Asian Studies* 44: 567–602.

Wade, R. 1990. *Governing the Market: Economic Theory and the Role of Government in East Asian Industrialization.* Princeton: Princeton University Press.

Weiner, M. 1967. *Party Building in a New Nation.* Chicago: University of Chicago.

——. 1991. *The Child and the State in India: Child Labor and Education Policy in Comparative Perspective.* Princeton: Princeton University Press.

Weintraub, A. R. 1966. "Prosperity versus Strikes: an Empirical Approach." *Industrial and Labor Relations Review* 19(1): 231–238.

Western, B. 1997. *Between Class and Market: Postwar Unionization in the Capitalist Democracies.* Princeton: Princeton University Press.

Wilkinson, S. 2006. "Explaining Changing Patterns of Party-Voter Linkages in India." In H. Kitschelt and S. Wilkinson, eds., *Patrons, Clients, and Policies.* Cambridge: Cambridge University Press: 110–140.

Wooldridge, J. 2003. "Cluster-Sample Methods in Applied Econometrics." *American Economic Review* 93(2): 133–138.

Yoder, D. 1938. "Seasonality in Strikes." *Journal of the American Statistical Association* 33(204): 687–693.

Government Publications

Government of India. 1976–1997. *Indian Labour Yearbook.* Ministry of Labour.

——. 2001. *Handbook of Industrial Policy and Statistics.* Ministry of Commerce and Industry.

——. Various years. *Employment Review.* Directorate General of Education and Training, Ministry of Labor.

——. Various years. *Statistical Report on General Elections to the Legislative Assemblies.* Election Commission of India.
——. Various years. *Trade Unions in India.*
Sri Lanka Board of Investment (BOI). 2000. "The BOI Sector: Statistical Abstract—2001." Colombo.
——. 2002. "Guidelines for the Formation and Operation of Employees' Councils." Colombo.

Online Databases

Cingranelli, D. L., and D. L. Richards. 2006. The Cingranelli-Richards (CIRI) Human Rights Dataset. http://ciri.binghamton.edu/.
ICFTU. 2004. Annual Survey of Violations of Trade Union Rights. http://www.icftu.org/survey2004.asp?language=EN.
ILO. 2003. Unpublished database on trade union membership in 45 countries. Available on request: http://www.ilo.org/public/english/bureau/stat/info/dbases.htm.
ILO Laborsta Online Database. Various years. http://laborsta.ilo.org.

Publications by International and Other Organizations

Confederation of Indian Industries (CII). 2004. *Labour Reforms in Southern Region States: Issues and Concerns.* Policy Primer No. 3, April. Accessed online at http://www.ciionline.org.
Freedom House. 2004. *Freedom in the World 2004: Selected Data from Freedom House's Survey of Political Rights and Civil Liberties.* Washington, DC: Freedom House.
World Bank. 1993. *The East Asian Miracle: Economic Growth and Public Policy.* Oxford: Oxford University Press.
——. 1995. *World Development Report, 1995: Workers in an Integrating World.* Washington, DC: World Bank.
——. 2000. *India: Reducing Poverty, Accelerating Development.* New Delhi: Oxford: University Press.
——. 2003. *Bangladesh Development Policy Review: Impressive Achievements but Continuing Challenges.* Report No. 26154-BD. Poverty Reduction and Economic Management Sector Unit, South Asia Region.
——. 2005. *World Development Report, 2005: A Better Investment Climate for Everyone.* Washington, DC: World Bank.
——. 2006. *Pakistan: Growth and Competitiveness.* Report No. 35499-PK. Poverty Reduction and Economic Management Sector Unit, South Asia Region.

Index